THE SAGA OF SEVEN SUNS: VEILED ALLIANCES

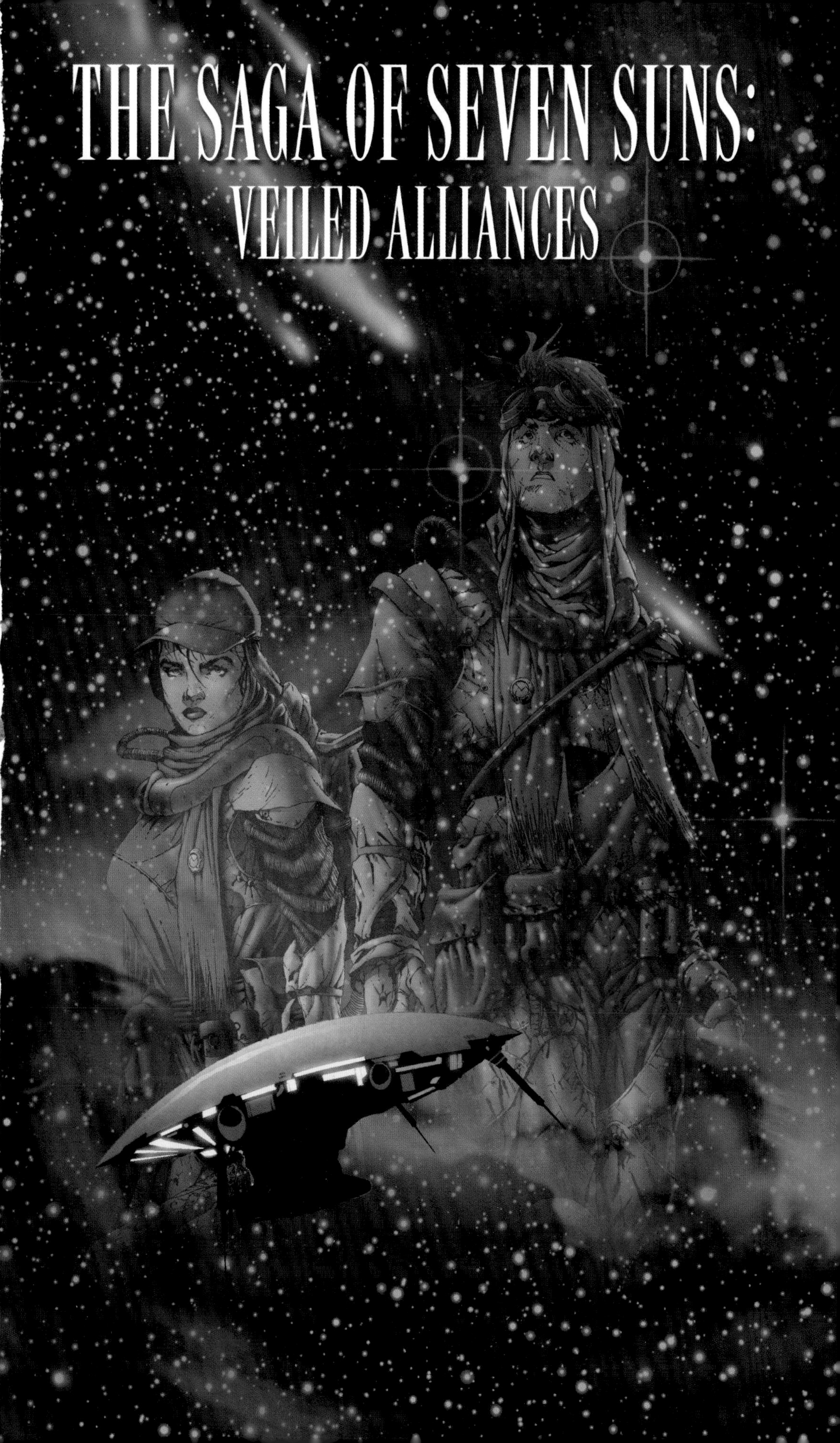

WRITER - Kevin J. Anderson

ARTIST - Robert Teranishi

COLORS - Wendy Fouts-Broome

LETTERS - Comicraft

COVER ART - Steven Youll

DESIGN - Ed Roeder

ASSISTANT EDITOR - Kristy Quinn

EDITORS - Ben Abernathy and Jeff Mariotte

Jim Lee, Editorial Director · John Nee, VP & General Manager · Scott Dunbier, Group Editor
Robbin Brosterman, Senior Art Director · Ed Roeder, Art Director · Paul Levitz, President & Publisher
Georg Brewer, VP—Design & Retail Product Development, · Richard Bruning, Senior VP—Creative Director
Patrick Caldon, Senior VP—Finance & Operations · Chris Caramalis, VP—Finance · Terri Cunningham, VP—Managing Editor
Dan DiDio, VP—Editorial · Alison Gill, VP—Manufacturing · Lillian Laserson, Senior VP & General Counsel
David McKillips, VP—Advertising & Custom Publishing · Cheryl Rubin, VP—Brand Management,
Bob Wayne, VP—Sales & Marketing

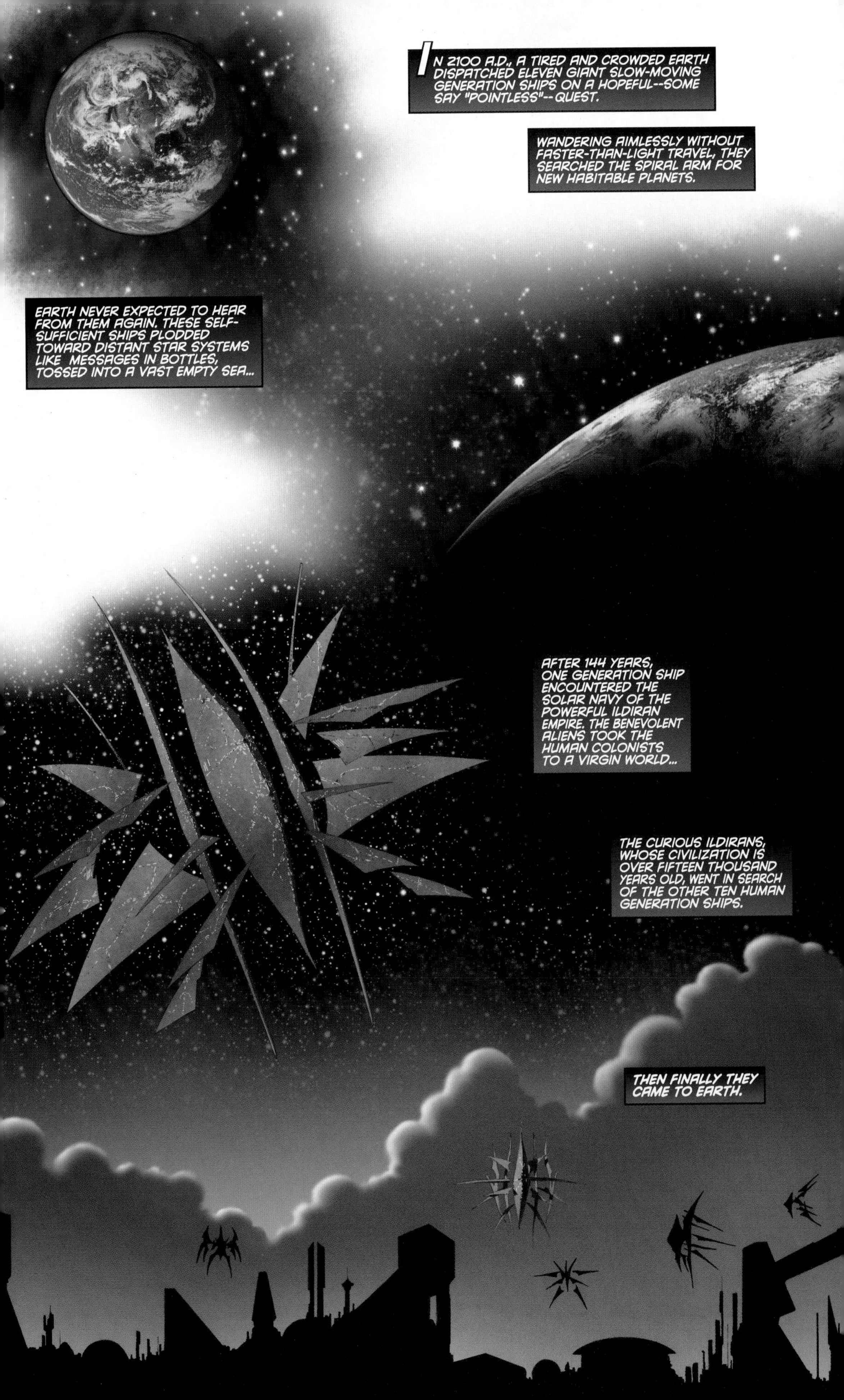
IN 2100 A.D., A TIRED AND CROWDED EARTH DISPATCHED ELEVEN GIANT SLOW-MOVING GENERATION SHIPS ON A HOPEFUL--SOME SAY "POINTLESS"--QUEST.
WANDERING AIMLESSLY WITHOUT FASTER-THAN-LIGHT TRAVEL, THEY SEARCHED THE SPIRAL ARM FOR NEW HABITABLE PLANETS.
EARTH NEVER EXPECTED TO HEAR FROM THEM AGAIN. THESE SELF-SUFFICIENT SHIPS PLODDED TOWARD DISTANT STAR SYSTEMS LIKE MESSAGES IN BOTTLES, TOSSED INTO A VAST EMPTY SEA...
AFTER 144 YEARS, ONE GENERATION SHIP ENCOUNTERED THE SOLAR NAVY OF THE POWERFUL ILDIRAN EMPIRE. THE BENEVOLENT ALIENS TOOK THE HUMAN COLONISTS TO A VIRGIN WORLD...
THE CURIOUS ILDIRANS, WHOSE CIVILIZATION IS OVER FIFTEEN THOUSAND YEARS OLD, WENT IN SEARCH OF THE OTHER TEN HUMAN GENERATION SHIPS.
THEN FINALLY THEY CAME TO EARTH.

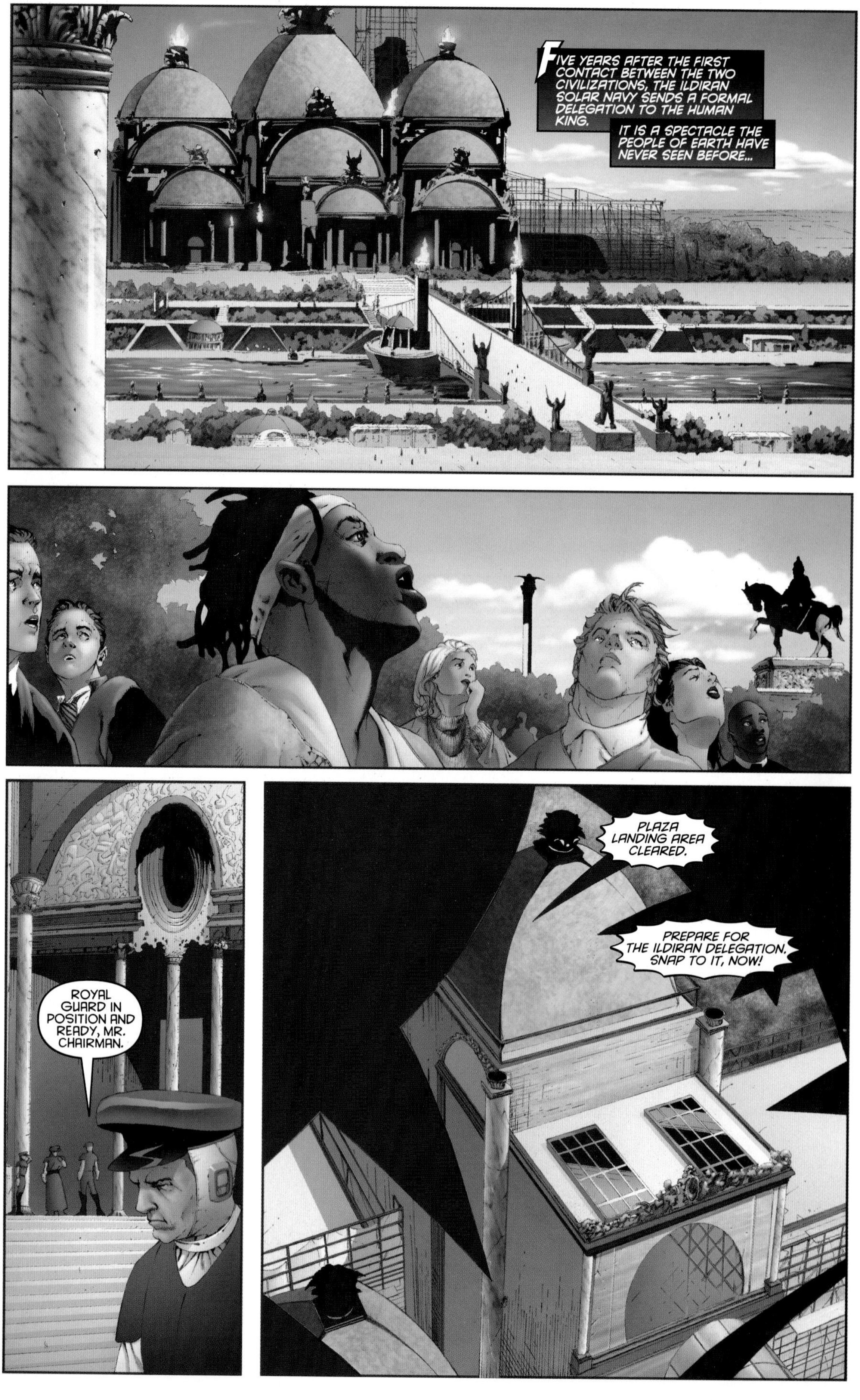
FIVE YEARS AFTER THE FIRST CONTACT BETWEEN THE TWO CIVILIZATIONS, THE ILDIRAN SOLAR NAVY SENDS A FORMAL DELEGATION TO THE HUMAN KING.
IT IS A SPECTACLE THE PEOPLE OF EARTH HAVE NEVER SEEN BEFORE...
ROYAL GUARD IN POSITION AND READY, MR. CHAIRMAN.
PLAZA LANDING AREA CLEARED.
PREPARE FOR THE ILDIRAN DELEGATION. SNAP TO IT, NOW!

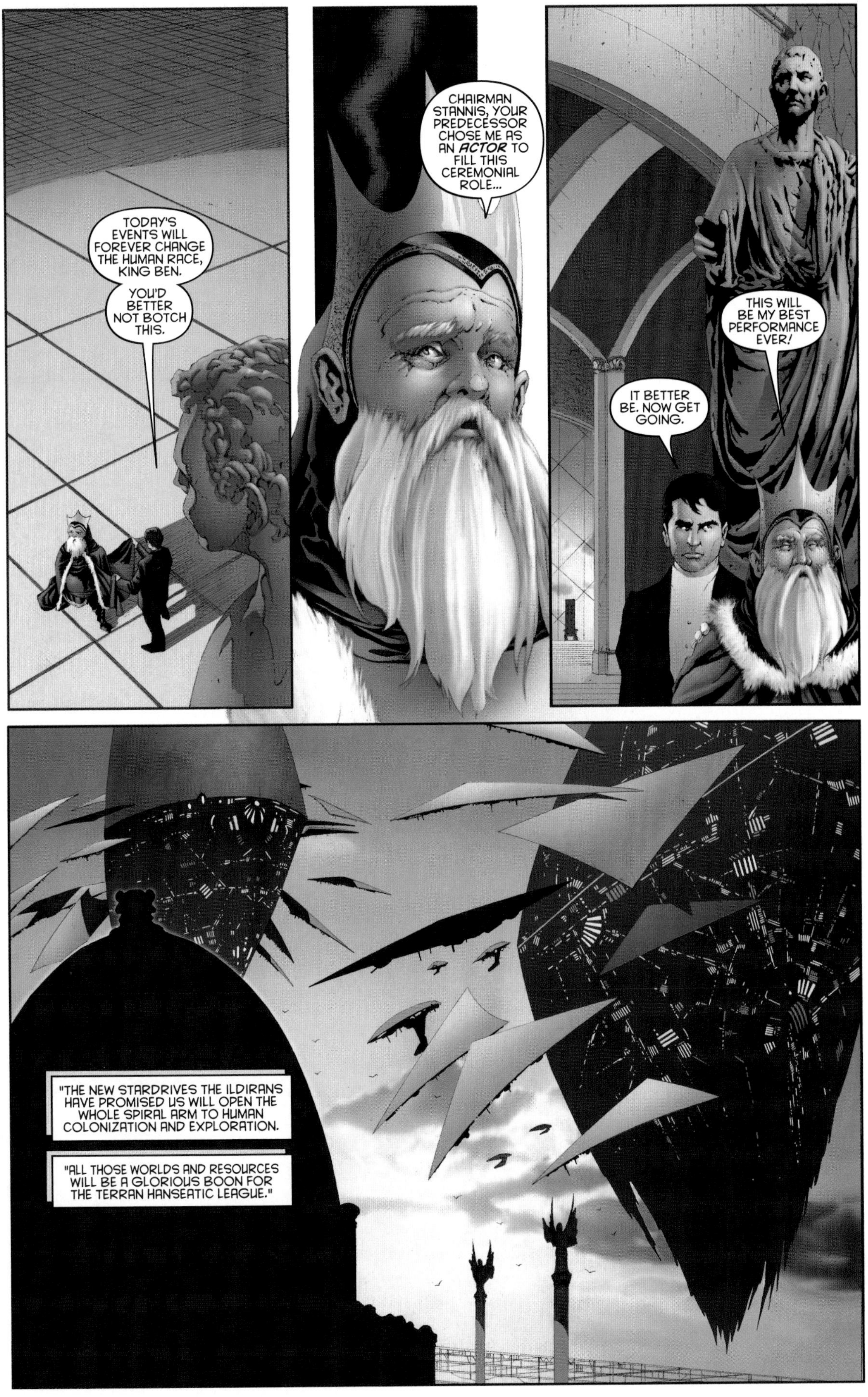
TODAY'S EVENTS WILL FOREVER CHANGE THE HUMAN RACE, KING BEN.
YOU'D BETTER NOT BOTCH THIS.
CHAIRMAN STANNIS, YOUR PREDECESSOR CHOSE ME AS AN *ACTOR* TO FILL THIS CEREMONIAL ROLE...
THIS WILL BE MY BEST PERFORMANCE EVER!
IT BETTER BE. NOW GET GOING.
"THE NEW STARDRIVES THE ILDIRANS HAVE PROMISED US WILL OPEN THE WHOLE SPIRAL ARM TO HUMAN COLONIZATION AND EXPLORATION.
"ALL THOSE WORLDS AND RESOURCES WILL BE A GLORIOUS BOON FOR THE TERRAN HANSEATIC LEAGUE."

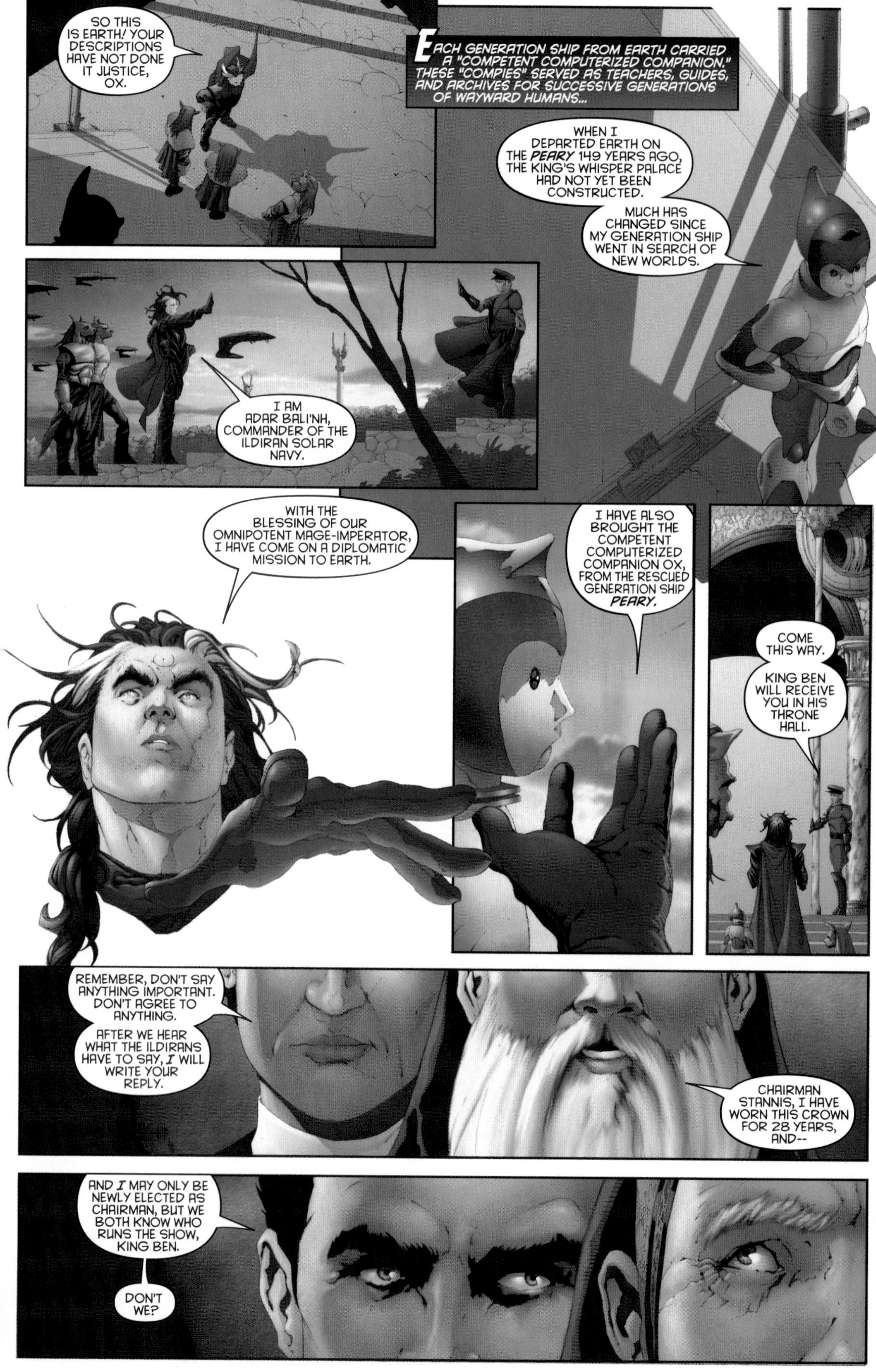
SO THIS IS EARTH! YOUR DESCRIPTIONS HAVE NOT DONE IT JUSTICE, OX.
EACH GENERATION SHIP FROM EARTH CARRIED A "COMPETENT COMPUTERIZED COMPANION." THESE "COMPIES" SERVED AS TEACHERS, GUIDES, AND ARCHIVES FOR SUCCESSIVE GENERATIONS OF WAYWARD HUMANS...
WHEN I DEPARTED EARTH ON THE PEARY 149 YEARS AGO, THE KING'S WHISPER PALACE HAD NOT YET BEEN CONSTRUCTED.
MUCH HAS CHANGED SINCE MY GENERATION SHIP WENT IN SEARCH OF NEW WORLDS.
I AM ADAR BALI'NH, COMMANDER OF THE ILDIRAN SOLAR NAVY.
WITH THE BLESSING OF OUR OMNIPOTENT MAGE-IMPERATOR, I HAVE COME ON A DIPLOMATIC MISSION TO EARTH.
I HAVE ALSO BROUGHT THE COMPETENT COMPUTERIZED COMPANION OX, FROM THE RESCUED GENERATION SHIP PEARY.
COME THIS WAY.
KING BEN WILL RECEIVE YOU IN HIS THRONE HALL.
REMEMBER, DON'T SAY ANYTHING IMPORTANT. DON'T AGREE TO ANYTHING.
AFTER WE HEAR WHAT THE ILDIRANS HAVE TO SAY, I WILL WRITE YOUR REPLY.
CHAIRMAN STANNIS, I HAVE WORN THIS CROWN FOR 28 YEARS, AND--
AND I MAY ONLY BE NEWLY ELECTED AS CHAIRMAN, BUT WE BOTH KNOW WHO RUNS THE SHOW, KING BEN.
DON'T WE?

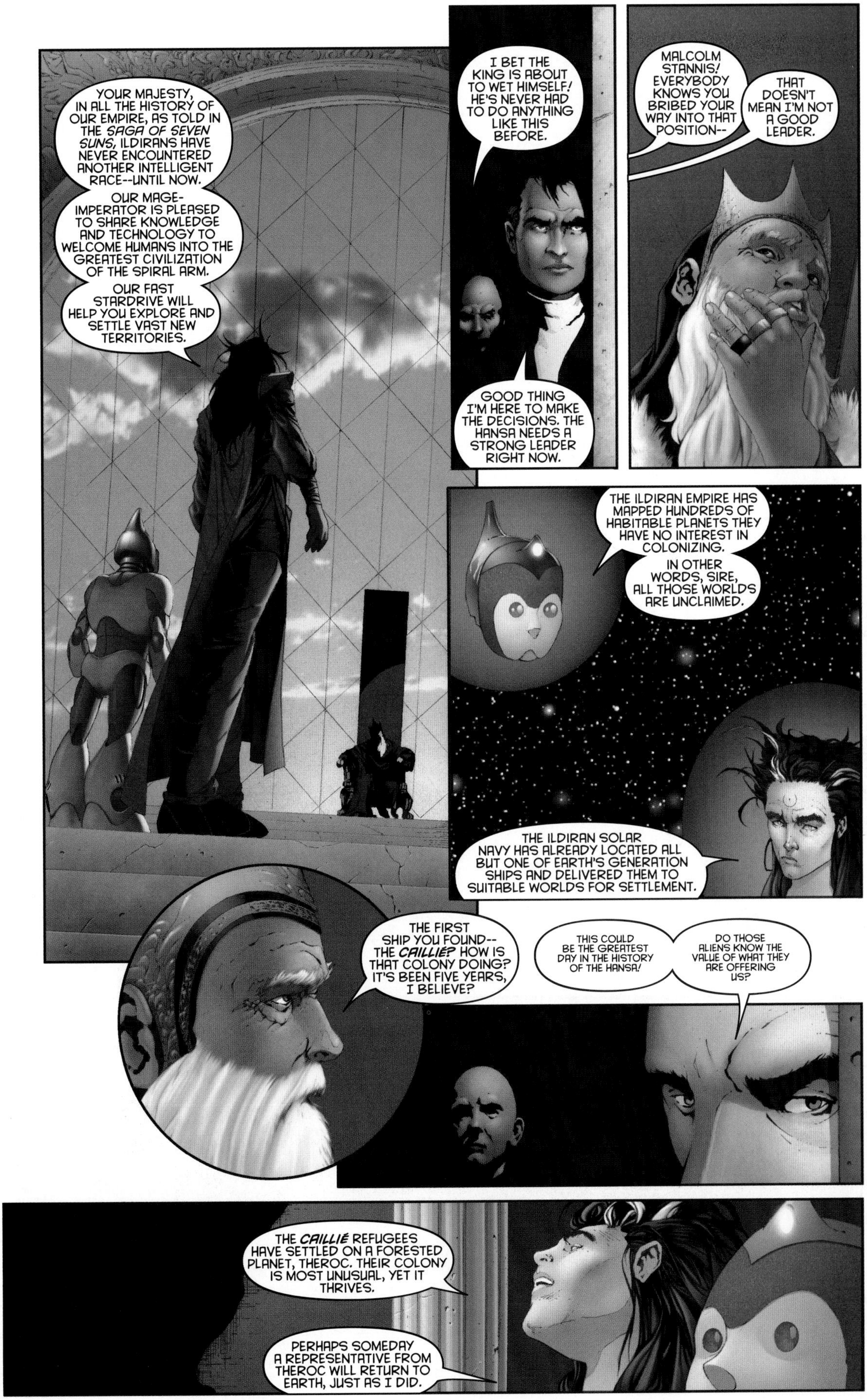
YOUR MAJESTY, IN ALL THE HISTORY OF OUR EMPIRE, AS TOLD IN THE SAGA OF SEVEN SUNS, ILDIRANS HAVE NEVER ENCOUNTERED ANOTHER INTELLIGENT RACE--UNTIL NOW.
OUR MAGE-IMPERATOR IS PLEASED TO SHARE KNOWLEDGE AND TECHNOLOGY TO WELCOME HUMANS INTO THE GREATEST CIVILIZATION OF THE SPIRAL ARM.
OUR FAST STARDRIVE WILL HELP YOU EXPLORE AND SETTLE VAST NEW TERRITORIES.
I BET THE KING IS ABOUT TO WET HIMSELF! HE'S NEVER HAD TO DO ANYTHING LIKE THIS BEFORE.
GOOD THING I'M HERE TO MAKE THE DECISIONS. THE HANSA NEEDS A STRONG LEADER RIGHT NOW.
MALCOLM STANNIS! EVERYBODY KNOWS YOU BRIBED YOUR WAY INTO THAT POSITION--
THAT DOESN'T MEAN I'M NOT A GOOD LEADER.
THE ILDIRAN EMPIRE HAS MAPPED HUNDREDS OF HABITABLE PLANETS THEY HAVE NO INTEREST IN COLONIZING.
IN OTHER WORDS, SIRE, ALL THOSE WORLDS ARE UNCLAIMED.
THE ILDIRAN SOLAR NAVY HAS ALREADY LOCATED ALL BUT ONE OF EARTH'S GENERATION SHIPS AND DELIVERED THEM TO SUITABLE WORLDS FOR SETTLEMENT.
THE FIRST SHIP YOU FOUND-- THE CAILLIE? HOW IS THAT COLONY DOING? IT'S BEEN FIVE YEARS, I BELIEVE?
THIS COULD BE THE GREATEST DAY IN THE HISTORY OF THE HANSA!
DO THOSE ALIENS KNOW THE VALUE OF WHAT THEY ARE OFFERING US?
THE CAILLIE REFUGEES HAVE SETTLED ON A FORESTED PLANET, THEROC. THEIR COLONY IS MOST UNUSUAL, YET IT THRIVES.
PERHAPS SOMEDAY A REPRESENTATIVE FROM THEROC WILL RETURN TO EARTH, JUST AS I DID.

THEROC

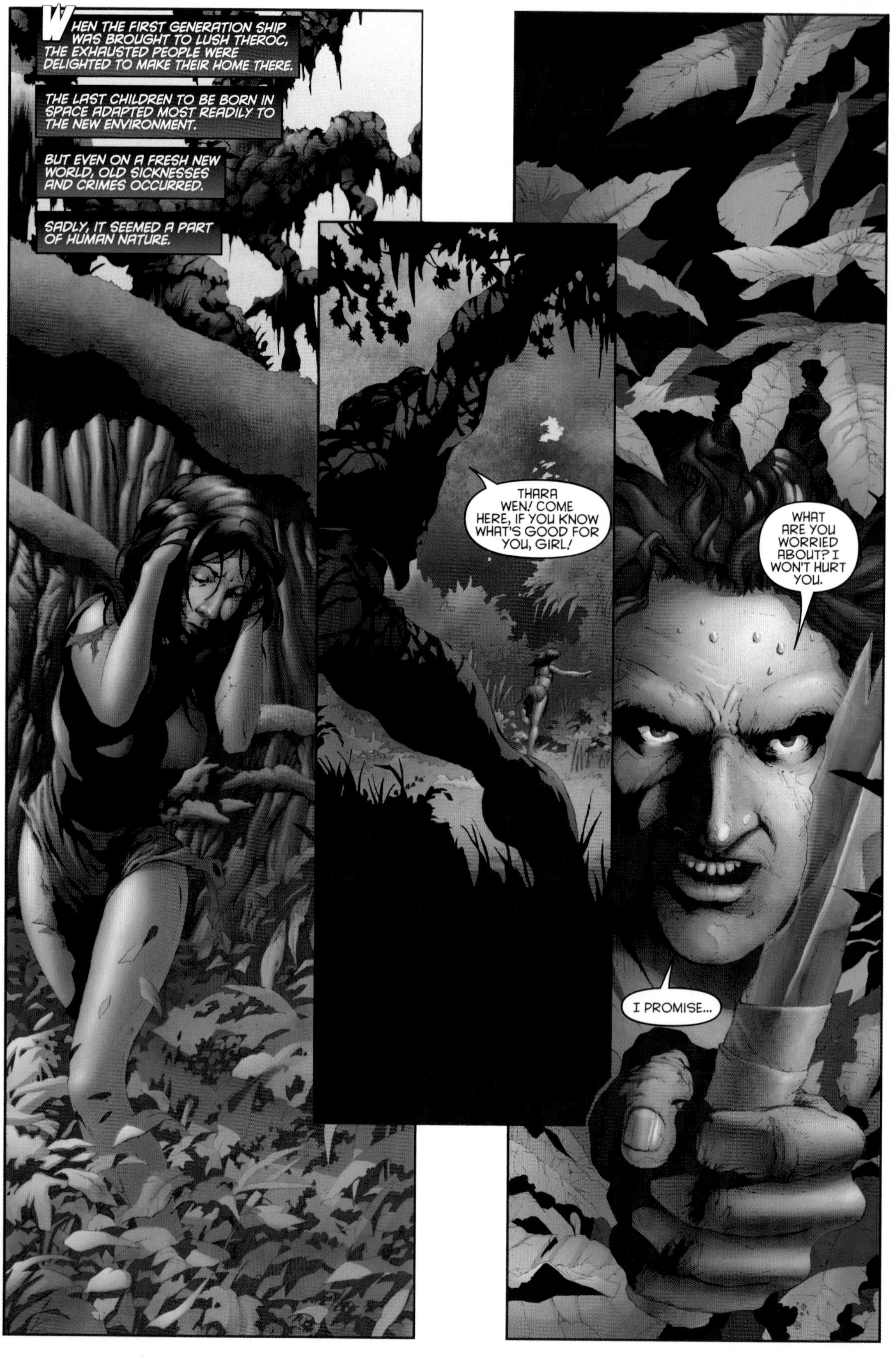
WHEN THE FIRST GENERATION SHIP WAS BROUGHT TO LUSH THEROC, THE EXHAUSTED PEOPLE WERE DELIGHTED TO MAKE THEIR HOME THERE.
THE LAST CHILDREN TO BE BORN IN SPACE ADAPTED MOST READILY TO THE NEW ENVIRONMENT.
BUT EVEN ON A FRESH NEW WORLD, OLD SICKNESSES AND CRIMES OCCURRED.
SADLY, IT SEEMED A PART OF HUMAN NATURE.
THARA WEN! COME HERE, IF YOU KNOW WHAT'S GOOD FOR YOU, GIRL!
WHAT ARE YOU WORRIED ABOUT? I WON'T HURT YOU.
I PROMISE...

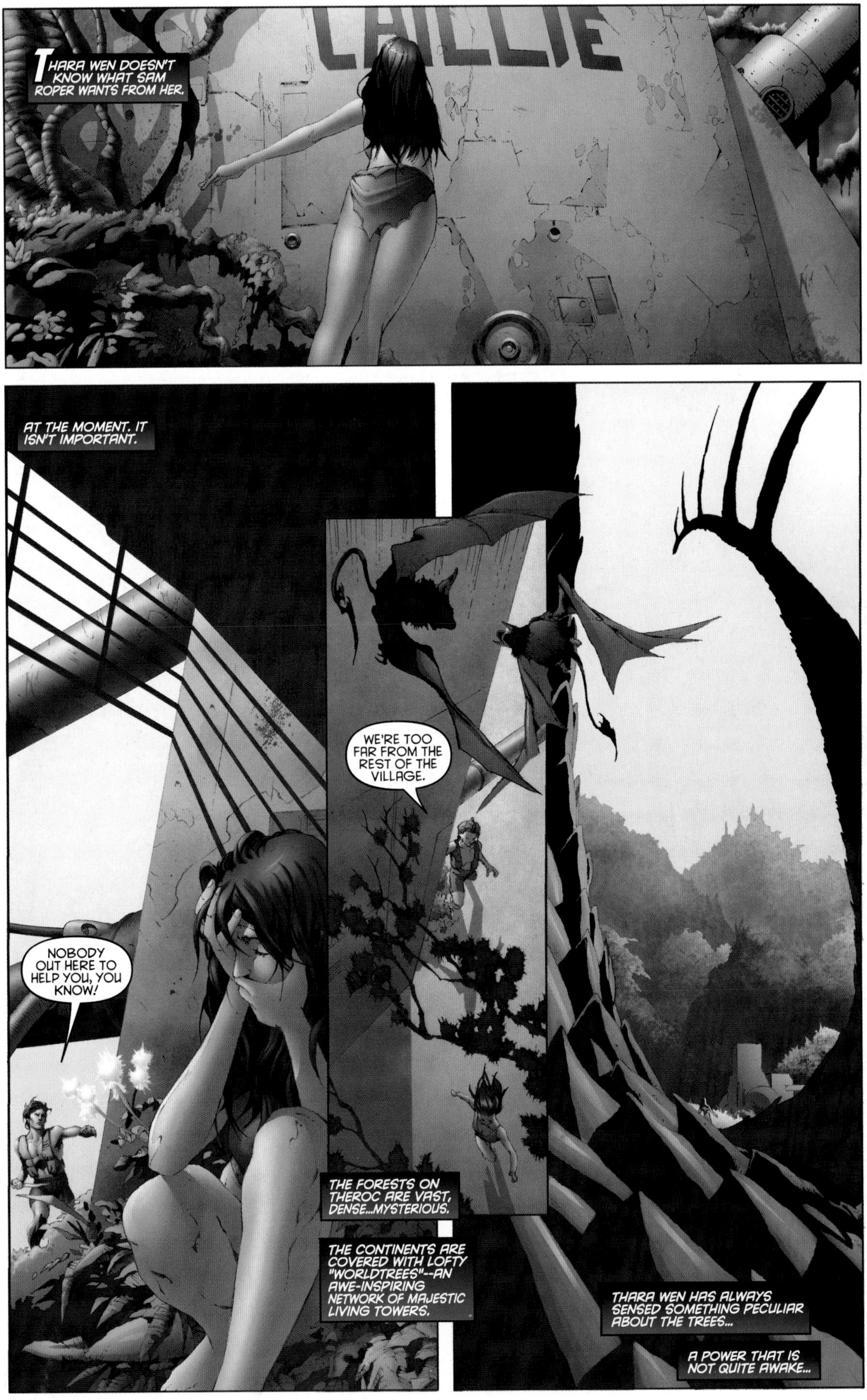
LAILLIE
THARA WEN DOESN'T KNOW WHAT SAM ROPER WANTS FROM HER.
AT THE MOMENT. IT ISN'T IMPORTANT.
NOBODY OUT HERE TO HELP YOU, YOU KNOW!
WE'RE TOO FAR FROM THE REST OF THE VILLAGE.
THE FORESTS ON THEROC ARE VAST, DENSE...MYSTERIOUS.
THE CONTINENTS ARE COVERED WITH LOFTY "WORLDTREES"--AN AWE-INSPIRING NETWORK OF MAJESTIC LIVING TOWERS.
THARA WEN HAS ALWAYS SENSED SOMETHING PECULIAR ABOUT THE TREES...
A POWER THAT IS NOT QUITE AWAKE...

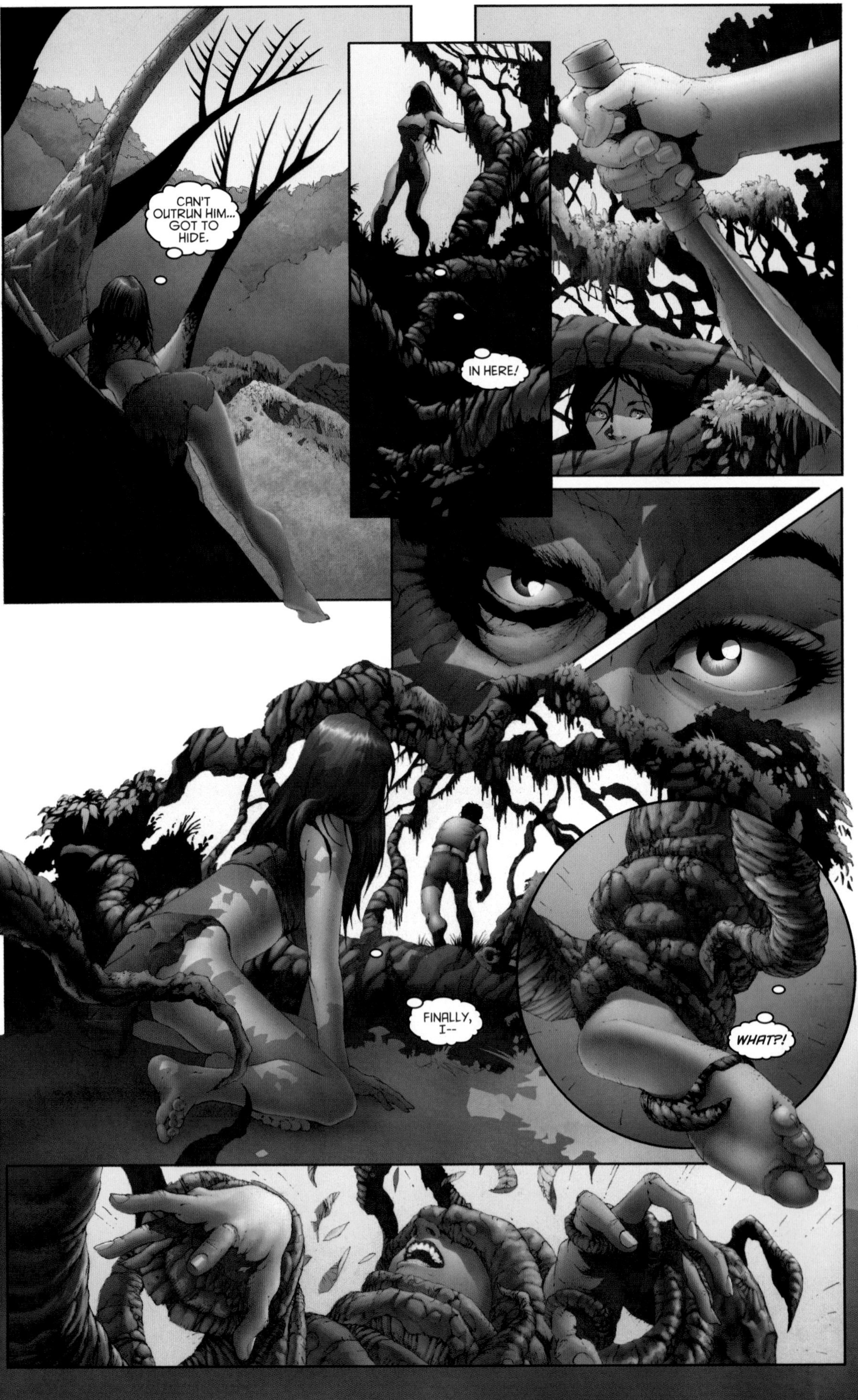
CAN'T OUTRUN HIM... GOT TO HIDE.
IN HERE!
FINALLY, I--
WHAT?!

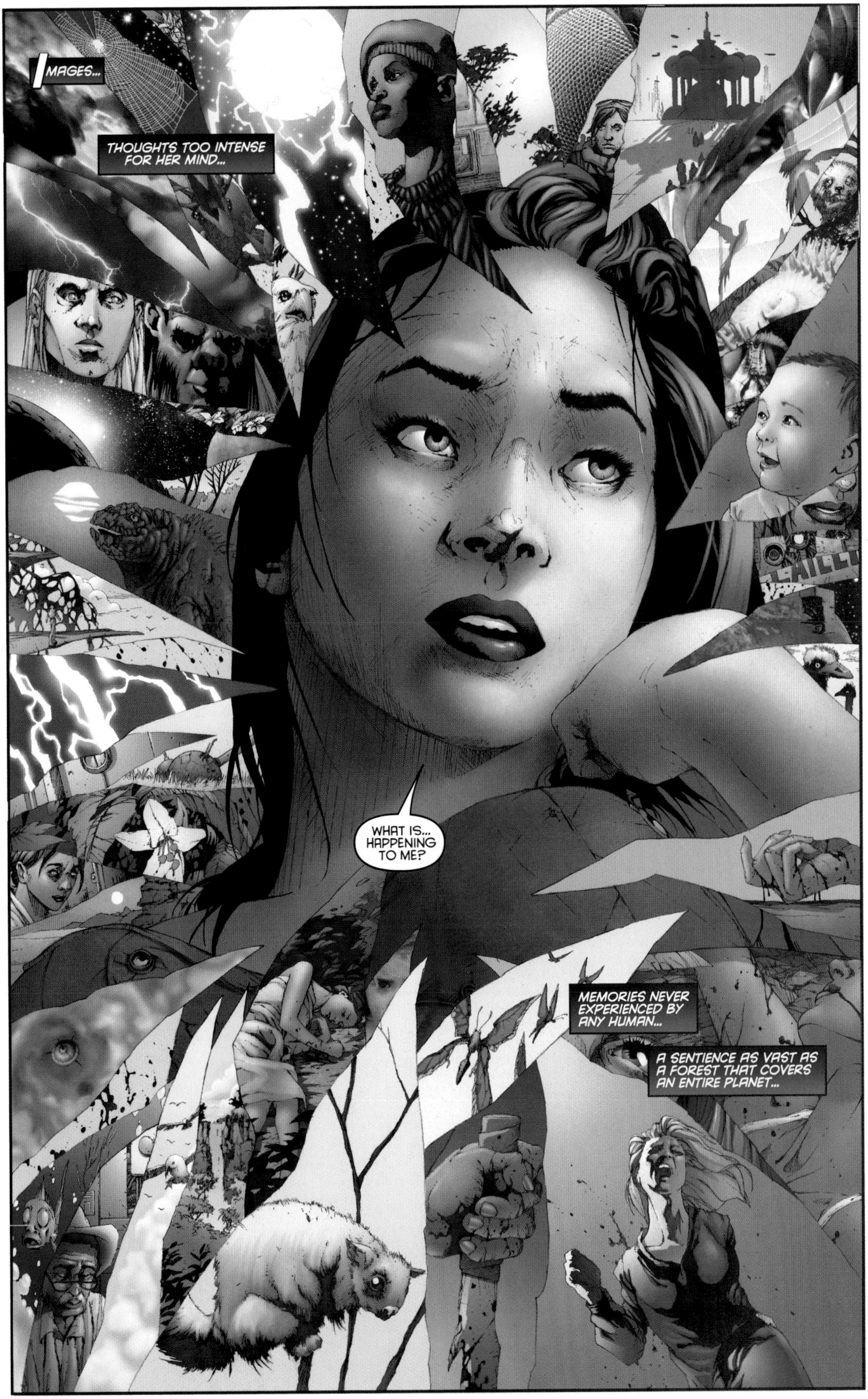
IMAGES...
THOUGHTS TOO INTENSE FOR HER MIND...
WHAT IS... HAPPENING TO ME?
MEMORIES NEVER EXPERIENCED BY ANY HUMAN...
A SENTIENCE AS VAST AS A FOREST THAT COVERS AN ENTIRE PLANET...

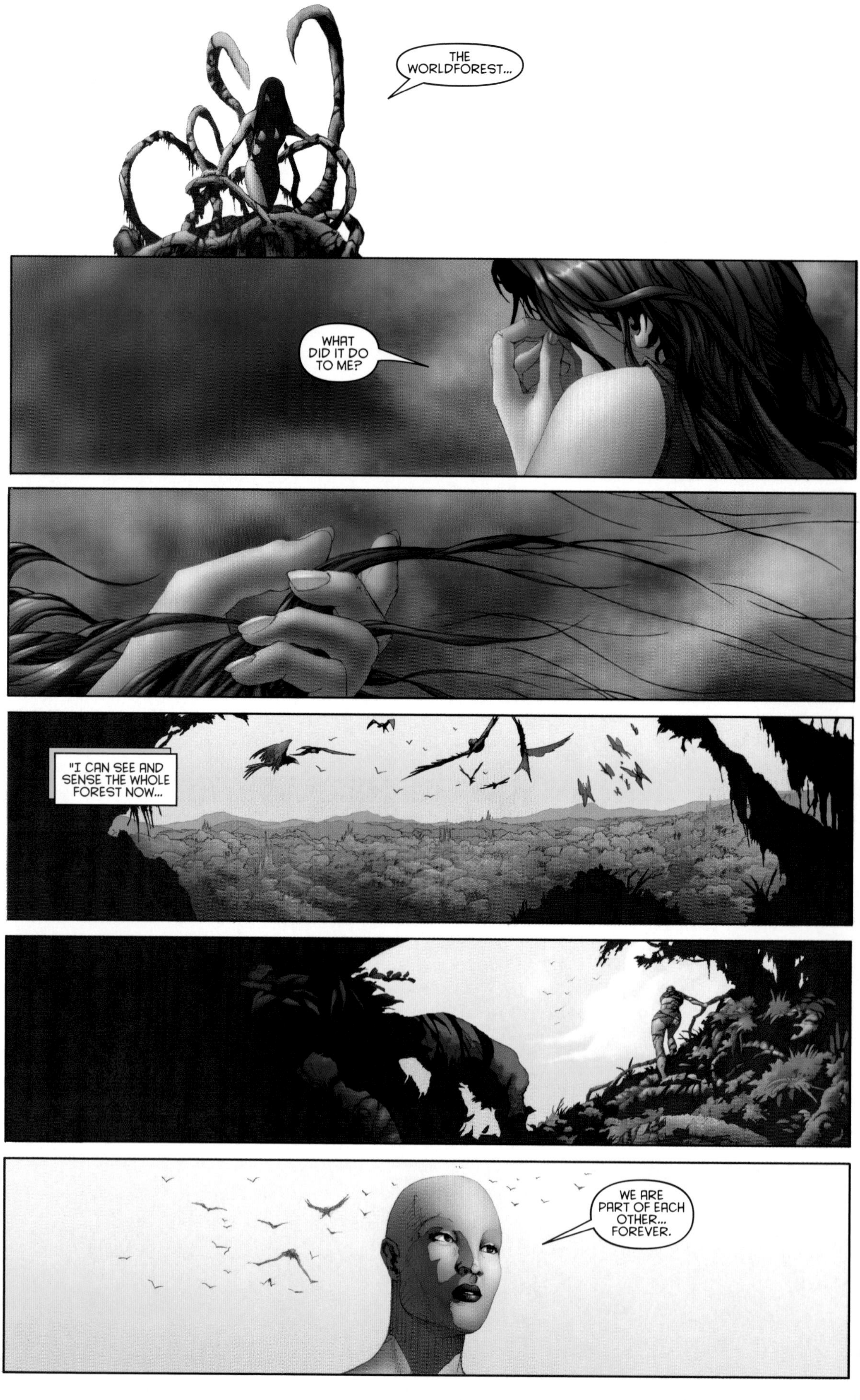
THE WORLDFOREST...
WHAT DID IT DO TO ME?
"I CAN SEE AND SENSE THE WHOLE FOREST NOW...
WE ARE PART OF EACH OTHER... FOREVER.

EARTH

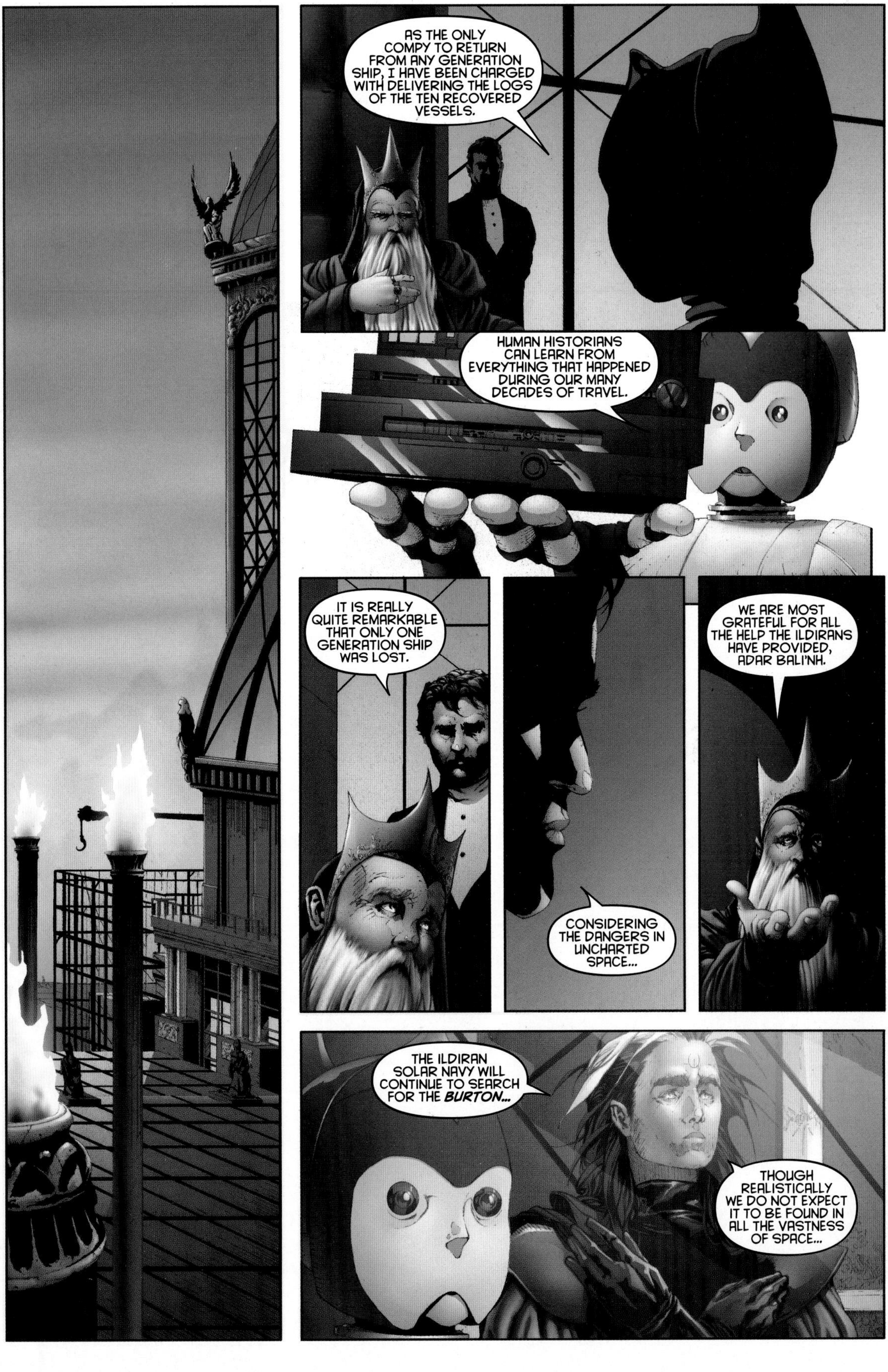
AS THE ONLY COMPY TO RETURN FROM ANY GENERATION SHIP, I HAVE BEEN CHARGED WITH DELIVERING THE LOGS OF THE TEN RECOVERED VESSELS.
HUMAN HISTORIANS CAN LEARN FROM EVERYTHING THAT HAPPENED DURING OUR MANY DECADES OF TRAVEL.
IT IS REALLY QUITE REMARKABLE THAT ONLY ONE GENERATION SHIP WAS LOST.
CONSIDERING THE DANGERS IN UNCHARTED SPACE...
WE ARE MOST GRATEFUL FOR ALL THE HELP THE ILDIRANS HAVE PROVIDED, ADAR BALI'NH.
THE ILDIRAN SOLAR NAVY WILL CONTINUE TO SEARCH FOR THE *BURTON*...
THOUGH REALISTICALLY WE DO NOT EXPECT IT TO BE FOUND IN ALL THE VASTNESS OF SPACE...

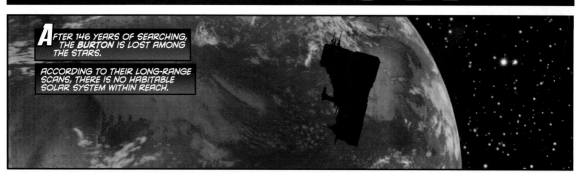

AFTER 146 YEARS OF SEARCHING, THE **BURTON** IS LOST AMONG THE STARS.

ACCORDING TO THEIR LONG-RANGE SCANS, THERE IS NO HABITABLE SOLAR SYSTEM WITHIN REACH.

THE **BURTON** HAS JUST PASSED THROUGH A DAMAGING ION STORM. SYSTEMS ARE BEGINNING TO FAIL, RESOURCES ARE DEPLETED...

...AND HOPE IS AT ITS FRAGILE END.

CHRYSTA LOGAN IS THE **BURTON'S** 21ST CAPTAIN. SHE HAS BEEN IN COMMAND FOR ONLY 4 YEARS... AND THINGS KEEP GETTING WORSE.

A CENTURY AGO, THEIR COMPY WAS DESTROYED IN AN ENGINE ACCIDENT, AND THE PEOPLE HAVE BEEN WITHOUT AN ANCHOR OR A TEACHER. SEVERAL PREVIOUS CAPTAINS WERE ASSASSINATED OR FORCED TO RESIGN.

SPIRITS ARE LOW, AND EMOTIONS RUN HIGH. NO ONE CAN CONTROL THE SHEER EMPTINESS OF SPACE...

A CAPTAIN USUALLY GETS A LITTLE MORE RESPECT THAN THIS.

NO, I DIDN'T THINK YOU'D LISTEN TO REASON.

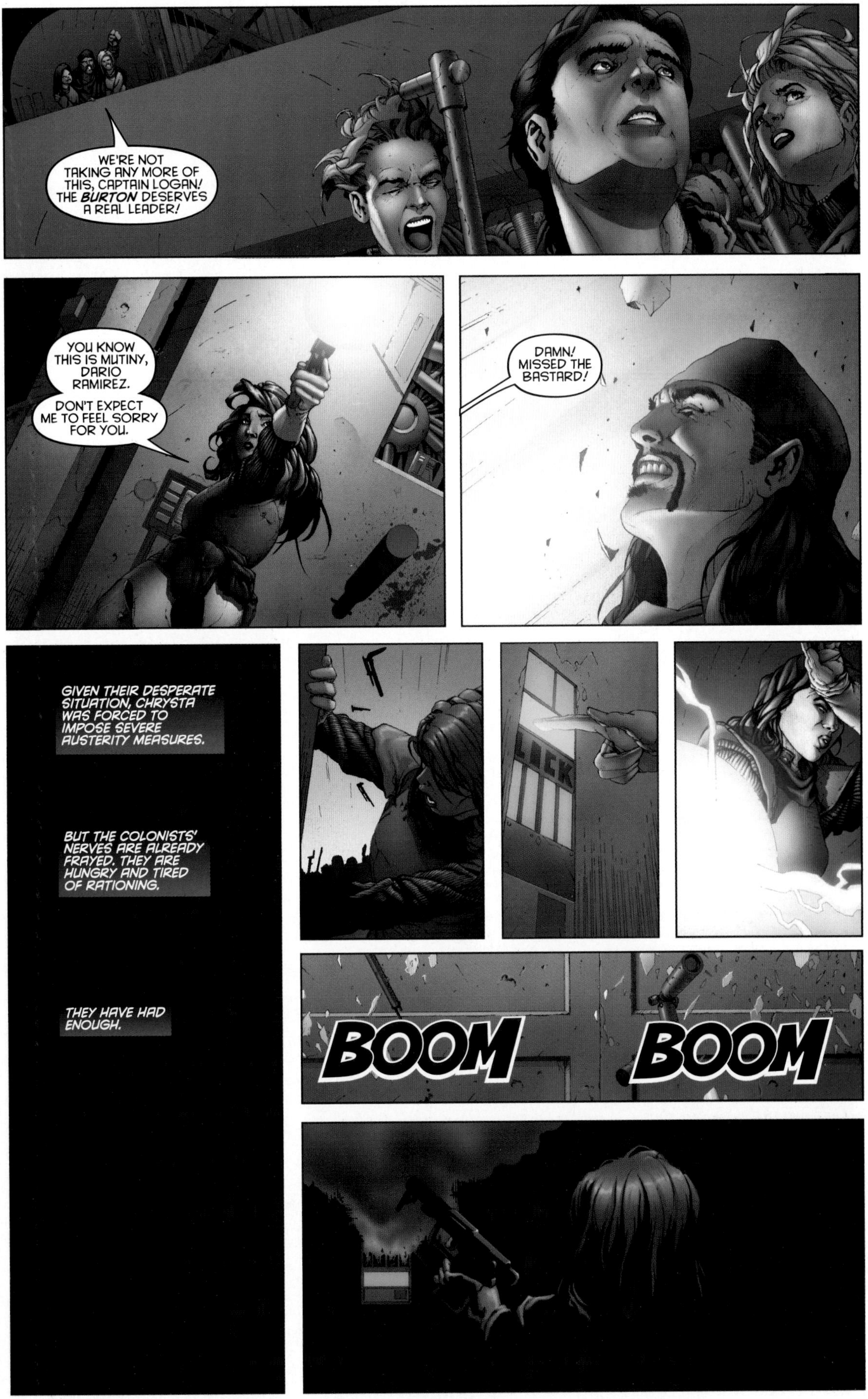
WE'RE NOT TAKING ANY MORE OF THIS, CAPTAIN LOGAN! THE BURTON DESERVES A REAL LEADER!
YOU KNOW THIS IS MUTINY, DARIO RAMIREZ.
DON'T EXPECT ME TO FEEL SORRY FOR YOU.
DAMN! MISSED THE BASTARD!
GIVEN THEIR DESPERATE SITUATION, CHRYSTA WAS FORCED TO IMPOSE SEVERE AUSTERITY MEASURES.
BUT THE COLONISTS' NERVES ARE ALREADY FRAYED. THEY ARE HUNGRY AND TIRED OF RATIONING.
THEY HAVE HAD ENOUGH.
BOOM
BOOM

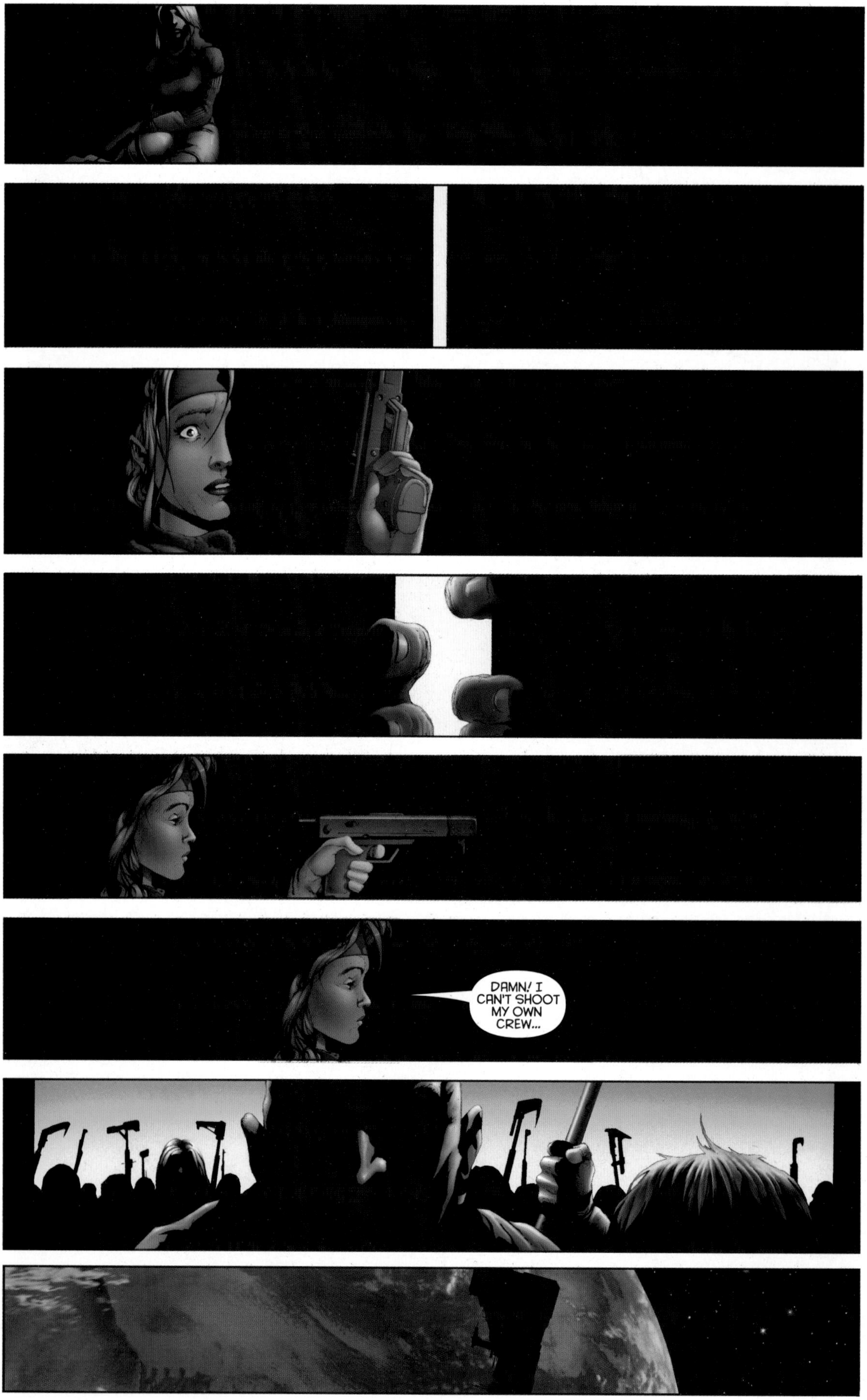
DAMN! I CAN'T SHOOT MY OWN CREW...

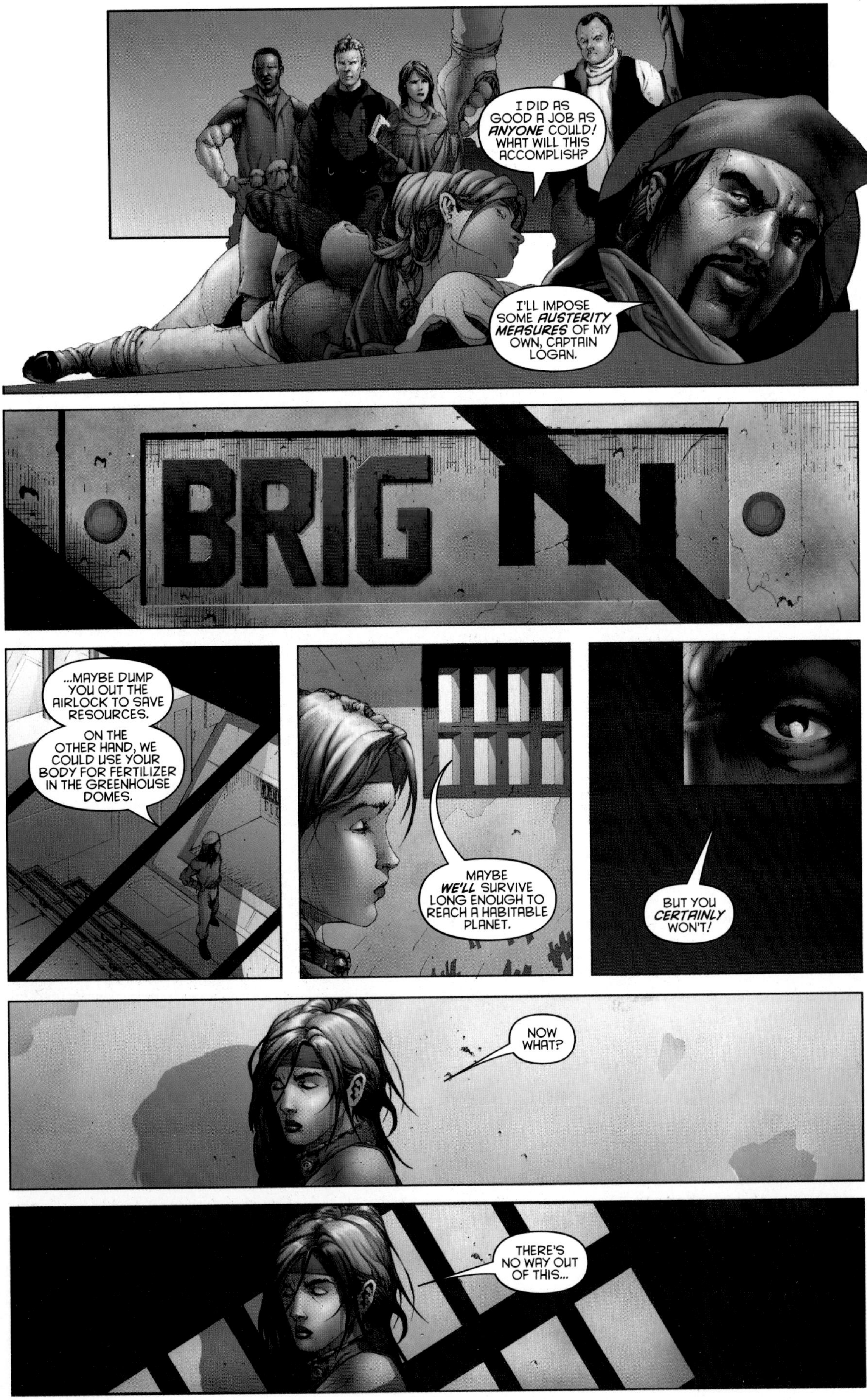
I DID AS GOOD A JOB AS ANYONE COULD! WHAT WILL THIS ACCOMPLISH?
I'LL IMPOSE SOME AUSTERITY MEASURES OF MY OWN, CAPTAIN LOGAN.
BRIG IN
...MAYBE DUMP YOU OUT THE AIRLOCK TO SAVE RESOURCES.
ON THE OTHER HAND, WE COULD USE YOUR BODY FOR FERTILIZER IN THE GREENHOUSE DOMES.
MAYBE WE'LL SURVIVE LONG ENOUGH TO REACH A HABITABLE PLANET.
BUT YOU CERTAINLY WON'T!
NOW WHAT?
THERE'S NO WAY OUT OF THIS...

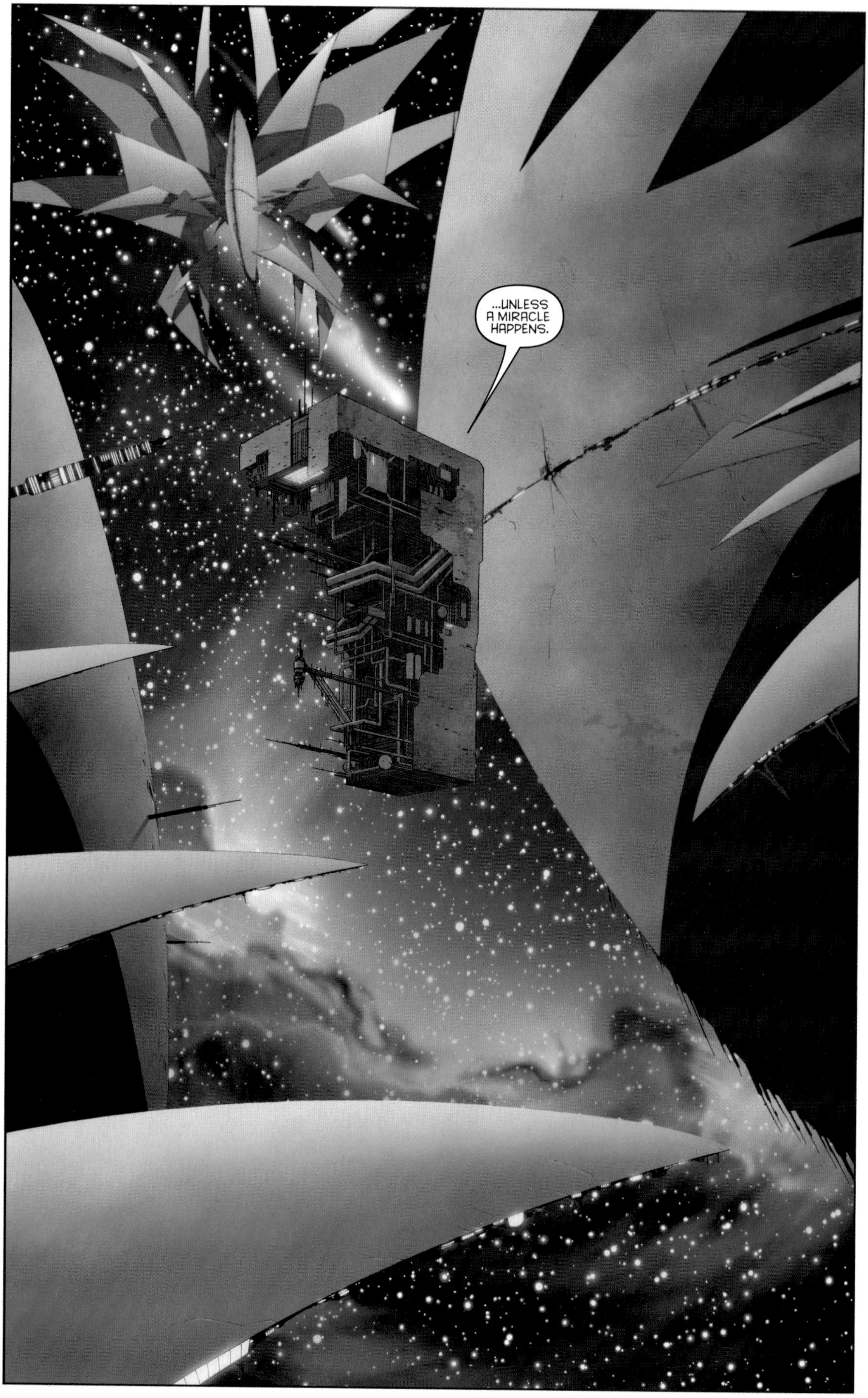
...UNLESS A MIRACLE HAPPENS.

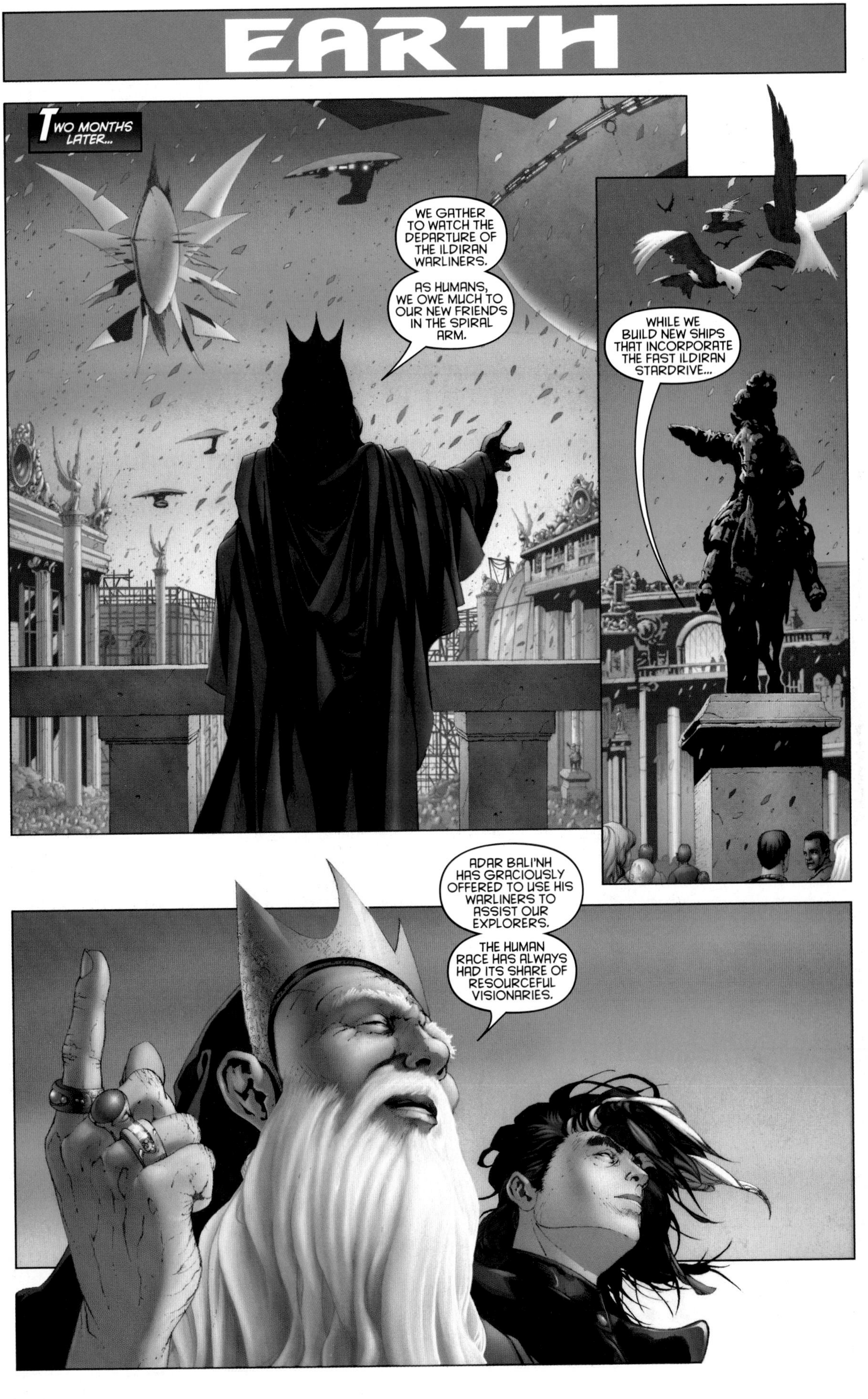
EARTH
TWO MONTHS LATER...
WE GATHER TO WATCH THE DEPARTURE OF THE ILDIRAN WARLINERS.
AS HUMANS, WE OWE MUCH TO OUR NEW FRIENDS IN THE SPIRAL ARM.
WHILE WE BUILD NEW SHIPS THAT INCORPORATE THE FAST ILDIRAN STARDRIVE...
ADAR BALI'NH HAS GRACIOUSLY OFFERED TO USE HIS WARLINERS TO ASSIST OUR EXPLORERS.
THE HUMAN RACE HAS ALWAYS HAD ITS SHARE OF RESOURCEFUL VISIONARIES.

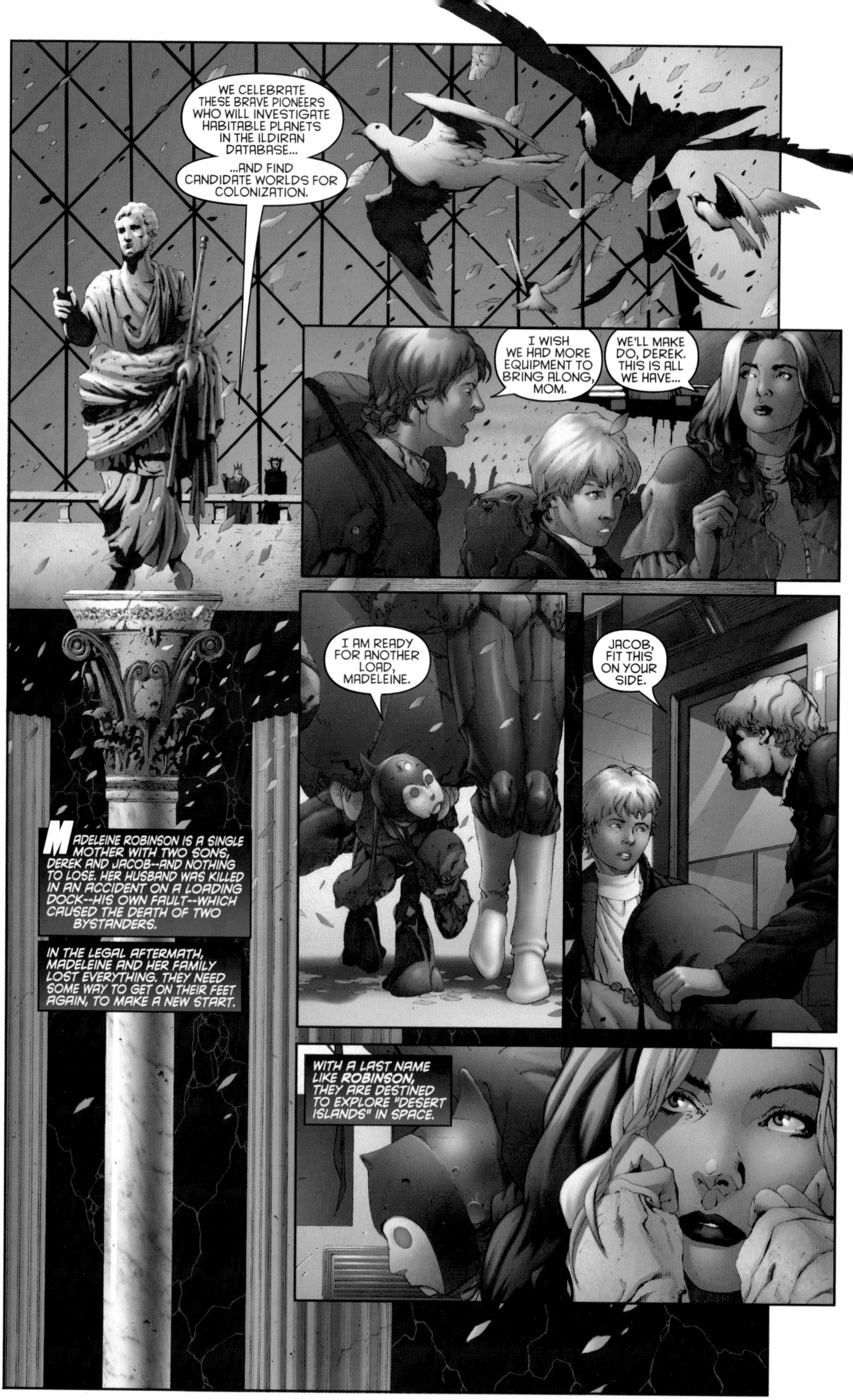
WE CELEBRATE THESE BRAVE PIONEERS WHO WILL INVESTIGATE HABITABLE PLANETS IN THE ILDIRAN DATABASE...
...AND FIND CANDIDATE WORLDS FOR COLONIZATION.
I WISH WE HAD MORE EQUIPMENT TO BRING ALONG, MOM.
WE'LL MAKE DO, DEREK. THIS IS ALL WE HAVE...
MADELEINE ROBINSON IS A SINGLE MOTHER WITH TWO SONS, DEREK AND JACOB--AND NOTHING TO LOSE. HER HUSBAND WAS KILLED IN AN ACCIDENT ON A LOADING DOCK--HIS OWN FAULT--WHICH CAUSED THE DEATH OF TWO BYSTANDERS.
IN THE LEGAL AFTERMATH, MADELEINE AND HER FAMILY LOST EVERYTHING. THEY NEED SOME WAY TO GET ON THEIR FEET AGAIN, TO MAKE A NEW START.
I AM READY FOR ANOTHER LOAD, MADELEINE.
JACOB, FIT THIS ON YOUR SIDE.
WITH A LAST NAME LIKE ROBINSON, THEY ARE DESTINED TO EXPLORE "DESERT ISLANDS" IN SPACE.

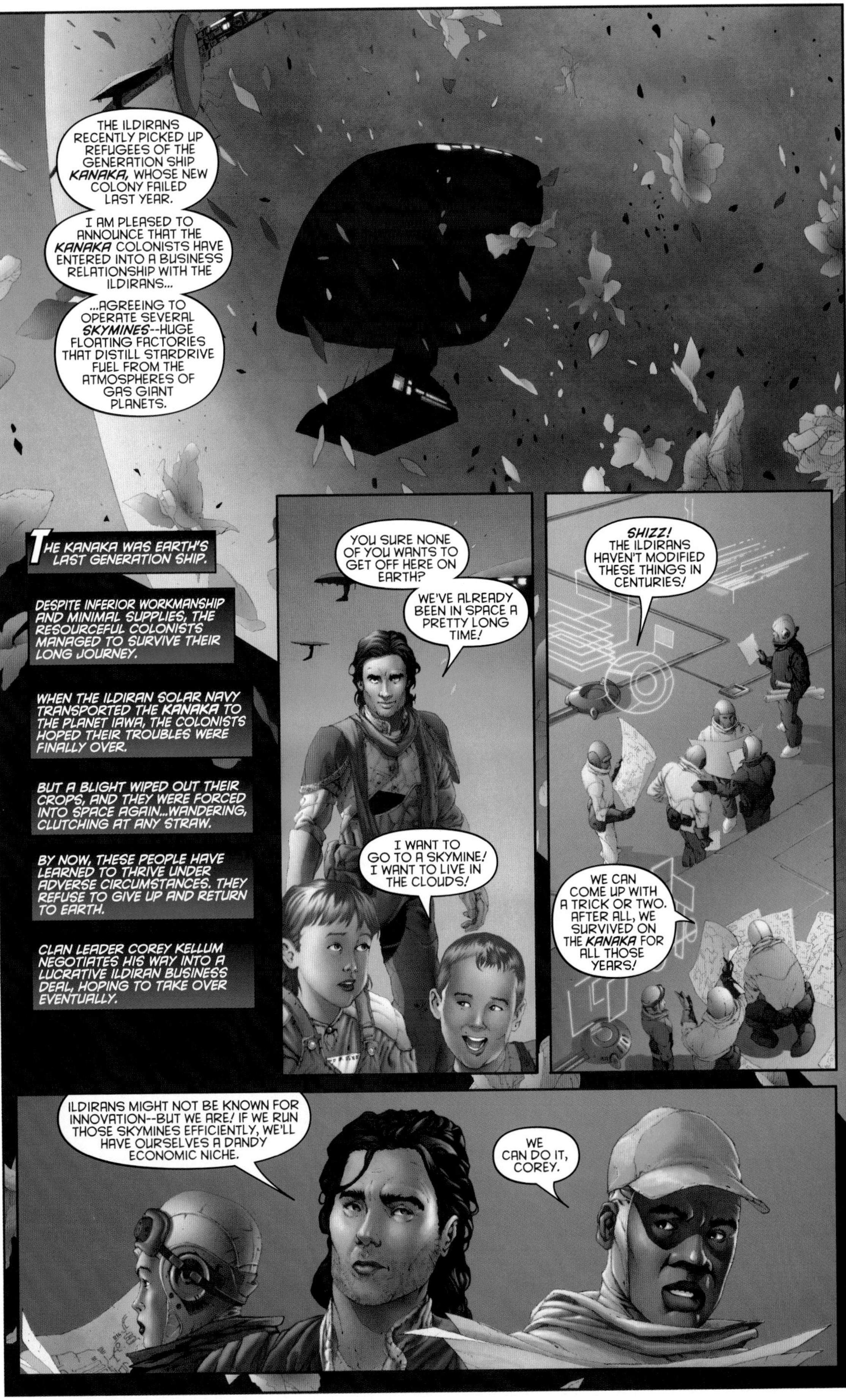

THE ILDIRANS RECENTLY PICKED UP REFUGEES OF THE GENERATION SHIP *KANAKA,* WHOSE NEW COLONY FAILED LAST YEAR.
I AM PLEASED TO ANNOUNCE THAT THE *KANAKA* COLONISTS HAVE ENTERED INTO A BUSINESS RELATIONSHIP WITH THE ILDIRANS...
...AGREEING TO OPERATE SEVERAL *SKYMINES*--HUGE FLOATING FACTORIES THAT DISTILL STARDRIVE FUEL FROM THE ATMOSPHERES OF GAS GIANT PLANETS.
THE KANAKA WAS EARTH'S LAST GENERATION SHIP.
DESPITE INFERIOR WORKMANSHIP AND MINIMAL SUPPLIES, THE RESOURCEFUL COLONISTS MANAGED TO SURVIVE THEIR LONG JOURNEY.
WHEN THE ILDIRAN SOLAR NAVY TRANSPORTED THE *KANAKA* TO THE PLANET IAWA, THE COLONISTS HOPED THEIR TROUBLES WERE FINALLY OVER.
BUT A BLIGHT WIPED OUT THEIR CROPS, AND THEY WERE FORCED INTO SPACE AGAIN...WANDERING, CLUTCHING AT ANY STRAW.
BY NOW, THESE PEOPLE HAVE LEARNED TO THRIVE UNDER ADVERSE CIRCUMSTANCES. THEY REFUSE TO GIVE UP AND RETURN TO EARTH.
CLAN LEADER COREY KELLUM NEGOTIATES HIS WAY INTO A LUCRATIVE ILDIRAN BUSINESS DEAL, HOPING TO TAKE OVER EVENTUALLY.
YOU SURE NONE OF YOU WANTS TO GET OFF HERE ON EARTH?
WE'VE ALREADY BEEN IN SPACE A PRETTY LONG TIME!
I WANT TO GO TO A SKYMINE! I WANT TO LIVE IN THE CLOUDS!
SHIZZ! THE ILDIRANS HAVEN'T MODIFIED THESE THINGS IN CENTURIES!
WE CAN COME UP WITH A TRICK OR TWO. AFTER ALL, WE SURVIVED ON THE *KANAKA* FOR ALL THOSE YEARS!
ILDIRANS MIGHT NOT BE KNOWN FOR INNOVATION--BUT WE ARE! IF WE RUN THOSE SKYMINES EFFICIENTLY, WE'LL HAVE OURSELVES A DANDY ECONOMIC NICHE.
WE CAN DO IT, COREY.

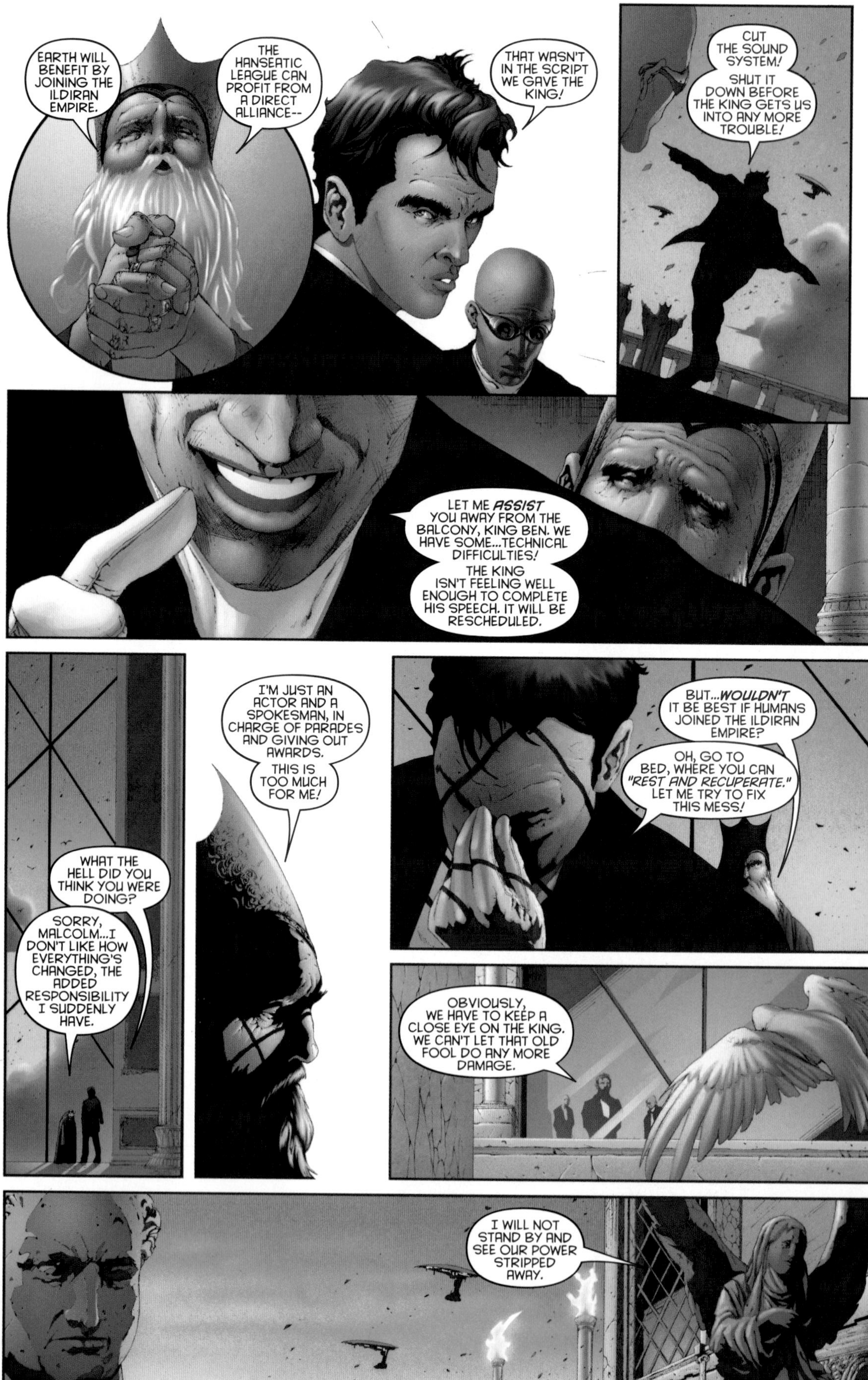
EARTH WILL BENEFIT BY JOINING THE ILDIRAN EMPIRE.
THE HANSEATIC LEAGUE CAN PROFIT FROM A DIRECT ALLIANCE--
THAT WASN'T IN THE SCRIPT WE GAVE THE KING!
CUT THE SOUND SYSTEM! SHUT IT DOWN BEFORE THE KING GETS US INTO ANY MORE TROUBLE!
LET ME ASSIST YOU AWAY FROM THE BALCONY, KING BEN. WE HAVE SOME...TECHNICAL DIFFICULTIES!
THE KING ISN'T FEELING WELL ENOUGH TO COMPLETE HIS SPEECH. IT WILL BE RESCHEDULED.
WHAT THE HELL DID YOU THINK YOU WERE DOING?
SORRY, MALCOLM...I DON'T LIKE HOW EVERYTHING'S CHANGED, THE ADDED RESPONSIBILITY I SUDDENLY HAVE.
I'M JUST AN ACTOR AND A SPOKESMAN, IN CHARGE OF PARADES AND GIVING OUT AWARDS.
THIS IS TOO MUCH FOR ME!
BUT...WOULDN'T IT BE BEST IF HUMANS JOINED THE ILDIRAN EMPIRE?
OH, GO TO BED, WHERE YOU CAN "REST AND RECUPERATE." LET ME TRY TO FIX THIS MESS!
OBVIOUSLY, WE HAVE TO KEEP A CLOSE EYE ON THE KING. WE CAN'T LET THAT OLD FOOL DO ANY MORE DAMAGE.
I WILL NOT STAND BY AND SEE OUR POWER STRIPPED AWAY.

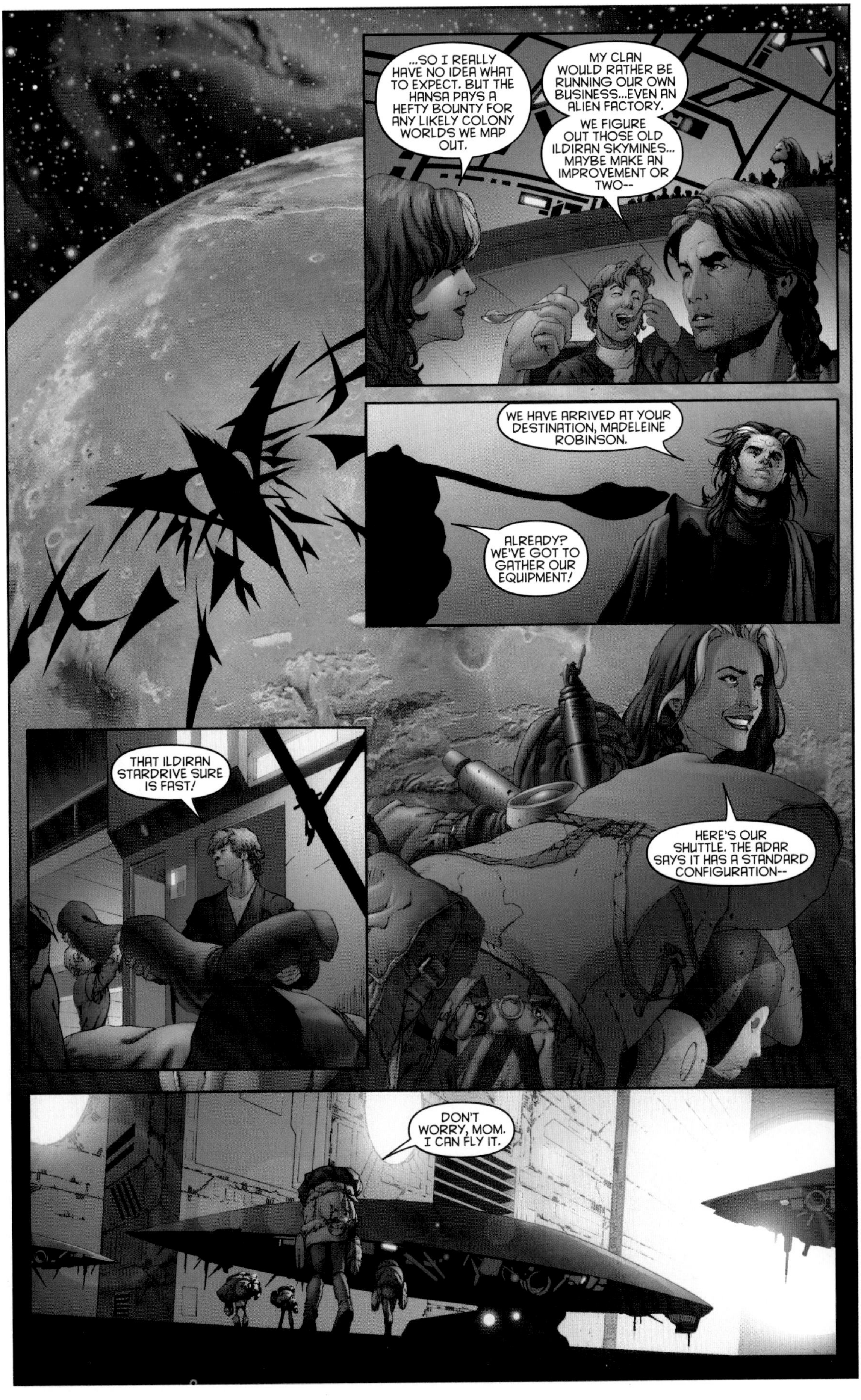
...SO I REALLY HAVE NO IDEA WHAT TO EXPECT. BUT THE HANSA PAYS A HEFTY BOUNTY FOR ANY LIKELY COLONY WORLDS WE MAP OUT.
MY CLAN WOULD RATHER BE RUNNING OUR OWN BUSINESS...EVEN AN ALIEN FACTORY.
WE FIGURE OUT THOSE OLD ILDIRAN SKYMINES... MAYBE MAKE AN IMPROVEMENT OR TWO--
WE HAVE ARRIVED AT YOUR DESTINATION, MADELEINE ROBINSON.
ALREADY? WE'VE GOT TO GATHER OUR EQUIPMENT!
THAT ILDIRAN STARDRIVE SURE IS FAST!
HERE'S OUR SHUTTLE. THE ADAR SAYS IT HAS A STANDARD CONFIGURATION--
DON'T WORRY, MOM. I CAN FLY IT.

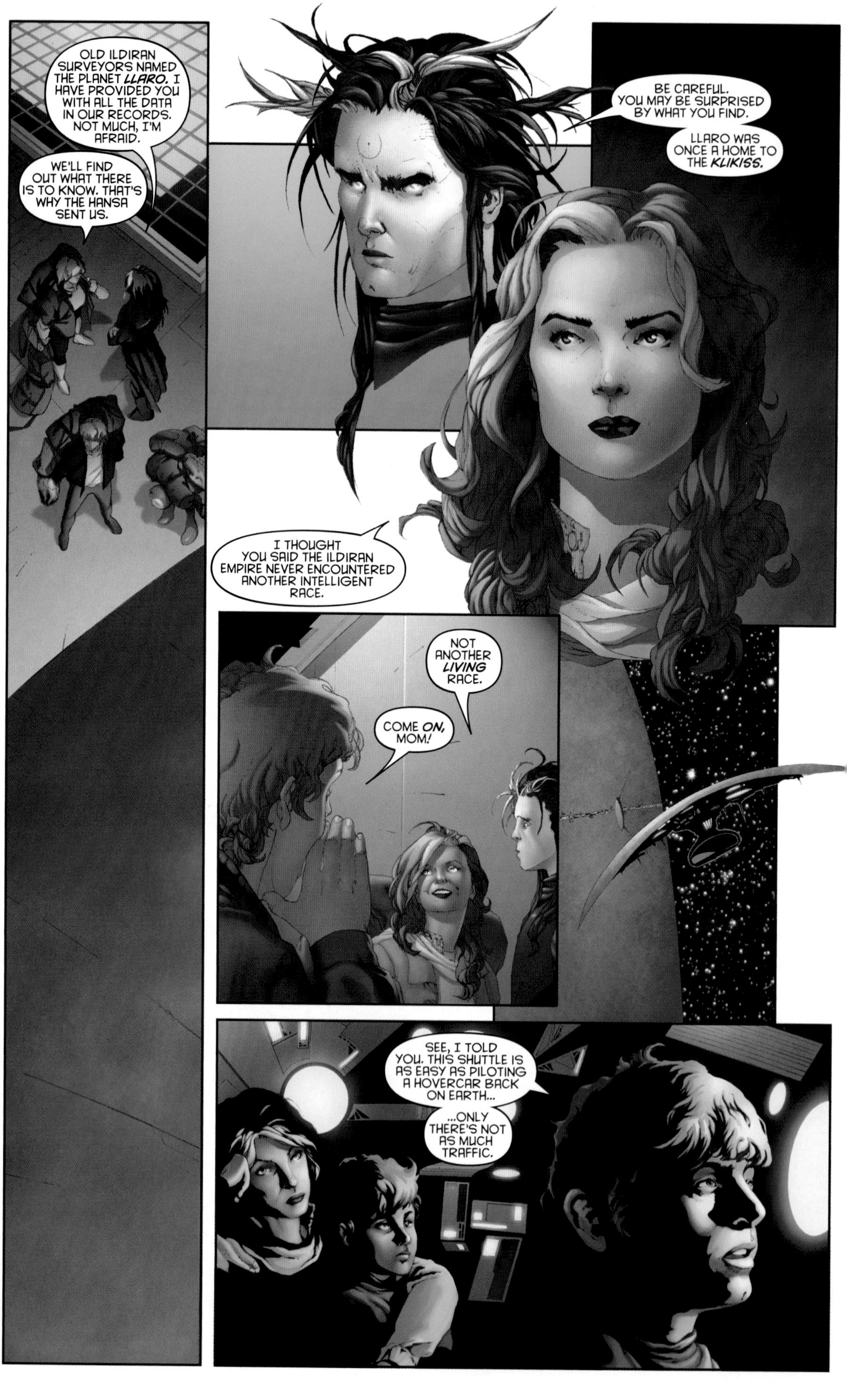
OLD ILDIRAN SURVEYORS NAMED THE PLANET LLARO. I HAVE PROVIDED YOU WITH ALL THE DATA IN OUR RECORDS. NOT MUCH, I'M AFRAID.
WE'LL FIND OUT WHAT THERE IS TO KNOW. THAT'S WHY THE HANSA SENT US.
BE CAREFUL. YOU MAY BE SURPRISED BY WHAT YOU FIND.
LLARO WAS ONCE A HOME TO THE KLIKISS.
I THOUGHT YOU SAID THE ILDIRAN EMPIRE NEVER ENCOUNTERED ANOTHER INTELLIGENT RACE.
NOT ANOTHER LIVING RACE.
COME ON, MOM!
SEE, I TOLD YOU. THIS SHUTTLE IS AS EASY AS PILOTING A HOVERCAR BACK ON EARTH...
...ONLY THERE'S NOT AS MUCH TRAFFIC.

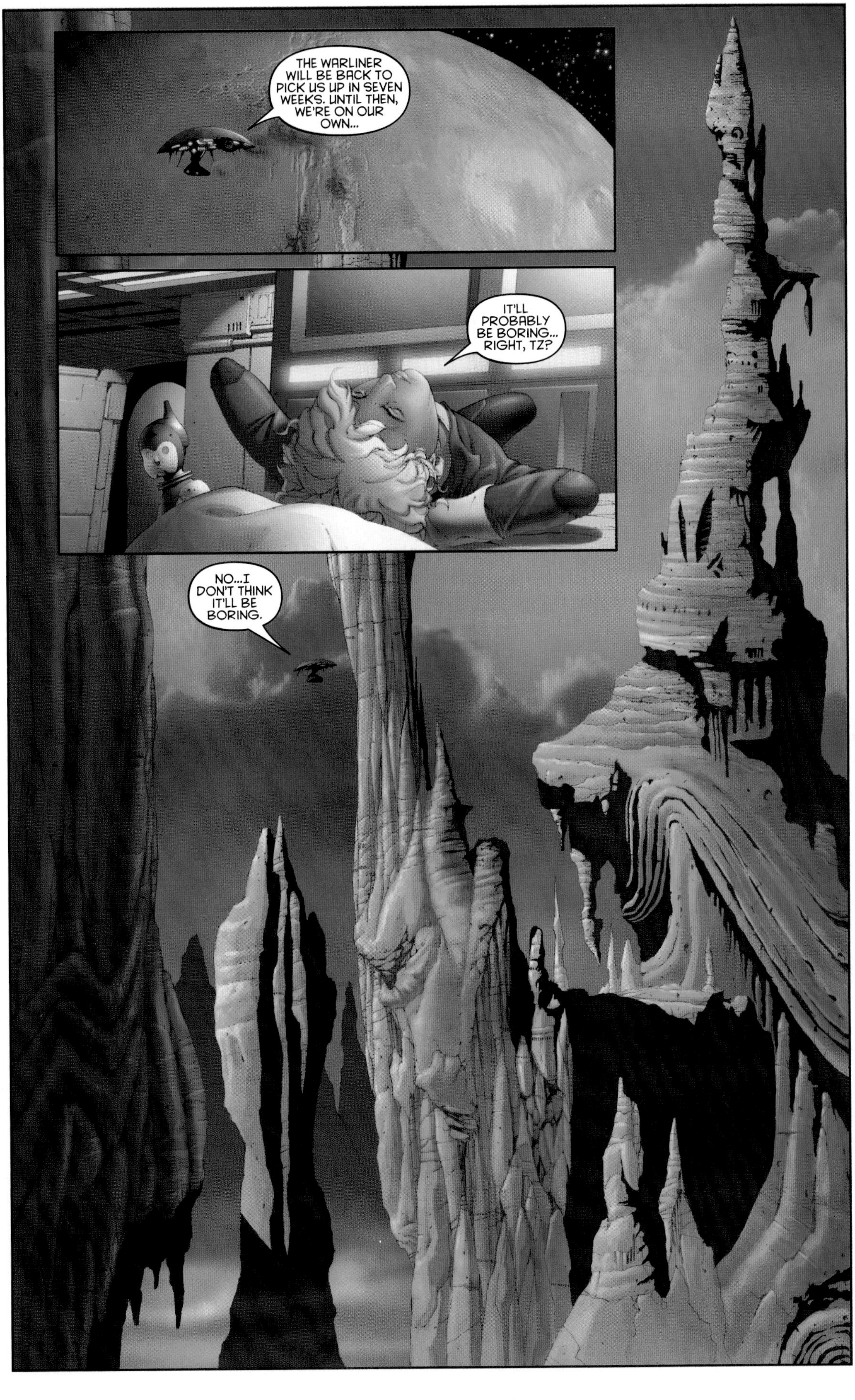

THE WARLINER WILL BE BACK TO PICK US UP IN SEVEN WEEKS. UNTIL THEN, WE'RE ON OUR OWN...
IT'LL PROBABLY BE BORING... RIGHT, TZ?
NO...I DON'T THINK IT'LL BE BORING.

DAYM

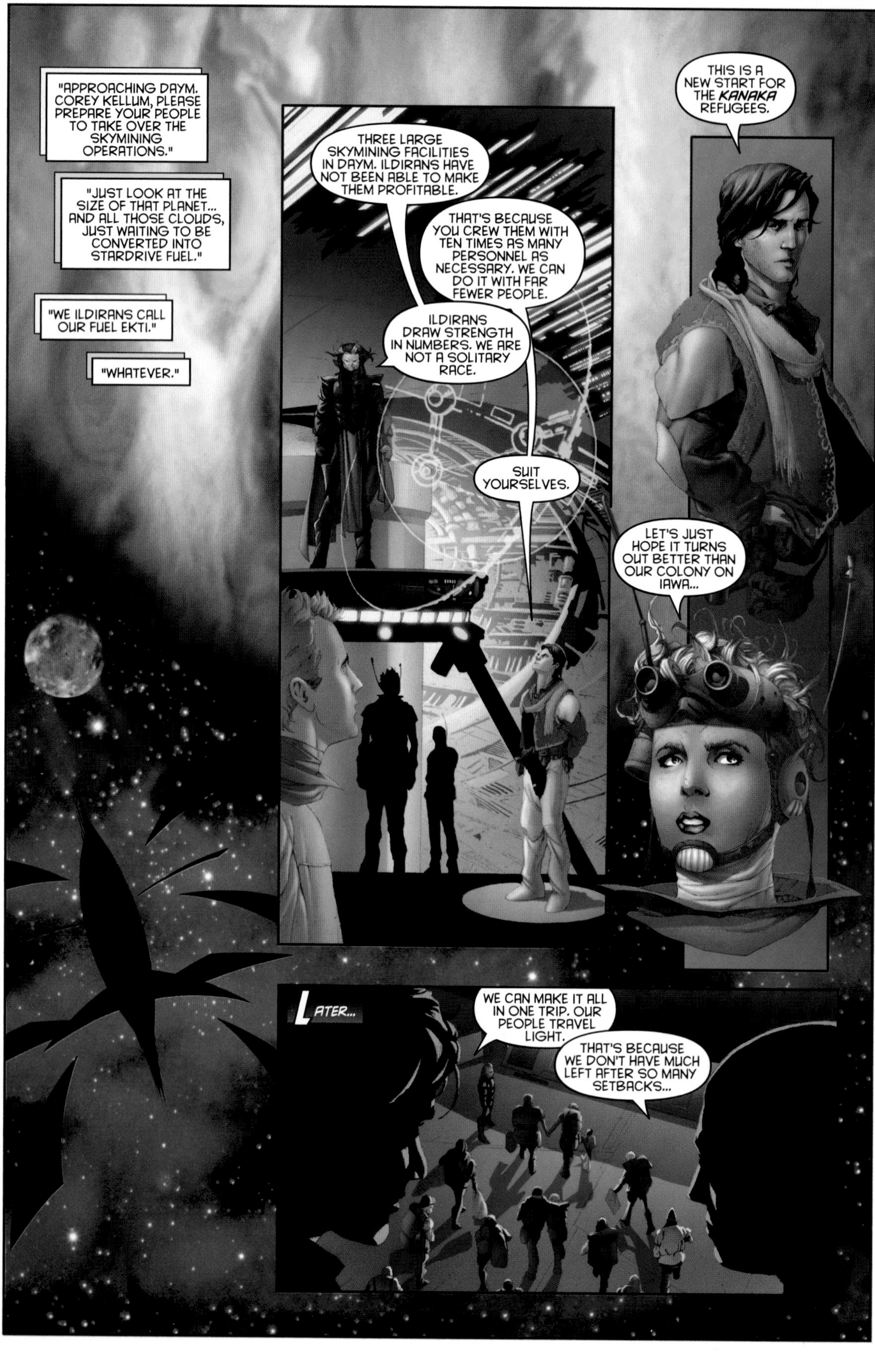
"APPROACHING DAYM. COREY KELLUM, PLEASE PREPARE YOUR PEOPLE TO TAKE OVER THE SKYMINING OPERATIONS."
"JUST LOOK AT THE SIZE OF THAT PLANET... AND ALL THOSE CLOUDS, JUST WAITING TO BE CONVERTED INTO STARDRIVE FUEL."
"WE ILDIRANS CALL OUR FUEL EKTI."
"WHATEVER."
THREE LARGE SKYMINING FACILITIES IN DAYM. ILDIRANS HAVE NOT BEEN ABLE TO MAKE THEM PROFITABLE.
THAT'S BECAUSE YOU CREW THEM WITH TEN TIMES AS MANY PERSONNEL AS NECESSARY. WE CAN DO IT WITH FAR FEWER PEOPLE.
ILDIRANS DRAW STRENGTH IN NUMBERS. WE ARE NOT A SOLITARY RACE.
SUIT YOURSELVES.
THIS IS A NEW START FOR THE *KANAKA* REFUGEES.
LET'S JUST HOPE IT TURNS OUT BETTER THAN OUR COLONY ON IAWA...
LATER...
WE CAN MAKE IT ALL IN ONE TRIP. OUR PEOPLE TRAVEL LIGHT.
THAT'S BECAUSE WE DON'T HAVE MUCH LEFT AFTER SO MANY SETBACKS...

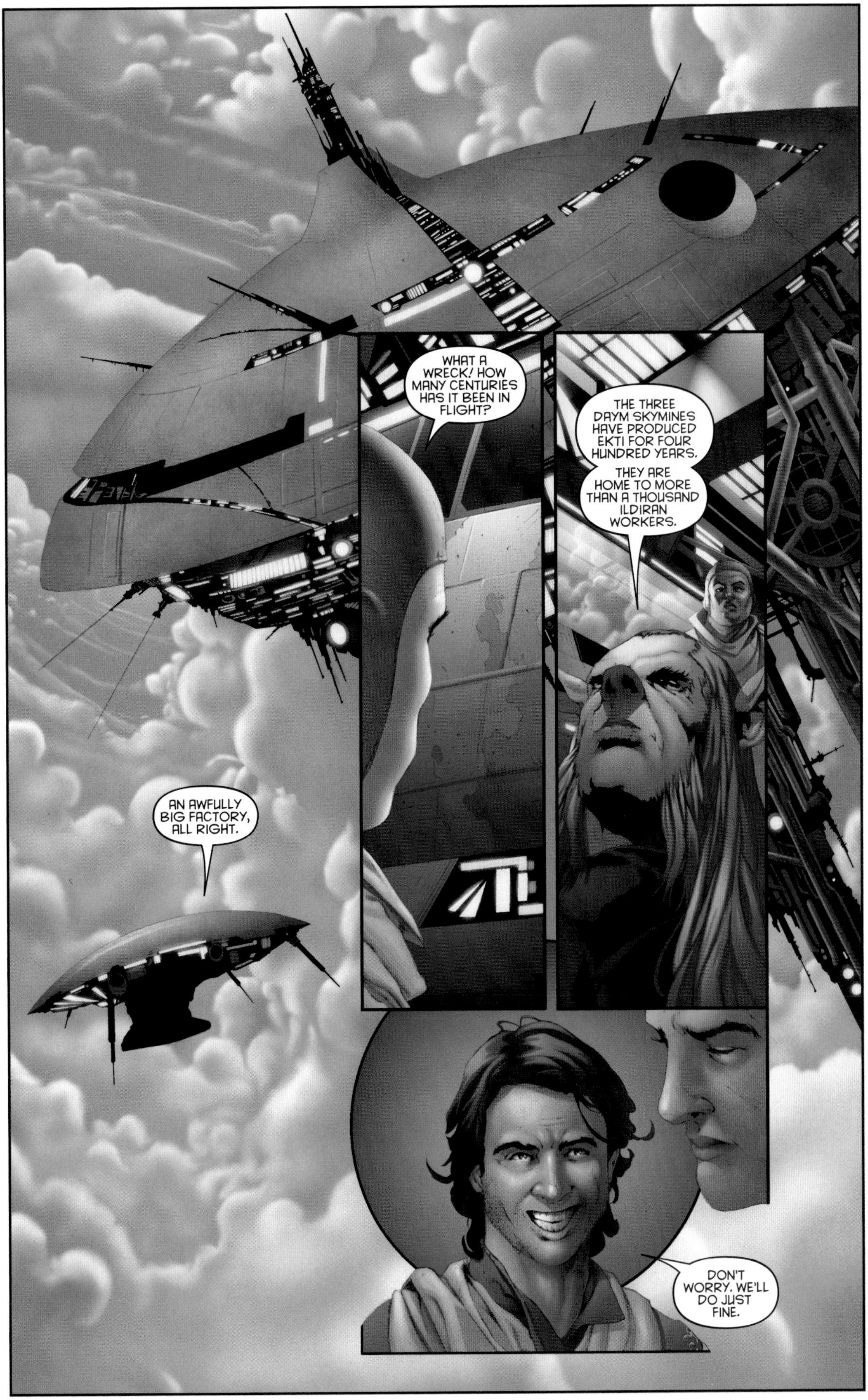
WHAT A WRECK! HOW MANY CENTURIES HAS IT BEEN IN FLIGHT?
THE THREE DAYM SKYMINES HAVE PRODUCED EKTI FOR FOUR HUNDRED YEARS.
THEY ARE HOME TO MORE THAN A THOUSAND ILDIRAN WORKERS.
AN AWFULLY BIG FACTORY, ALL RIGHT.
DON'T WORRY. WE'LL DO JUST FINE.

CAPTAIN KELLUM, WE ARE HAPPY TO CEDE CONTROL OF THIS FACILITY TO HUMAN OPERATORS.

AND WE'RE HAPPY FOR THE OPPORTUNITY, SIR.

"MY PEOPLE HAVEN'T HAD A HOME FOR A LONG TIME.

"THESE SKYMINES AREN'T MUCH DIFFERENT FROM OUR OLD GENERATION SHIP... EXCEPT THIS TIME WE'LL BE MAKING A PROFIT."

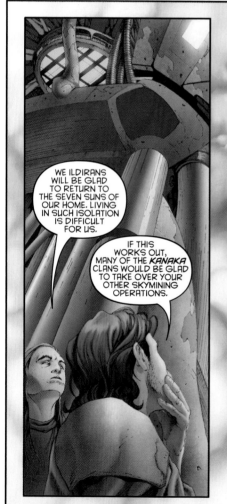

WE ILDIRANS WILL BE GLAD TO RETURN TO THE SEVEN SUNS OF OUR HOME. LIVING IN SUCH ISOLATION IS DIFFICULT FOR US.

IF THIS WORKS OUT, MANY OF THE KANAKA CLANS WOULD BE GLAD TO TAKE OVER YOUR OTHER SKYMINING OPERATIONS.

"...COULD BE THE START OF A WHOLE NEW CAREER FOR US."

DO YOU SUPPOSE THE ILDIRANS HAVE ANY IDEA WHAT A GOLDEN GOOSE THEY'VE JUST GIVEN US?

PROBABLY NOT A CLUE. AND THAT SUITS ME JUST FINE.

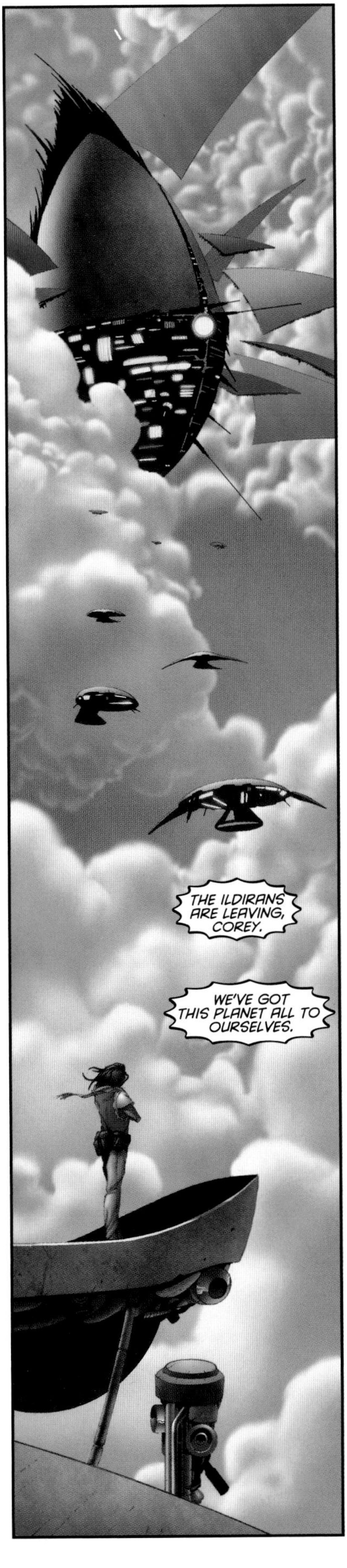
THE ILDIRANS ARE LEAVING, COREY.
WE'VE GOT THIS PLANET ALL TO OURSELVES.
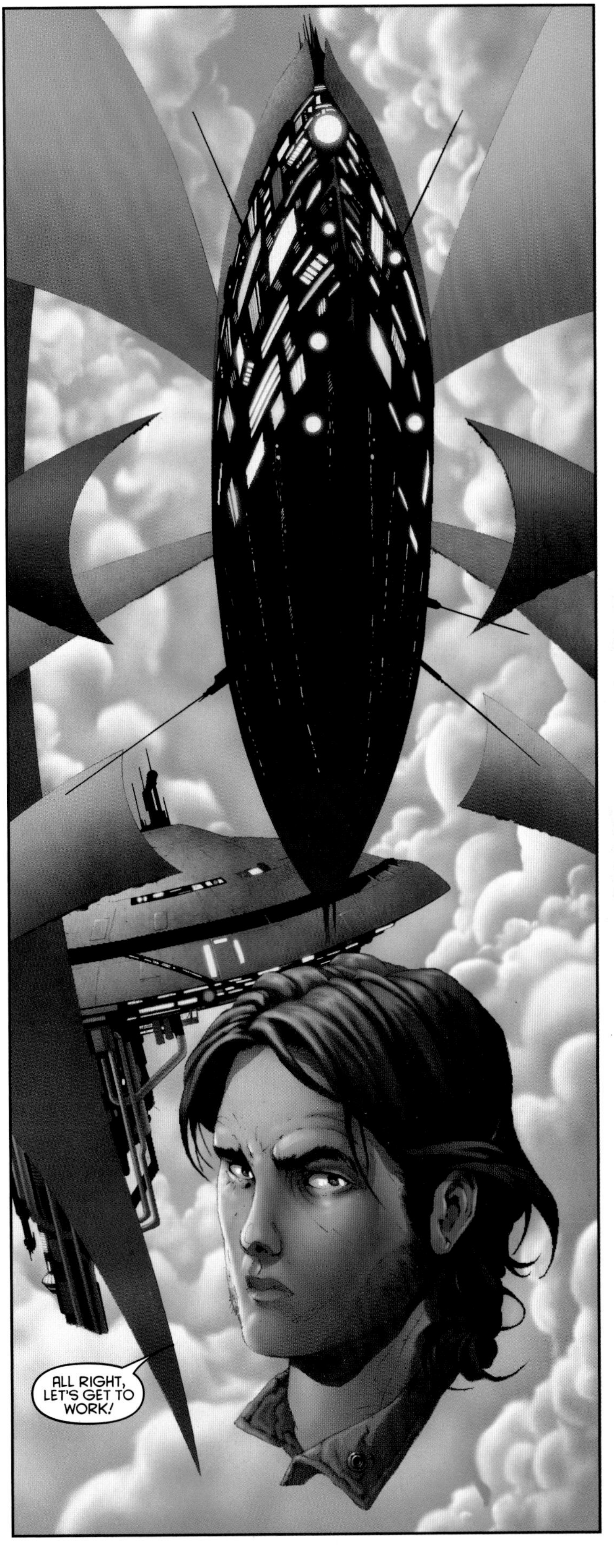
ALL RIGHT, LET'S GET TO WORK!

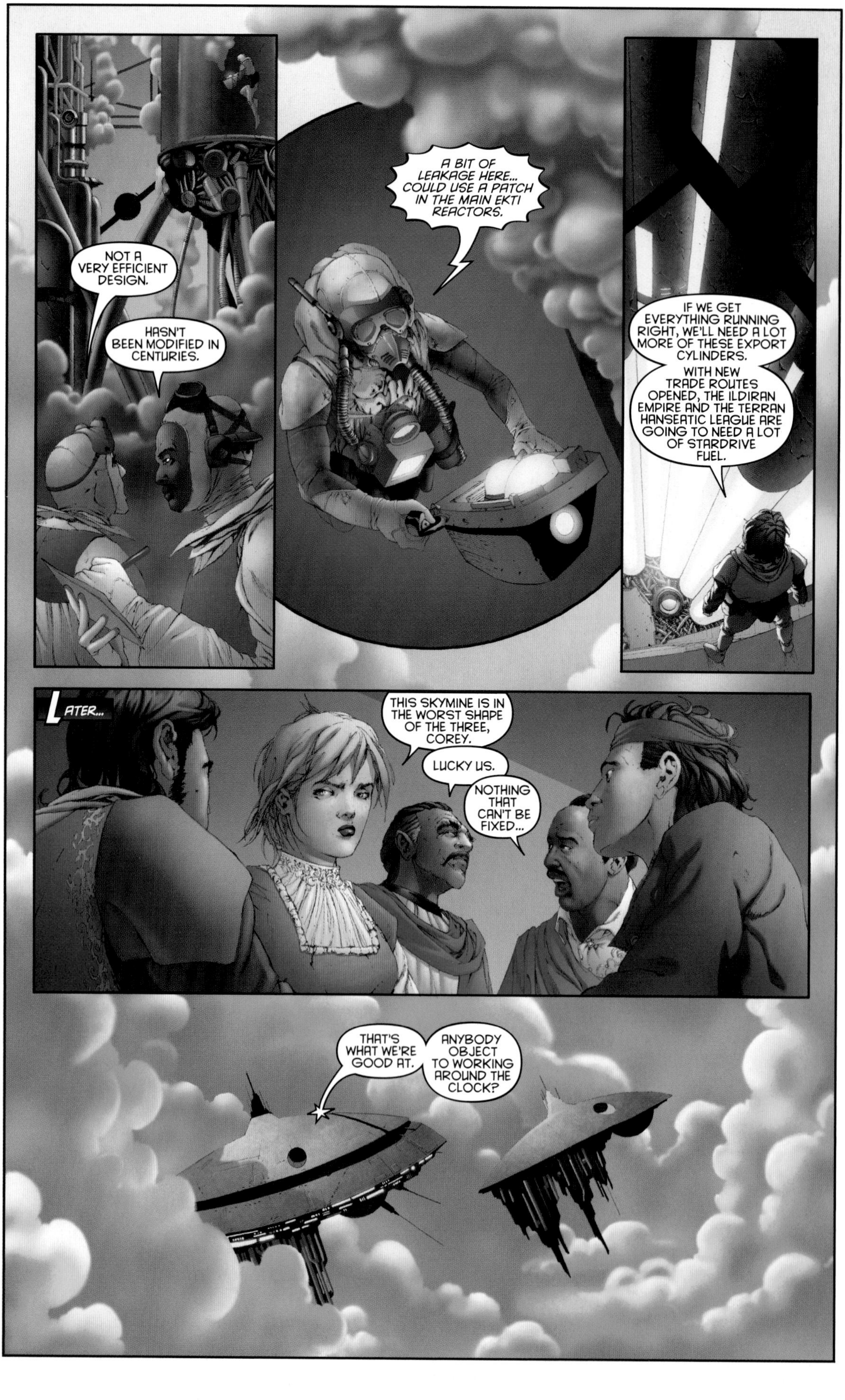
NOT A VERY EFFICIENT DESIGN.
HASN'T BEEN MODIFIED IN CENTURIES.
A BIT OF LEAKAGE HERE... COULD USE A PATCH IN THE MAIN EKTI REACTORS.
IF WE GET EVERYTHING RUNNING RIGHT, WE'LL NEED A LOT MORE OF THESE EXPORT CYLINDERS.
WITH NEW TRADE ROUTES OPENED, THE ILDIRAN EMPIRE AND THE TERRAN HANSEATIC LEAGUE ARE GOING TO NEED A LOT OF STARDRIVE FUEL.
LATER...
THIS SKYMINE IS IN THE WORST SHAPE OF THE THREE, COREY.
LUCKY US.
NOTHING THAT CAN'T BE FIXED...
THAT'S WHAT WE'RE GOOD AT.
ANYBODY OBJECT TO WORKING AROUND THE CLOCK?

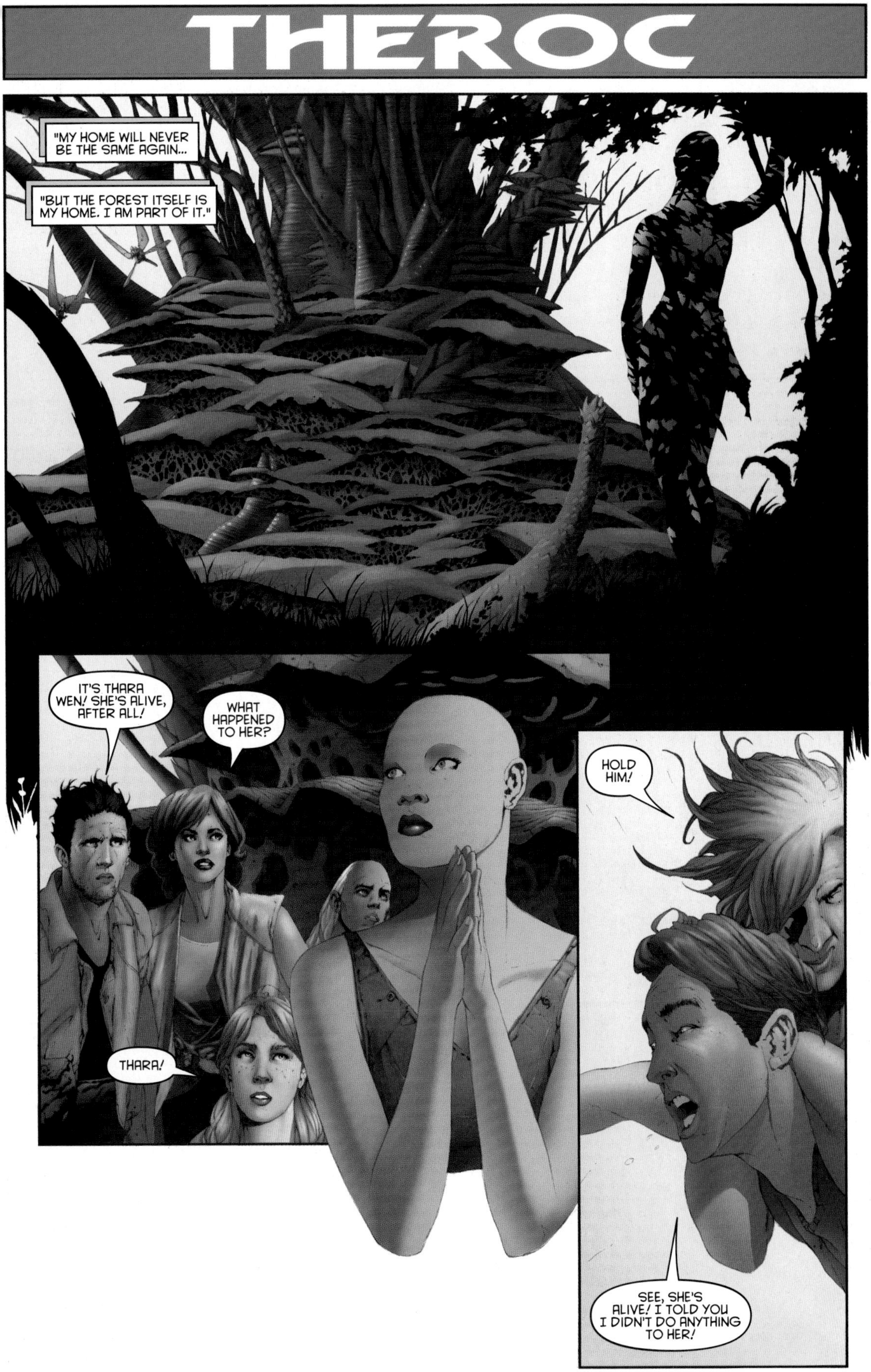
THEROC
"MY HOME WILL NEVER BE THE SAME AGAIN...
"BUT THE FOREST ITSELF IS MY HOME. I AM PART OF IT."
IT'S THARA WEN! SHE'S ALIVE, AFTER ALL!
WHAT HAPPENED TO HER?
THARA!
HOLD HIM!
SEE, SHE'S ALIVE! I TOLD YOU I DIDN'T DO ANYTHING TO HER!

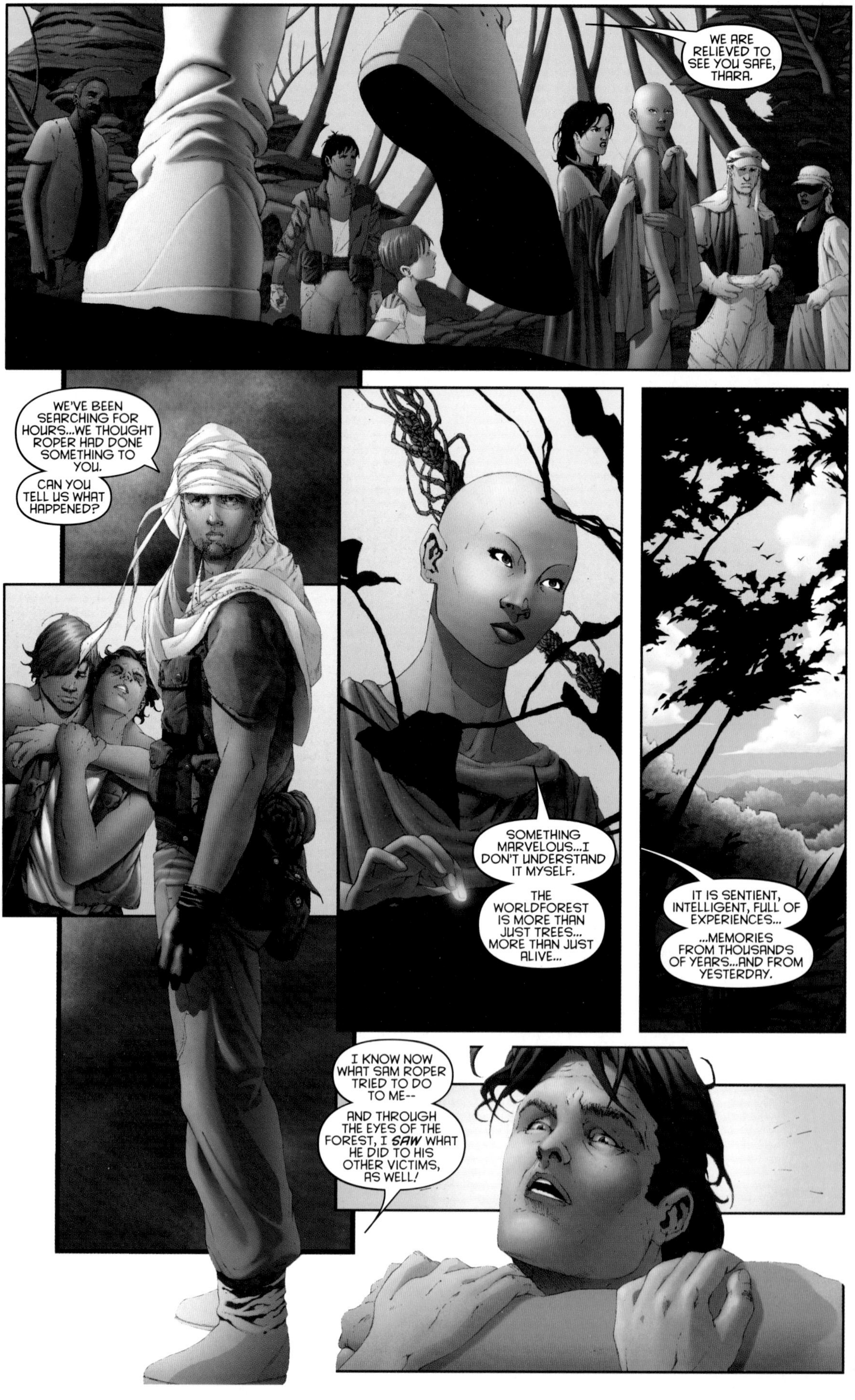
WE ARE RELIEVED TO SEE YOU SAFE, THARA.
WE'VE BEEN SEARCHING FOR HOURS...WE THOUGHT ROPER HAD DONE SOMETHING TO YOU.
CAN YOU TELL US WHAT HAPPENED?
SOMETHING MARVELOUS...I DON'T UNDERSTAND IT MYSELF.
THE WORLDFOREST IS MORE THAN JUST TREES... MORE THAN JUST ALIVE...
IT IS SENTIENT, INTELLIGENT, FULL OF EXPERIENCES...
...MEMORIES FROM THOUSANDS OF YEARS...AND FROM YESTERDAY.
I KNOW NOW WHAT SAM ROPER TRIED TO DO TO ME--
AND THROUGH THE EYES OF THE FOREST, I SAW WHAT HE DID TO HIS OTHER VICTIMS, AS WELL!

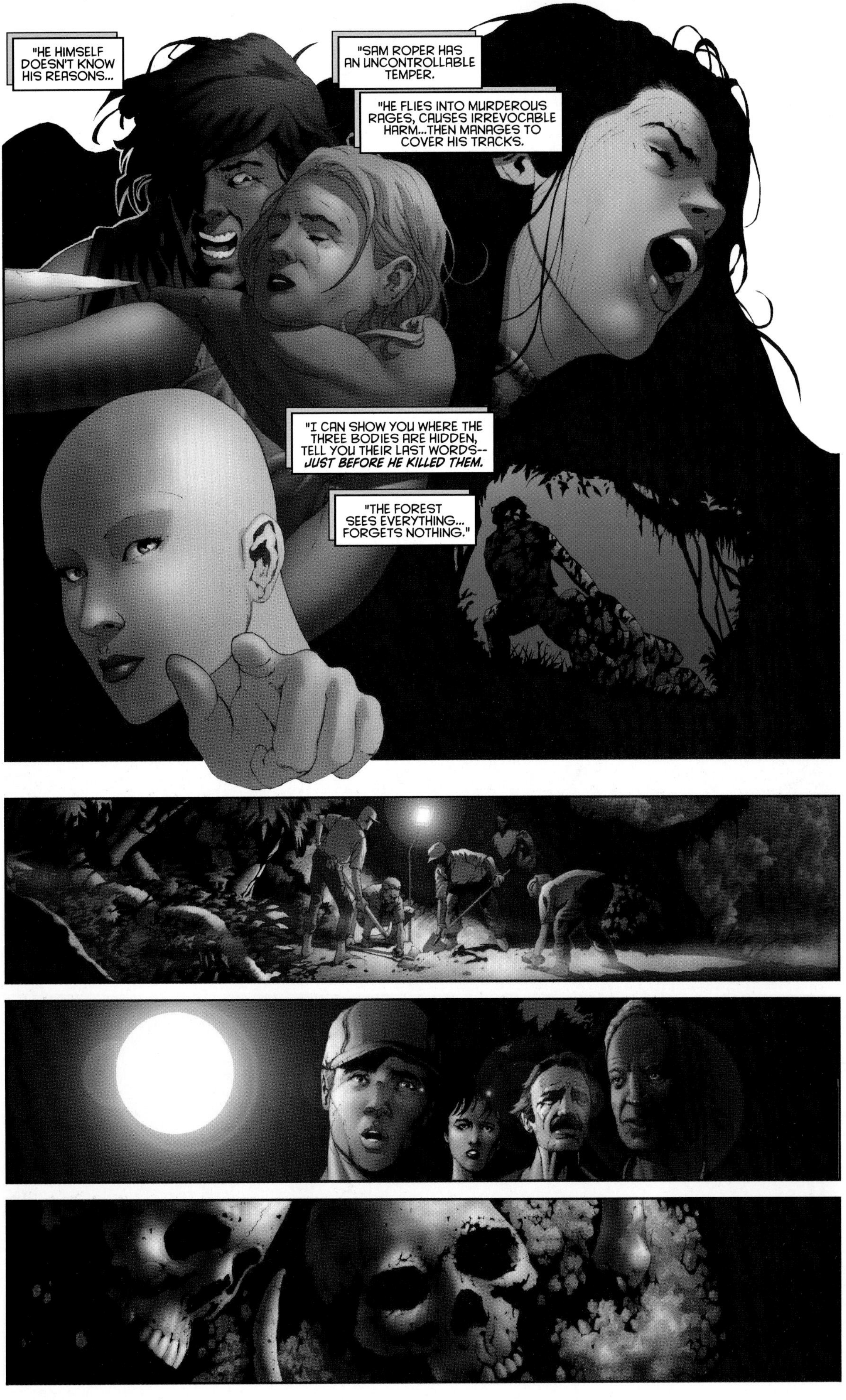
"HE HIMSELF DOESN'T KNOW HIS REASONS...
"SAM ROPER HAS AN UNCONTROLLABLE TEMPER.
"HE FLIES INTO MURDEROUS RAGES, CAUSES IRREVOCABLE HARM...THEN MANAGES TO COVER HIS TRACKS.
"I CAN SHOW YOU WHERE THE THREE BODIES ARE HIDDEN, TELL YOU THEIR LAST WORDS--*JUST BEFORE HE KILLED THEM.*
"THE FOREST SEES EVERYTHING... FORGETS NOTHING."

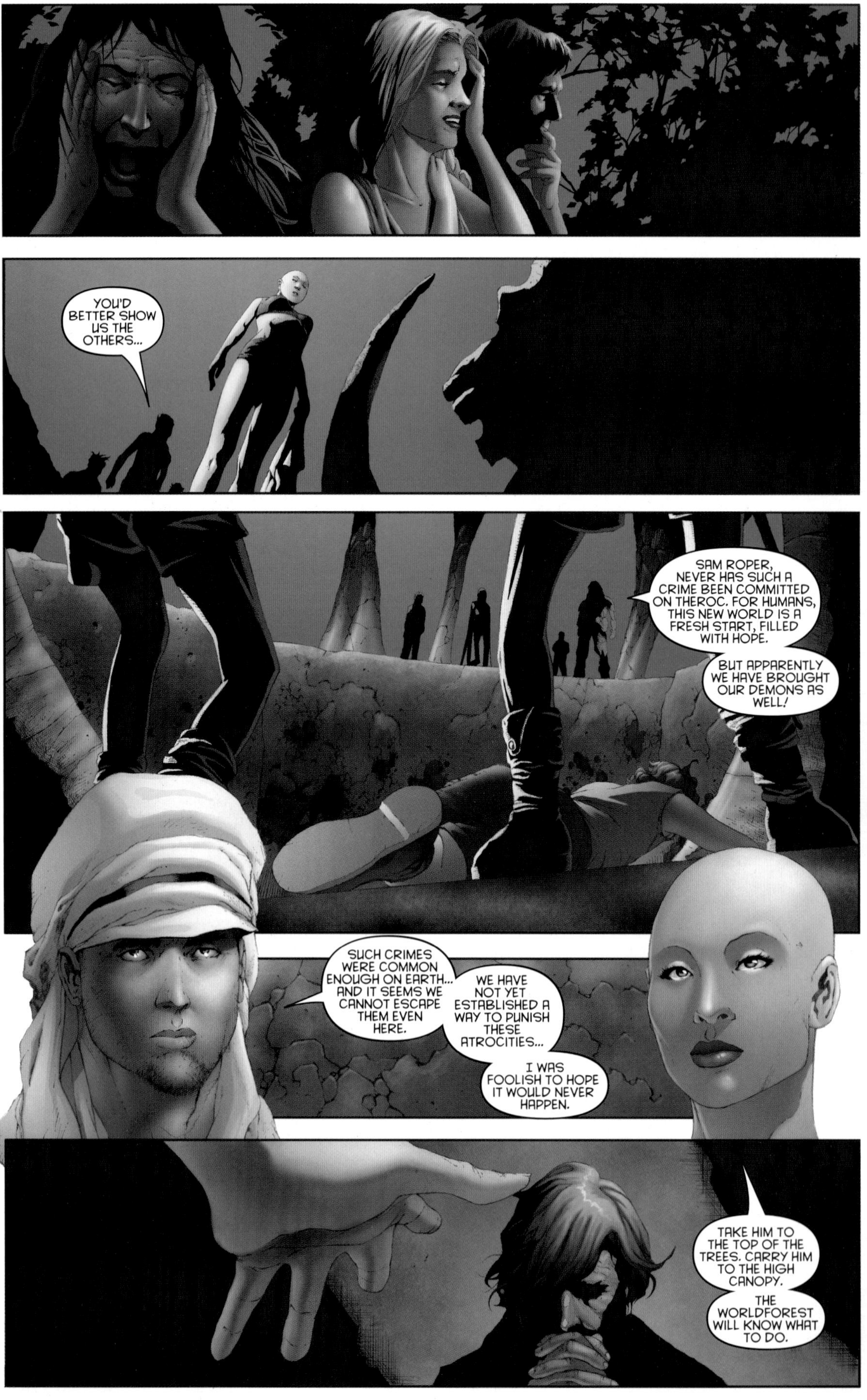
YOU'D BETTER SHOW US THE OTHERS...
SAM ROPER, NEVER HAS SUCH A CRIME BEEN COMMITTED ON THEROC. FOR HUMANS, THIS NEW WORLD IS A FRESH START, FILLED WITH HOPE.
BUT APPARENTLY WE HAVE BROUGHT OUR DEMONS AS WELL!
SUCH CRIMES WERE COMMON ENOUGH ON EARTH... AND IT SEEMS WE CANNOT ESCAPE THEM EVEN HERE.
WE HAVE NOT YET ESTABLISHED A WAY TO PUNISH THESE ATROCITIES...
I WAS FOOLISH TO HOPE IT WOULD NEVER HAPPEN.
TAKE HIM TO THE TOP OF THE TREES. CARRY HIM TO THE HIGH CANOPY.
THE WORLDFOREST WILL KNOW WHAT TO DO.

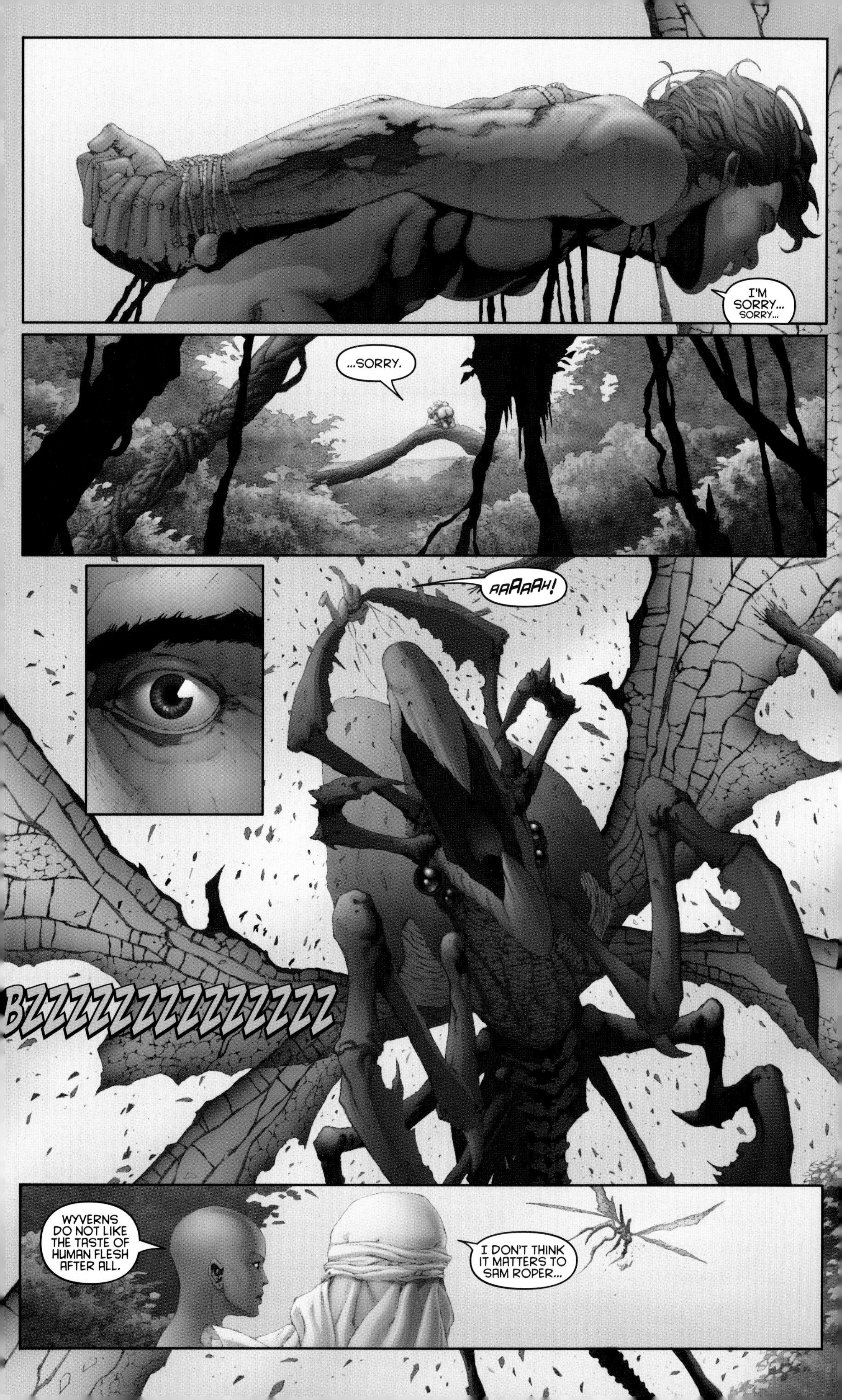
I'M SORRY... SORRY...
...SORRY.
AAAAAH!
BZZZZZZZZZZZZZZ
WYVERNS DO NOT LIKE THE TASTE OF HUMAN FLESH AFTER ALL.
I DON'T THINK IT MATTERS TO SAM ROPER...

I AM HAPPY TO SERVE THE HANSEATIC LEAGUE AND THE KING.

YOU ARE AWARE FROM HISTORY, OX, THAT THE HANSA'S GREAT KING HAS ALWAYS BEEN A MERE SPOKESMAN...

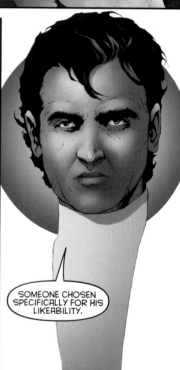

SOMEONE CHOSEN SPECIFICALLY FOR HIS LIKEABILITY.

YOU'VE SERVED HUMANITY FOR MANY YEARS ON THE *PEARY*, OX...

NOW I HAVE OTHER TASKS FOR YOU IN THE WHISPER PALACE.

MY PROGRAMMING IS EASILY ADAPTABLE, CHAIRMAN STANNIS.

WITH SO MANY THINGS CHANGING, IT'S TIME TO TRAIN A NEW PRINCE.

WE SELECTED THIS ONE FROM A LARGE POOL OF CANDIDATES.

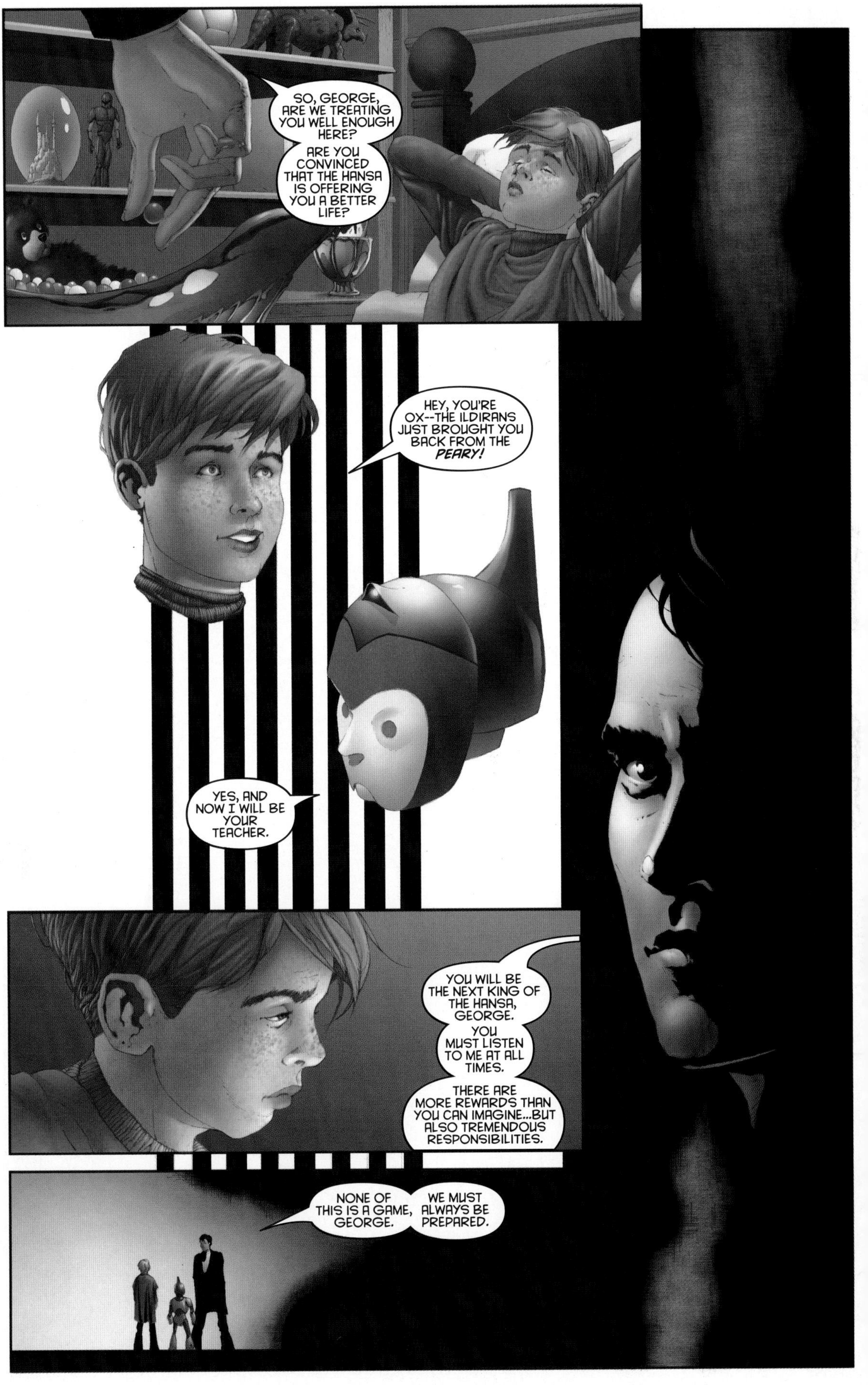
SO, GEORGE, ARE WE TREATING YOU WELL ENOUGH HERE?
ARE YOU CONVINCED THAT THE HANSA IS OFFERING YOU A BETTER LIFE?
HEY, YOU'RE OX--THE ILDIRANS JUST BROUGHT YOU BACK FROM THE *PEARY!*
YES, AND NOW I WILL BE YOUR TEACHER.
YOU WILL BE THE NEXT KING OF THE HANSA, GEORGE.
YOU MUST LISTEN TO ME AT ALL TIMES.
THERE ARE MORE REWARDS THAN YOU CAN IMAGINE...BUT ALSO TREMENDOUS RESPONSIBILITIES.
NONE OF THIS IS A GAME, GEORGE.
WE MUST ALWAYS BE PREPARED.

DOBRO

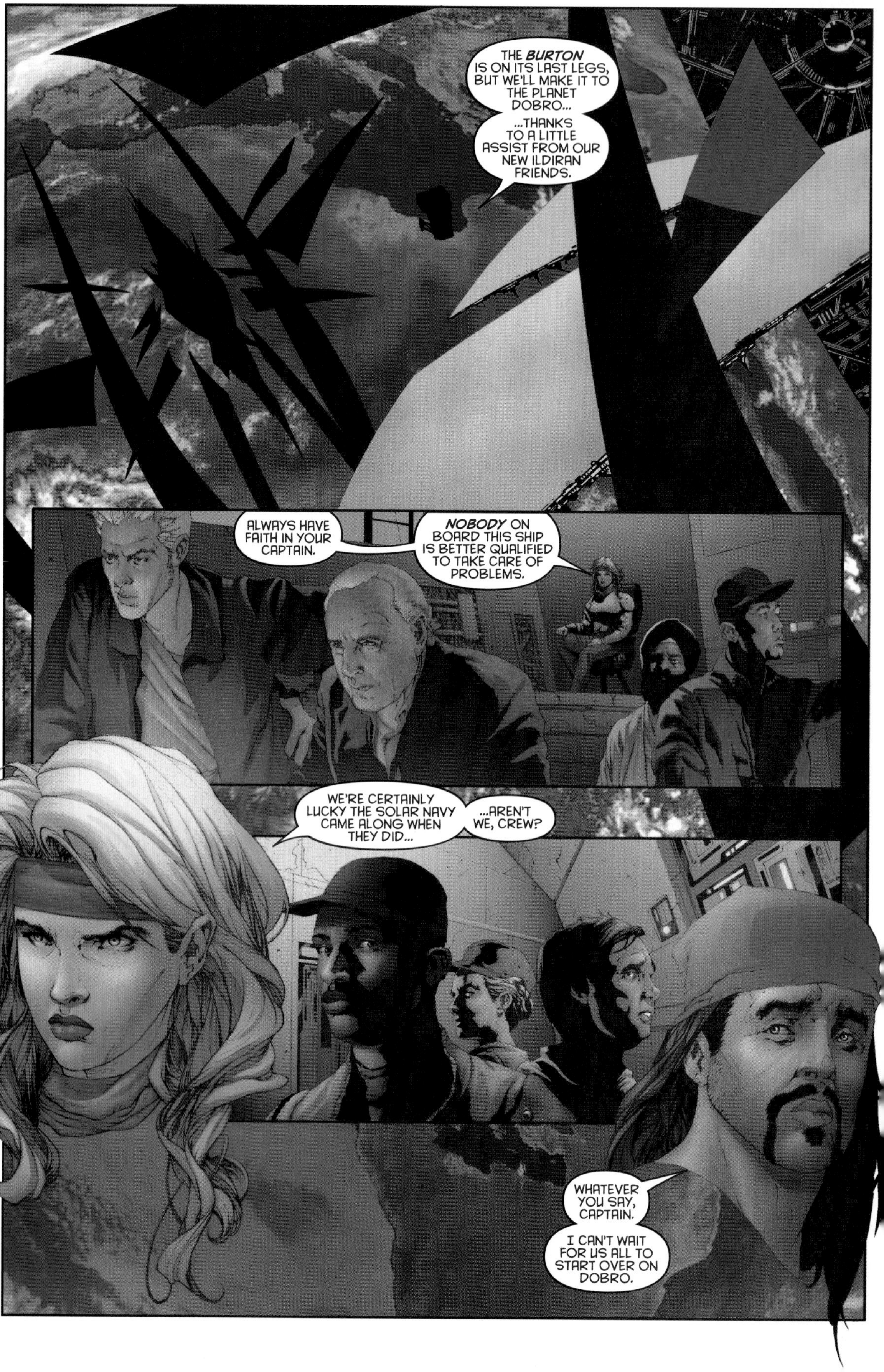
THE *BURTON* IS ON ITS LAST LEGS, BUT WE'LL MAKE IT TO THE PLANET DOBRO...
...THANKS TO A LITTLE ASSIST FROM OUR NEW ILDIRAN FRIENDS.
ALWAYS HAVE FAITH IN YOUR CAPTAIN.
NOBODY ON BOARD THIS SHIP IS BETTER QUALIFIED TO TAKE CARE OF PROBLEMS.
WE'RE CERTAINLY LUCKY THE SOLAR NAVY CAME ALONG WHEN THEY DID...
...AREN'T WE, CREW?
WHATEVER YOU SAY, CAPTAIN.
I CAN'T WAIT FOR US ALL TO START OVER ON DOBRO.

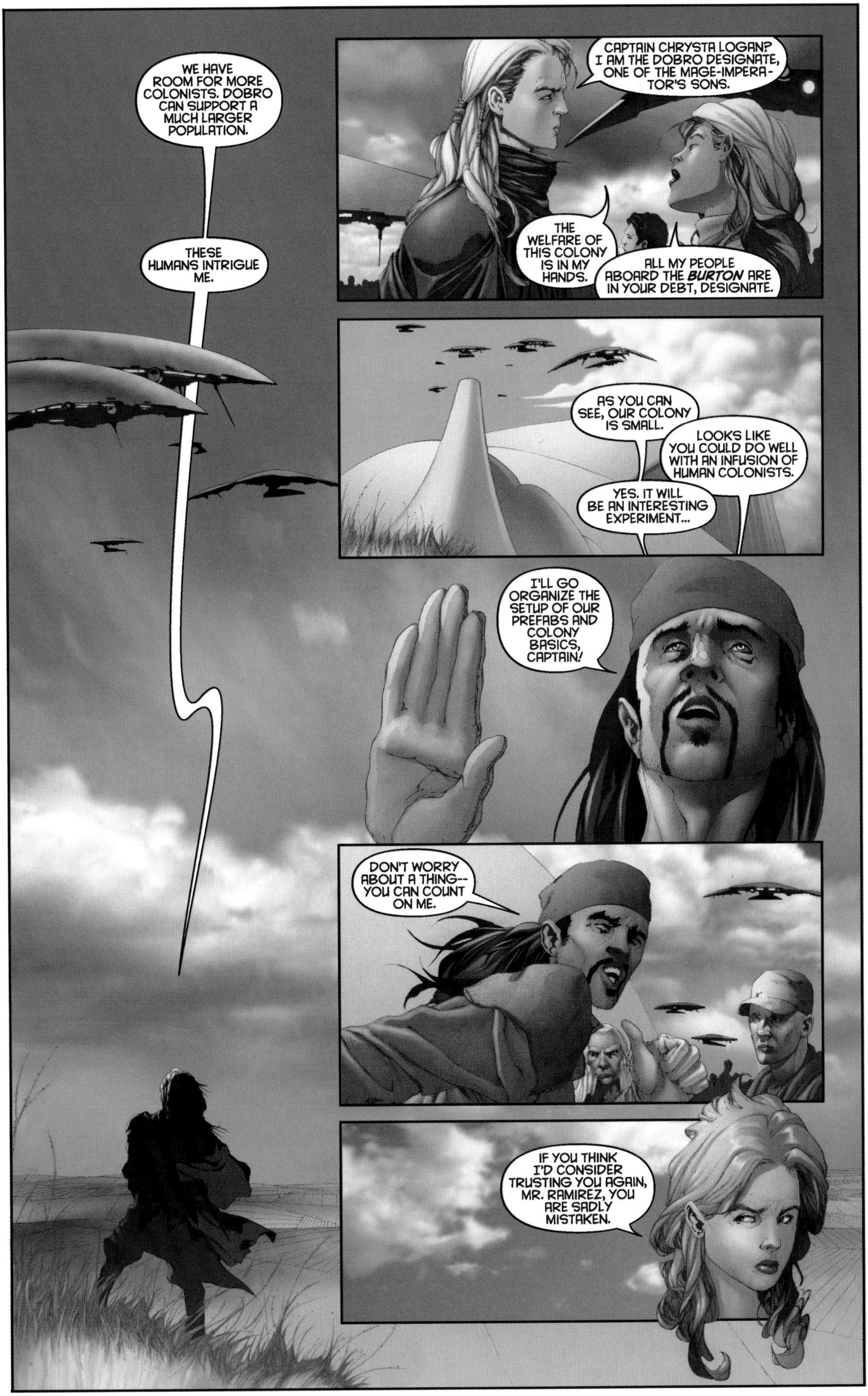
WE HAVE ROOM FOR MORE COLONISTS. DOBRO CAN SUPPORT A MUCH LARGER POPULATION.
THESE HUMANS INTRIGUE ME.
CAPTAIN CHRYSTA LOGAN? I AM THE DOBRO DESIGNATE, ONE OF THE MAGE-IMPERATOR'S SONS.
THE WELFARE OF THIS COLONY IS IN MY HANDS.
ALL MY PEOPLE ABOARD THE BURTON ARE IN YOUR DEBT, DESIGNATE.
AS YOU CAN SEE, OUR COLONY IS SMALL.
LOOKS LIKE YOU COULD DO WELL WITH AN INFUSION OF HUMAN COLONISTS.
YES. IT WILL BE AN INTERESTING EXPERIMENT...
I'LL GO ORGANIZE THE SETUP OF OUR PREFABS AND COLONY BASICS, CAPTAIN!
DON'T WORRY ABOUT A THING-- YOU CAN COUNT ON ME.
IF YOU THINK I'D CONSIDER TRUSTING YOU AGAIN, MR. RAMIREZ, YOU ARE SADLY MISTAKEN.

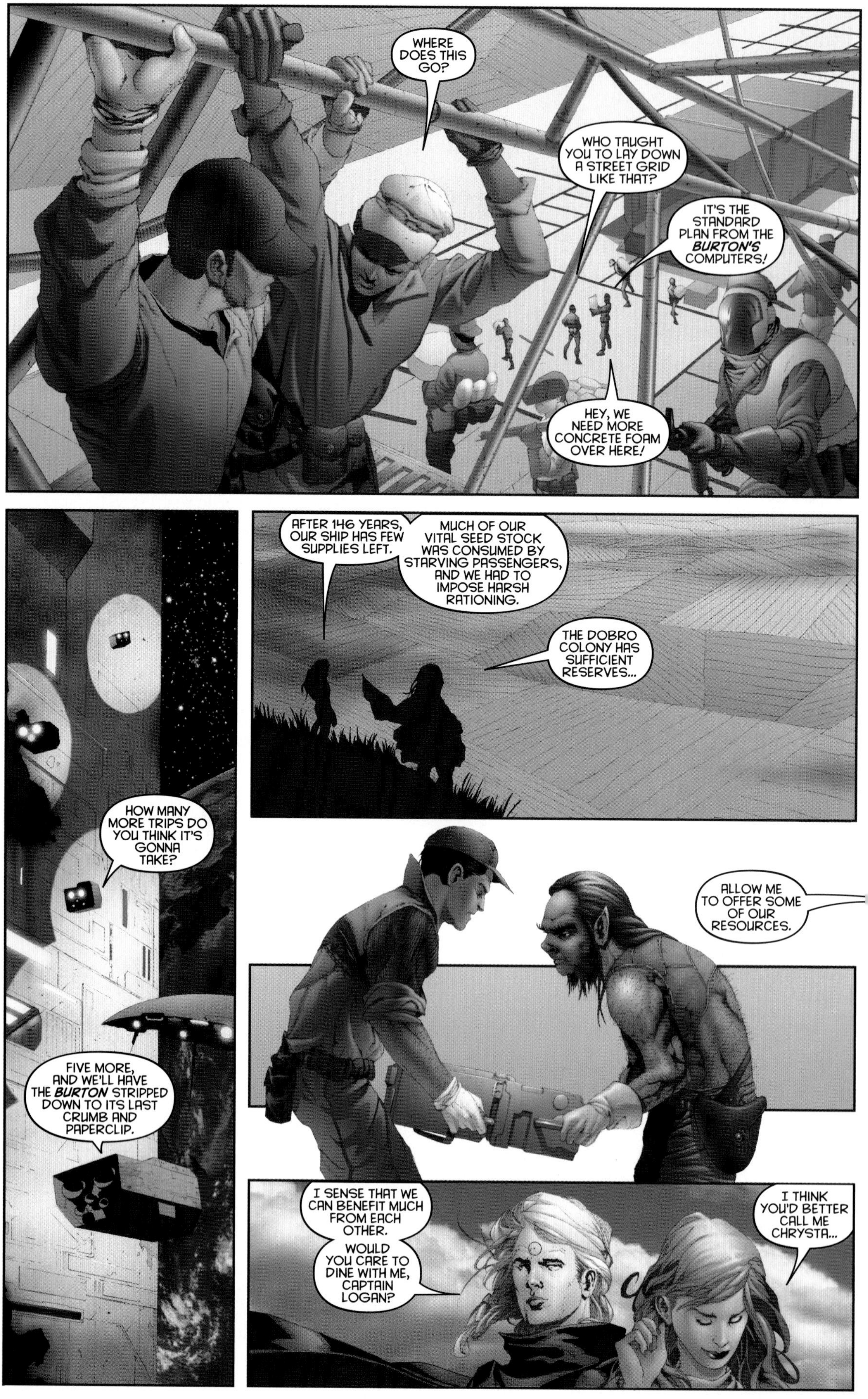

WHERE DOES THIS GO?
WHO TAUGHT YOU TO LAY DOWN A STREET GRID LIKE THAT?
IT'S THE STANDARD PLAN FROM THE *BURTON'S* COMPUTERS!
HEY, WE NEED MORE CONCRETE FOAM OVER HERE!
HOW MANY MORE TRIPS DO YOU THINK IT'S GONNA TAKE?
FIVE MORE, AND WE'LL HAVE THE *BURTON* STRIPPED DOWN TO ITS LAST CRUMB AND PAPERCLIP.
AFTER 146 YEARS, OUR SHIP HAS FEW SUPPLIES LEFT.
MUCH OF OUR VITAL SEED STOCK WAS CONSUMED BY STARVING PASSENGERS, AND WE HAD TO IMPOSE HARSH RATIONING.
THE DOBRO COLONY HAS SUFFICIENT RESERVES...
ALLOW ME TO OFFER SOME OF OUR RESOURCES.
I SENSE THAT WE CAN BENEFIT MUCH FROM EACH OTHER.
WOULD YOU CARE TO DINE WITH ME, CAPTAIN LOGAN?
I THINK YOU'D BETTER CALL ME CHRYSTA...

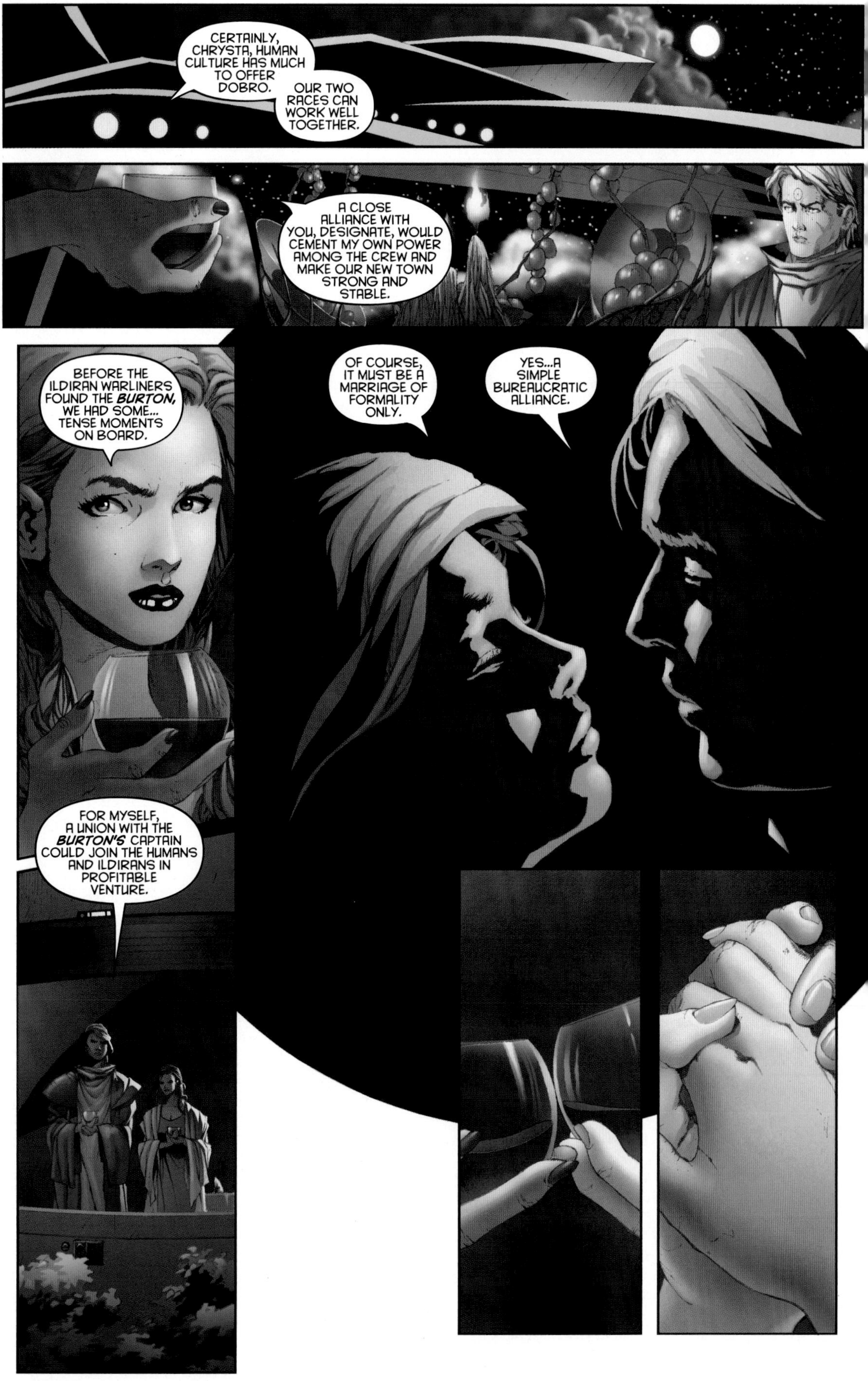
CERTAINLY, CHRYSTA, HUMAN CULTURE HAS MUCH TO OFFER DOBRO.
OUR TWO RACES CAN WORK WELL TOGETHER.
A CLOSE ALLIANCE WITH YOU, DESIGNATE, WOULD CEMENT MY OWN POWER AMONG THE CREW AND MAKE OUR NEW TOWN STRONG AND STABLE.
BEFORE THE ILDIRAN WARLINERS FOUND THE *BURTON,* WE HAD SOME... TENSE MOMENTS ON BOARD.
FOR MYSELF, A UNION WITH THE *BURTON'S* CAPTAIN COULD JOIN THE HUMANS AND ILDIRANS IN PROFITABLE VENTURE.
OF COURSE, IT MUST BE A MARRIAGE OF FORMALITY ONLY.
YES...A SIMPLE BUREAUCRATIC ALLIANCE.

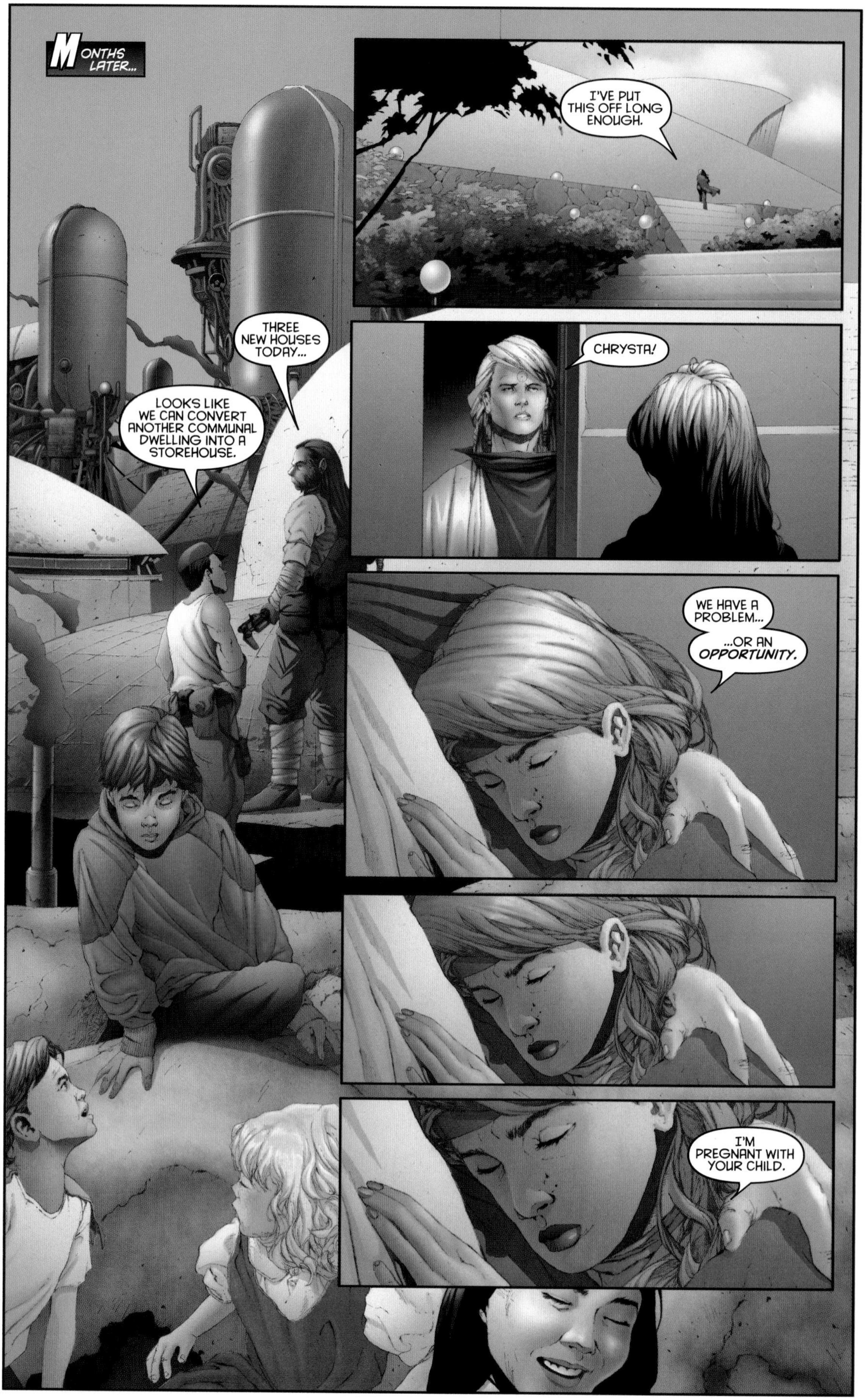
MONTHS LATER...
I'VE PUT THIS OFF LONG ENOUGH.
THREE NEW HOUSES TODAY...
LOOKS LIKE WE CAN CONVERT ANOTHER COMMUNAL DWELLING INTO A STOREHOUSE.
CHRYSTA!
WE HAVE A PROBLEM...
...OR AN OPPORTUNITY.
I'M PREGNANT WITH YOUR CHILD.

*T*HE PRISM PALACE...

THE MAGE-IMPERATOR'S GRAND RESIDENCE UNDER THE SEVEN SUNS OF ILDIRA.

PRIME DESIGNATE CYROC'H!

WELCOME BACK TO ILDIRA, BROTHER. YOU CAN BASK IN ILDIRA'S BRIGHT LIGHT. YOU'VE SPENT TOO LONG IN DOBRO'S DIM SUNSHINE.

DOBRO IS MY HOME, CYROC'H, DESPITE ITS FAILINGS...

AND MUCH HAS CHANGED IN RECENT MONTHS, SINCE THE ARRIVAL OF THE HUMANS.

THE MAGE-IMPERATOR ALREADY SEES AND FEELS EVERYTHING IN OUR EMPIRE.

EVEN SO, FATHER WILL BE GLAD TO HEAR YOUR REPORT.

WELCOME, DESIGNATE.

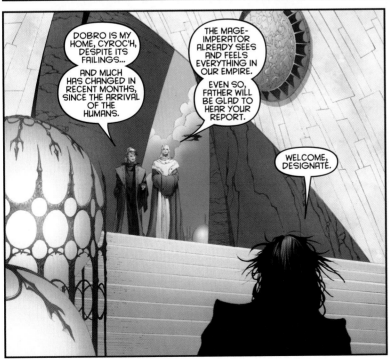

THE MAGE-IMPERATOR IS EAGER TO LEARN MORE ABOUT YOUR EXPERIENCES WITH THE *BURTON* REFUGEES.

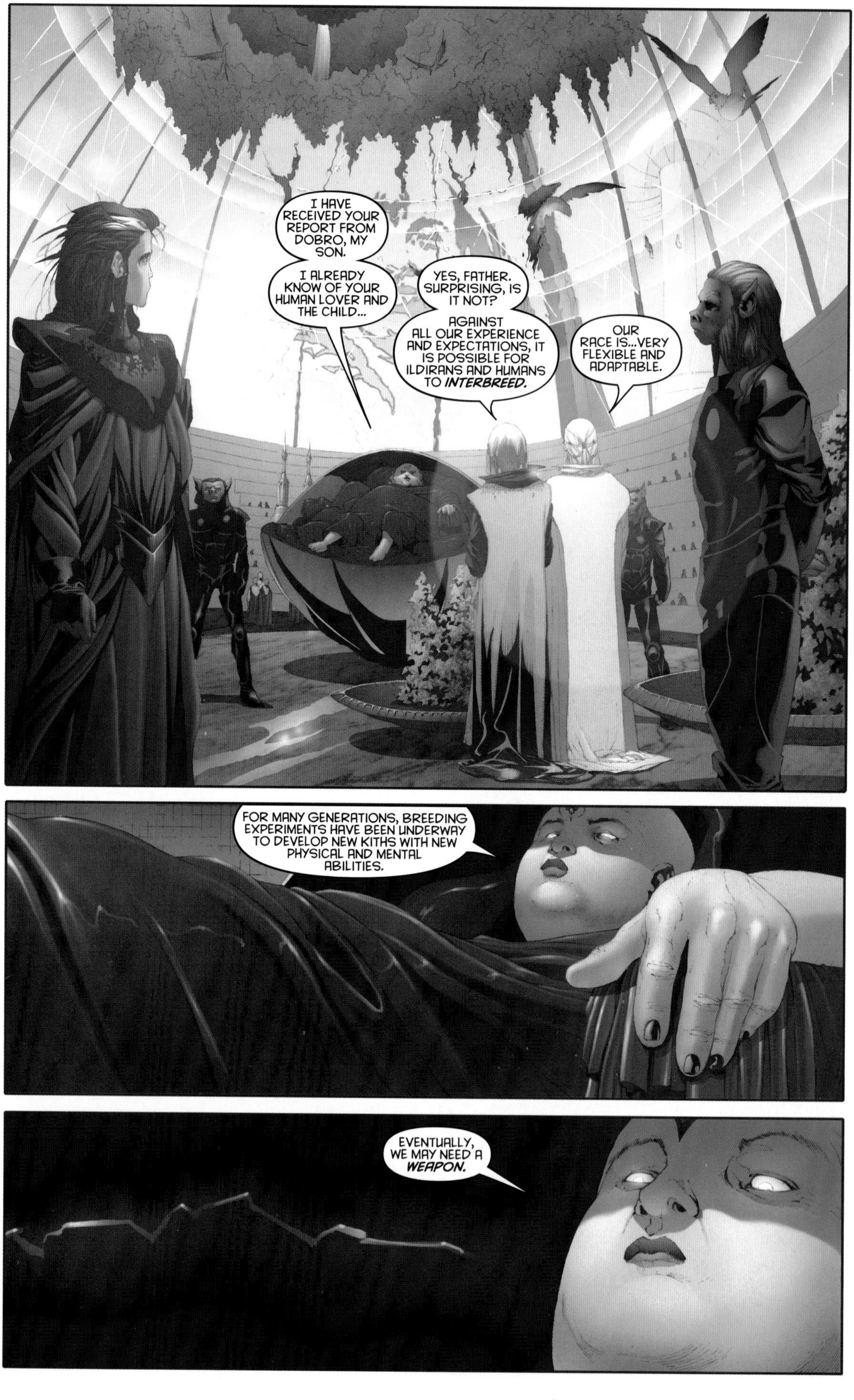

I HAVE RECEIVED YOUR REPORT FROM DOBRO, MY SON.
I ALREADY KNOW OF YOUR HUMAN LOVER AND THE CHILD...
YES, FATHER. SURPRISING, IS IT NOT?
AGAINST ALL OUR EXPERIENCE AND EXPECTATIONS, IT IS POSSIBLE FOR ILDIRANS AND HUMANS TO *INTERBREED.*
OUR RACE IS...VERY FLEXIBLE AND ADAPTABLE.
FOR MANY GENERATIONS, BREEDING EXPERIMENTS HAVE BEEN UNDERWAY TO DEVELOP NEW KITHS WITH NEW PHYSICAL AND MENTAL ABILITIES.
EVENTUALLY, WE MAY NEED A *WEAPON.*

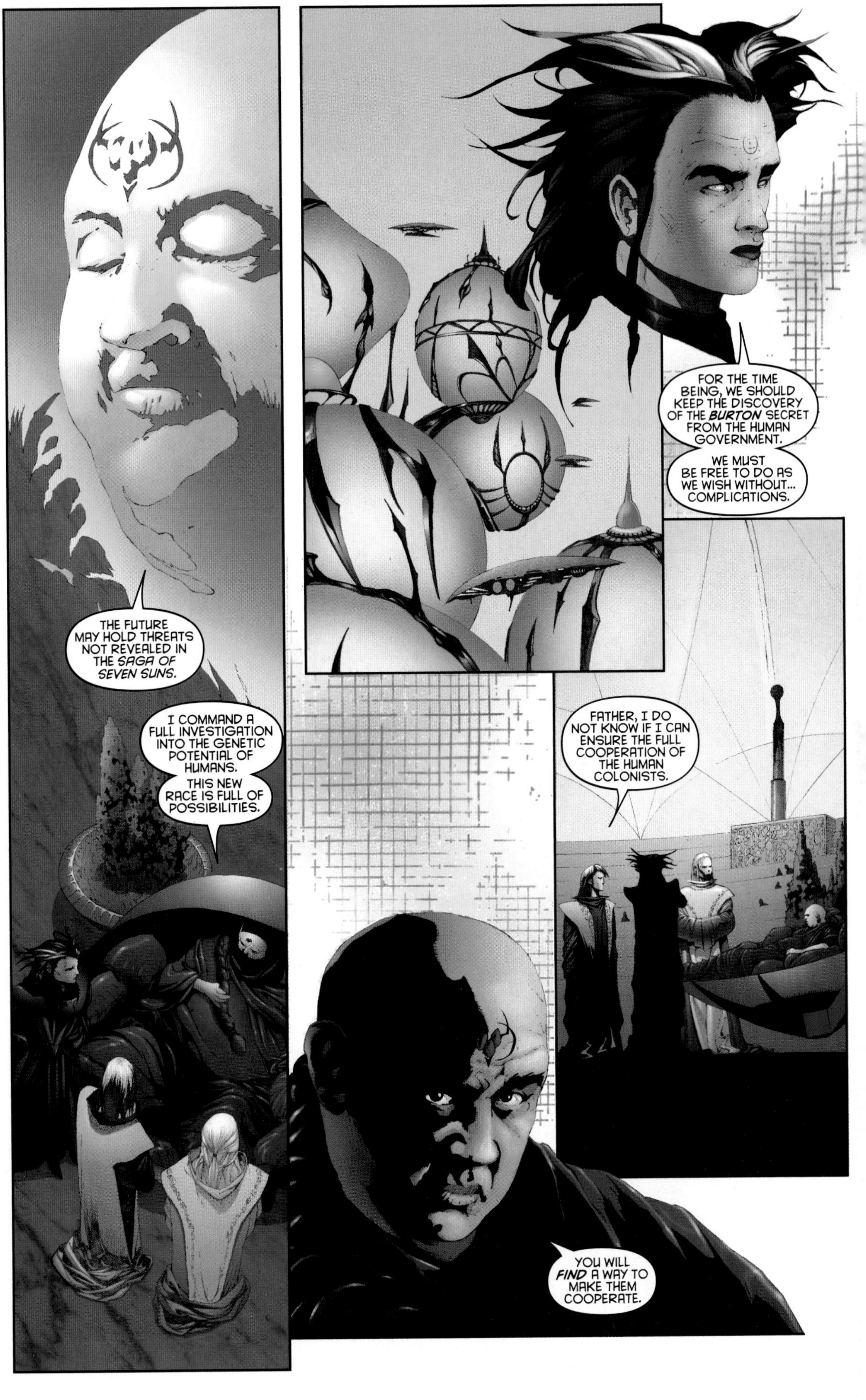
THE FUTURE MAY HOLD THREATS NOT REVEALED IN THE *SAGA OF SEVEN SUNS*.
I COMMAND A FULL INVESTIGATION INTO THE GENETIC POTENTIAL OF HUMANS.
THIS NEW RACE IS FULL OF POSSIBILITIES.
FOR THE TIME BEING, WE SHOULD KEEP THE DISCOVERY OF THE ***BURTON*** SECRET FROM THE HUMAN GOVERNMENT.
WE MUST BE FREE TO DO AS WE WISH WITHOUT... COMPLICATIONS.
FATHER, I DO NOT KNOW IF I CAN ENSURE THE FULL COOPERATION OF THE HUMAN COLONISTS.
YOU WILL ***FIND*** A WAY TO MAKE THEM COOPERATE.

DAYM

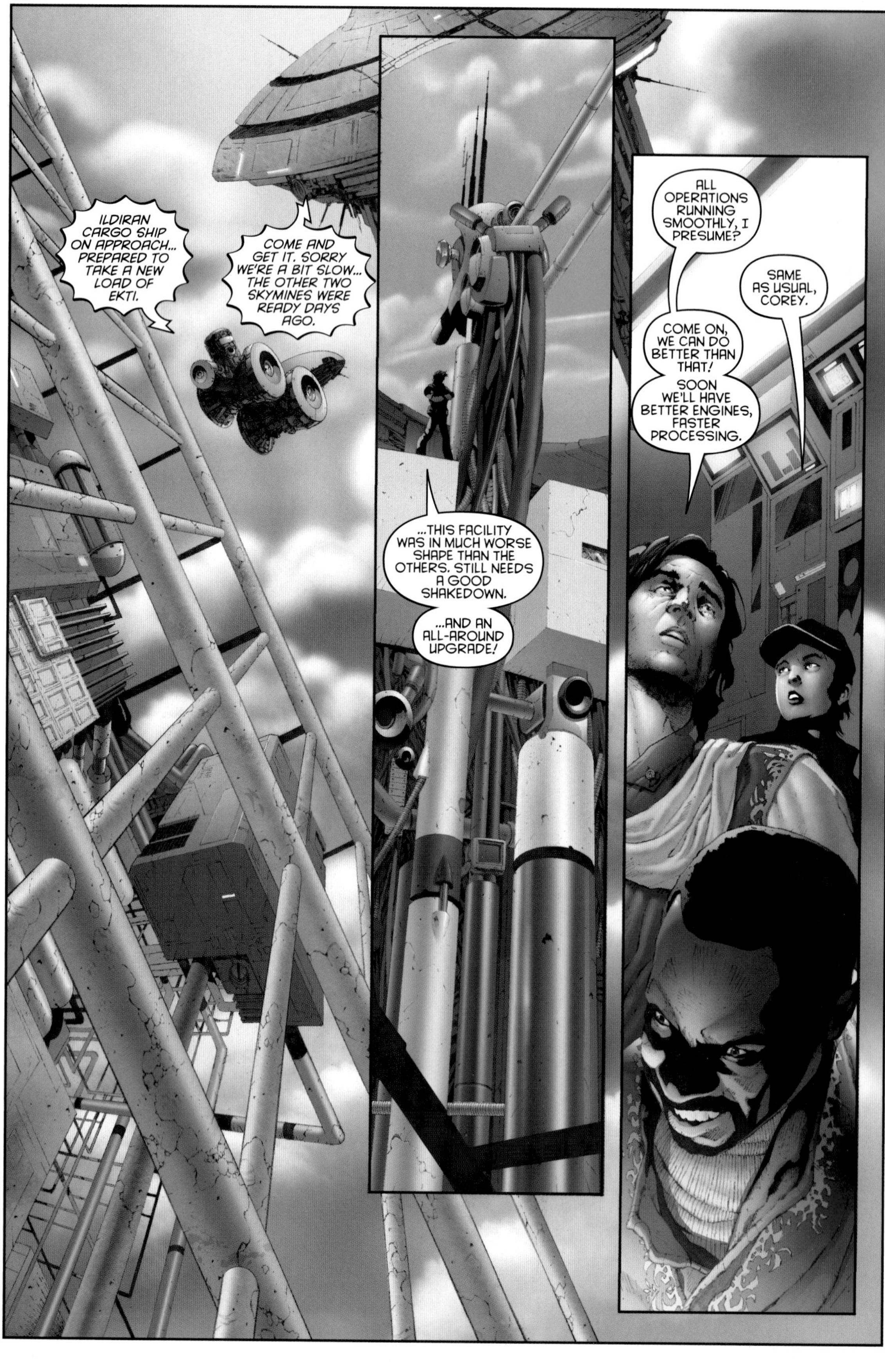

ILDIRAN CARGO SHIP ON APPROACH... PREPARED TO TAKE A NEW LOAD OF EKTI.
COME AND GET IT. SORRY WE'RE A BIT SLOW... THE OTHER TWO SKYMINES WERE READY DAYS AGO.
...THIS FACILITY WAS IN MUCH WORSE SHAPE THAN THE OTHERS. STILL NEEDS A GOOD SHAKEDOWN.
...AND AN ALL-AROUND UPGRADE!
ALL OPERATIONS RUNNING SMOOTHLY, I PRESUME?
SAME AS USUAL, COREY.
COME ON, WE CAN DO BETTER THAN THAT!
SOON WE'LL HAVE BETTER ENGINES, FASTER PROCESSING.

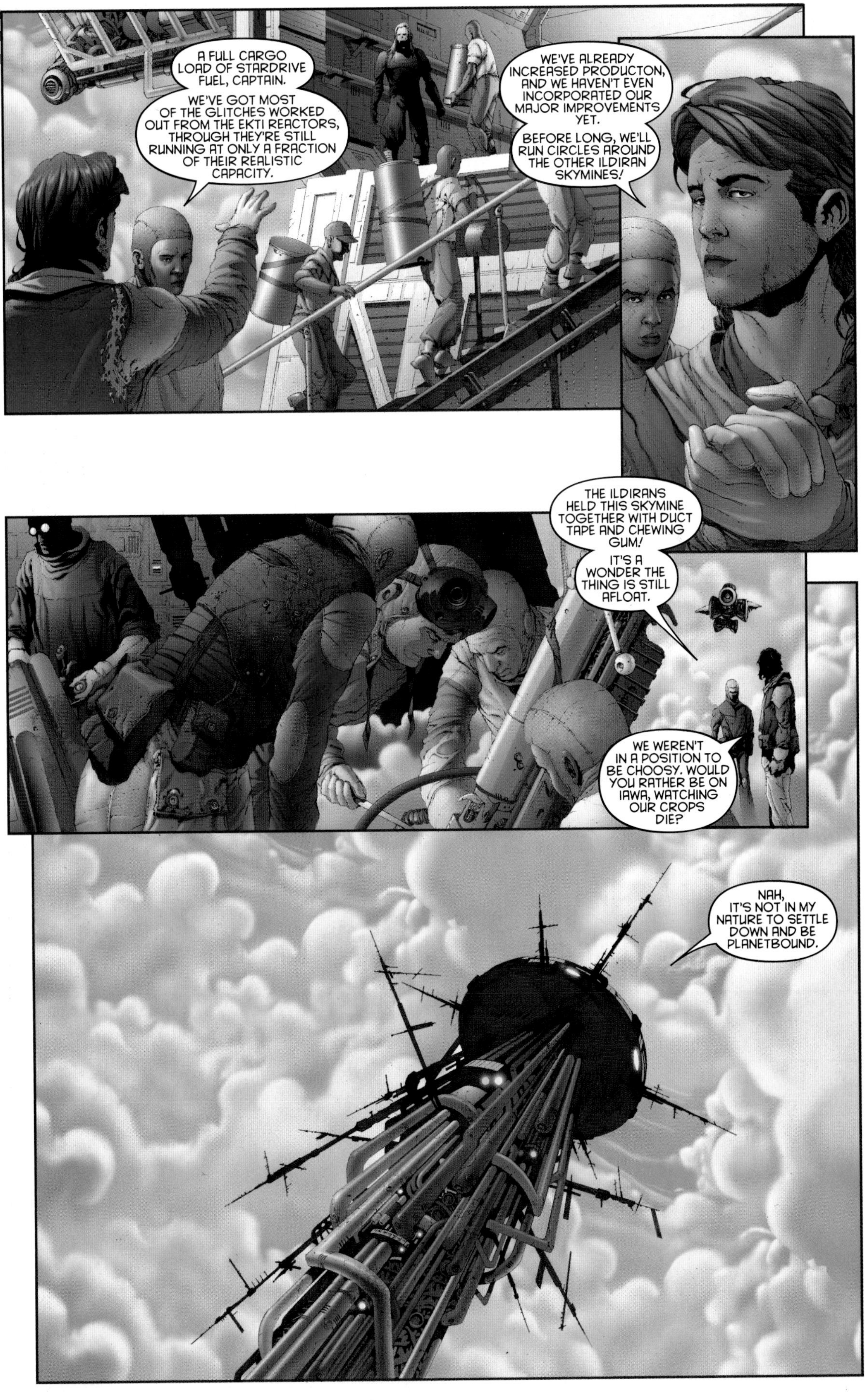
A FULL CARGO LOAD OF STARDRIVE FUEL, CAPTAIN.
WE'VE GOT MOST OF THE GLITCHES WORKED OUT FROM THE EKTI REACTORS, THROUGH THEY'RE STILL RUNNING AT ONLY A FRACTION OF THEIR REALISTIC CAPACITY.
WE'VE ALREADY INCREASED PRODUCTON, AND WE HAVEN'T EVEN INCORPORATED OUR MAJOR IMPROVEMENTS YET.
BEFORE LONG, WE'LL RUN CIRCLES AROUND THE OTHER ILDIRAN SKYMINES!
THE ILDIRANS HELD THIS SKYMINE TOGETHER WITH DUCT TAPE AND CHEWING GUM!
IT'S A WONDER THE THING IS STILL AFLOAT.
WE WEREN'T IN A POSITION TO BE CHOOSY. WOULD YOU RATHER BE ON IAWA, WATCHING OUR CROPS DIE?
NAH, IT'S NOT IN MY NATURE TO SETTLE DOWN AND BE PLANETBOUND.

A WEEK LATER...

READY FOR THE FULL-POWER TEST? MY TEAM DID MORE THAN GIVE THIS OLD SKYMINE A FACELIFT--IT'S GOT A WHOLE NEW HEART!

HERE WE GO!

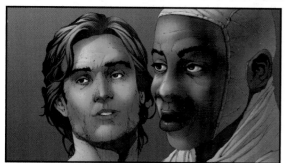

DAMN! THE REACTOR THROUGHPUT WAS TOO MUCH!

THOSE WERE THE LEVITATION ENGINES! SOUND THE ALARMS!

MAJOR INSTABILITIES! CAN'T WE LOCK IT DOWN?

LOSING ALTITUDE!

STUPID ILDIRAN TECHNOLOGY! CAN'T FIGURE HOW TO BRING IT UNDER CONTROL!

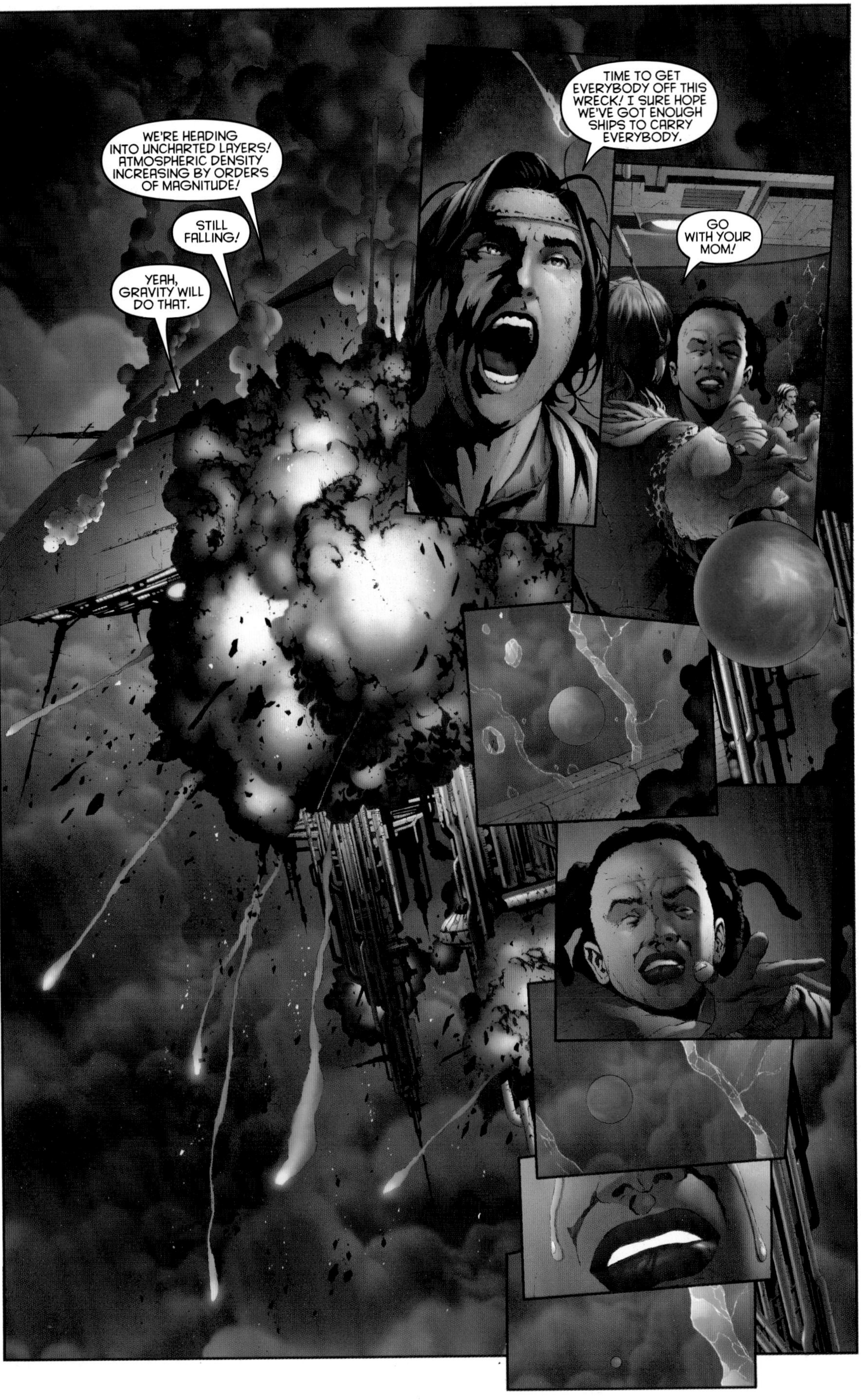
WE'RE HEADING INTO UNCHARTED LAYERS! ATMOSPHERIC DENSITY INCREASING BY ORDERS OF MAGNITUDE!
STILL FALLING!
YEAH, GRAVITY WILL DO THAT.
TIME TO GET EVERYBODY OFF THIS WRECK! I SURE HOPE WE'VE GOT ENOUGH SHIPS TO CARRY EVERYBODY.
GO WITH YOUR MOM!

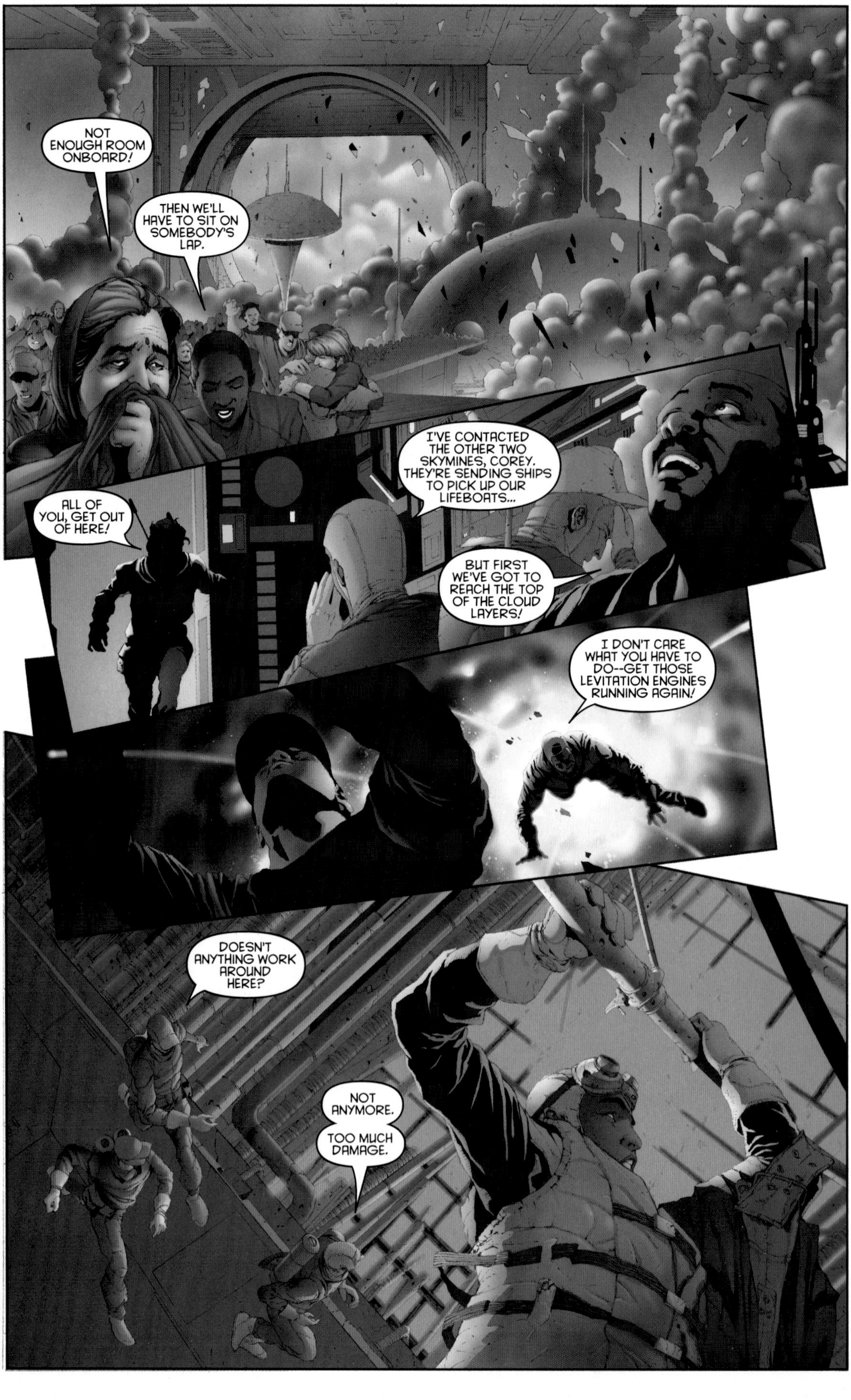
NOT ENOUGH ROOM ONBOARD!
THEN WE'LL HAVE TO SIT ON SOMEBODY'S LAP.
I'VE CONTACTED THE OTHER TWO SKYMINES, COREY. THEY'RE SENDING SHIPS TO PICK UP OUR LIFEBOATS...
ALL OF YOU, GET OUT OF HERE!
BUT FIRST WE'VE GOT TO REACH THE TOP OF THE CLOUD LAYERS!
I DON'T CARE WHAT YOU HAVE TO DO--GET THOSE LEVITATION ENGINES RUNNING AGAIN!
DOESN'T ANYTHING WORK AROUND HERE?
NOT ANYMORE.
TOO MUCH DAMAGE.

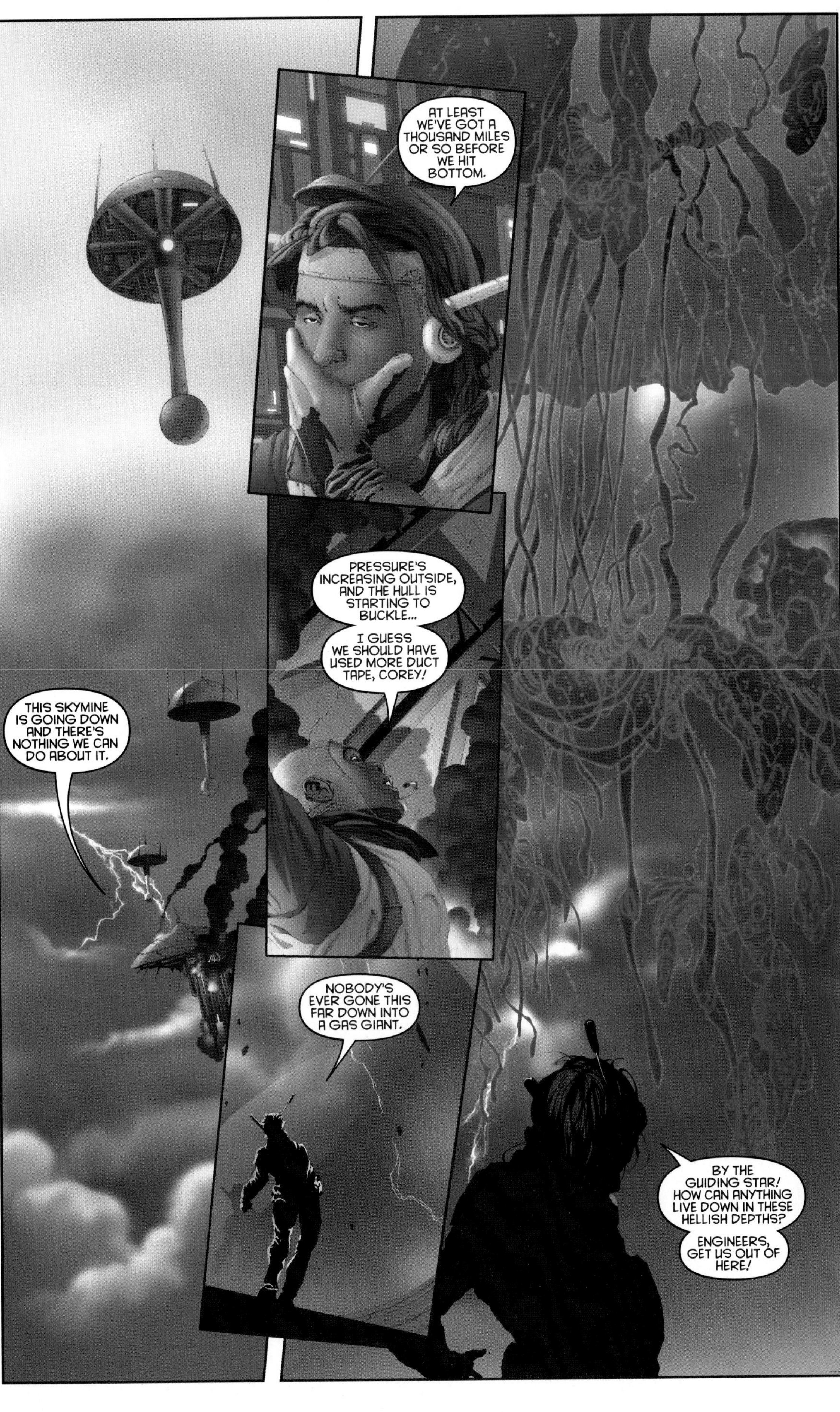
AT LEAST WE'VE GOT A THOUSAND MILES OR SO BEFORE WE HIT BOTTOM.
PRESSURE'S INCREASING OUTSIDE, AND THE HULL IS STARTING TO BUCKLE...
I GUESS WE SHOULD HAVE USED MORE DUCT TAPE, COREY!
THIS SKYMINE IS GOING DOWN AND THERE'S NOTHING WE CAN DO ABOUT IT.
NOBODY'S EVER GONE THIS FAR DOWN INTO A GAS GIANT.
BY THE GUIDING STAR! HOW CAN ANYTHING LIVE DOWN IN THESE HELLISH DEPTHS?
ENGINEERS, GET US OUT OF HERE!

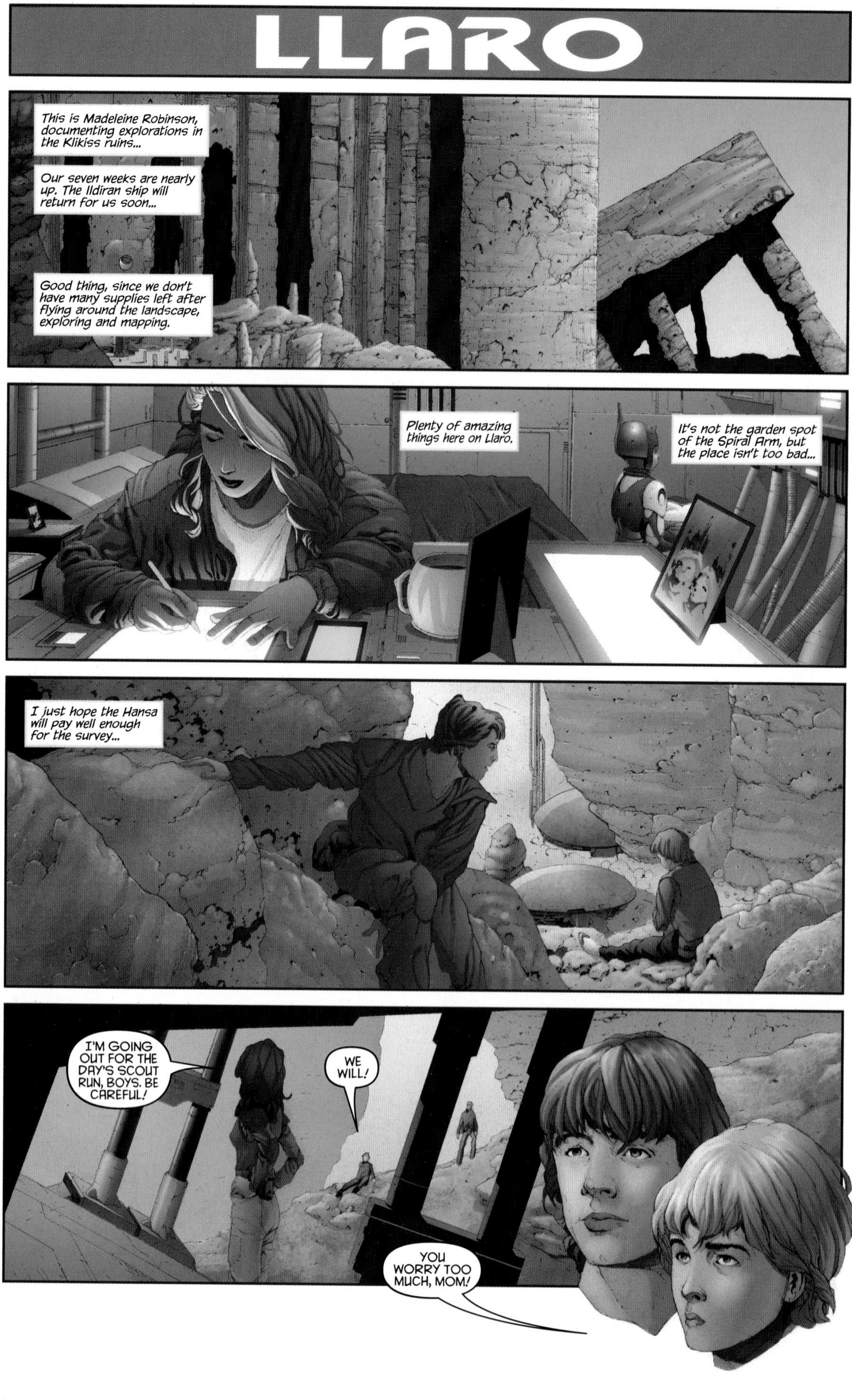
LLARO
This is Madeleine Robinson, documenting explorations in the Klikiss ruins...
Our seven weeks are nearly up. The Ildiran ship will return for us soon...
Good thing, since we don't have many supplies left after flying around the landscape, exploring and mapping.
Plenty of amazing things here on Llaro.
It's not the garden spot of the Spiral Arm, but the place isn't too bad...
I just hope the Hansa will pay well enough for the survey...
I'M GOING OUT FOR THE DAY'S SCOUT RUN, BOYS. BE CAREFUL!
WE WILL!
YOU WORRY TOO MUCH, MOM!

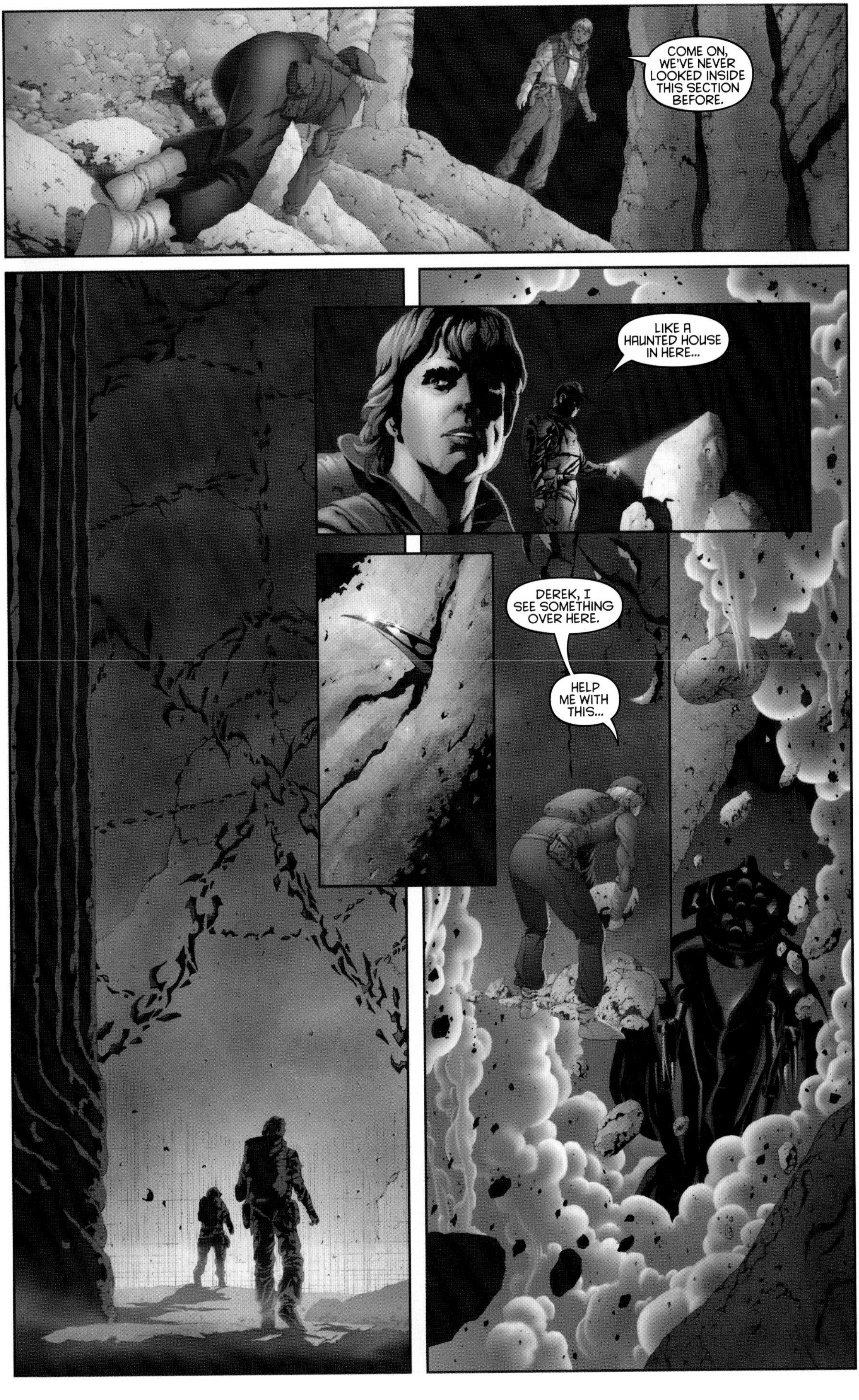
COME ON, WE'VE NEVER LOOKED INSIDE THIS SECTION BEFORE.
LIKE A HAUNTED HOUSE IN HERE...
DEREK, I SEE SOMETHING OVER HERE.
HELP ME WITH THIS...

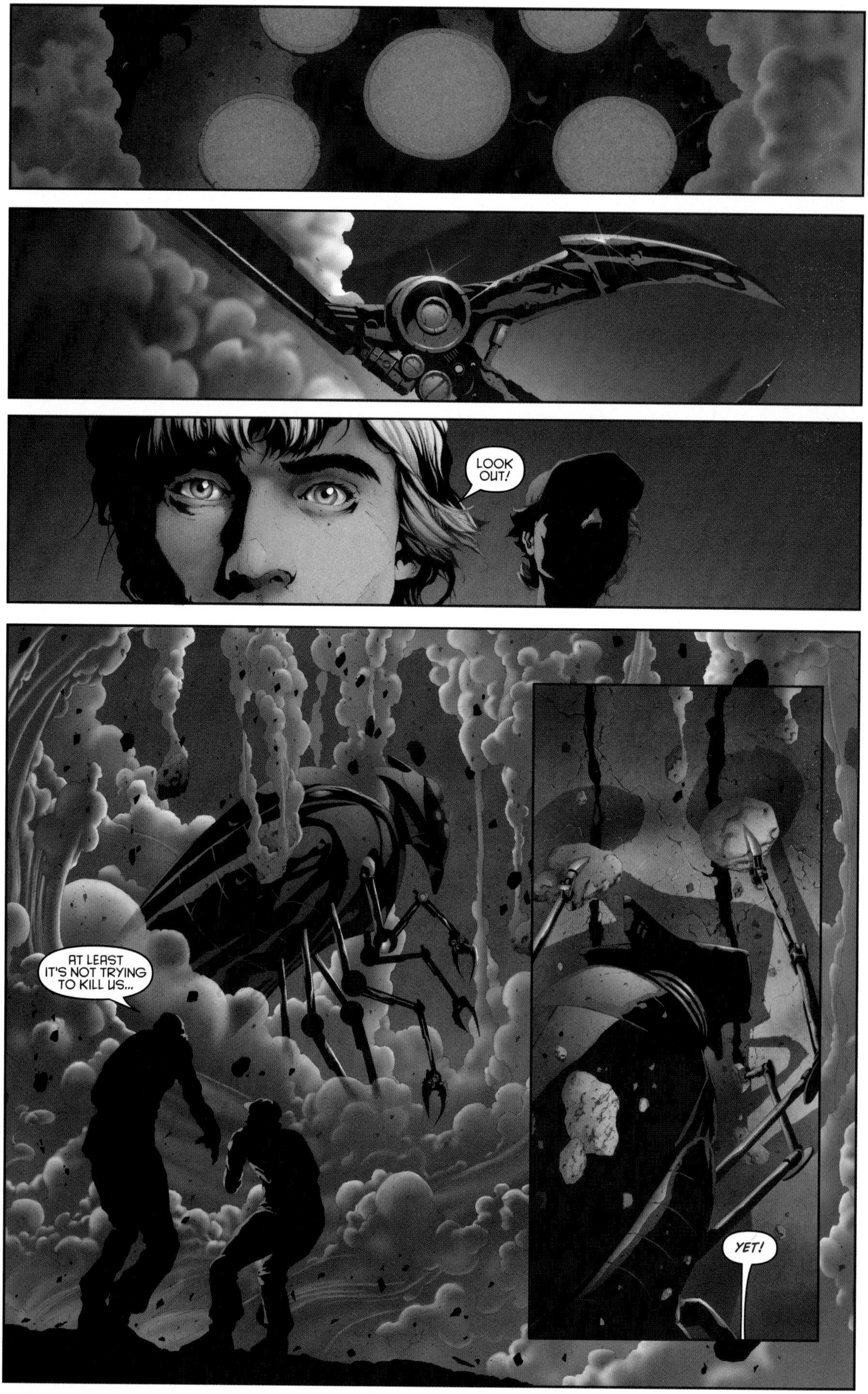
LOOK OUT!
AT LEAST IT'S NOT TRYING TO KILL US...
YET!

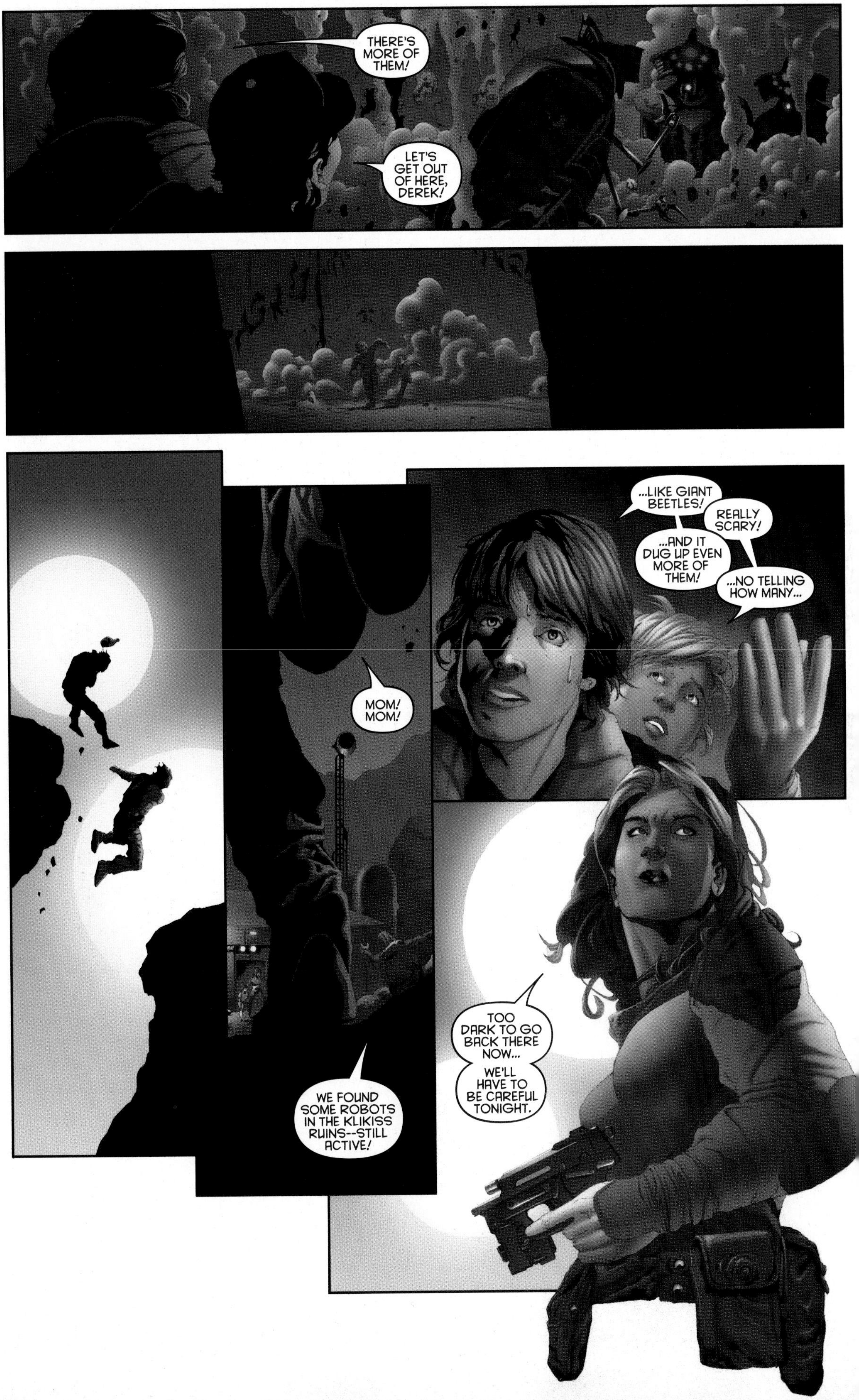
THERE'S MORE OF THEM!
LET'S GET OUT OF HERE, DEREK!
MOM! MOM!
WE FOUND SOME ROBOTS IN THE KLIKISS RUINS--STILL ACTIVE!
...LIKE GIANT BEETLES!
...AND IT DUG UP EVEN MORE OF THEM!
REALLY SCARY!
...NO TELLING HOW MANY...
TOO DARK TO GO BACK THERE NOW...
WE'LL HAVE TO BE CAREFUL TONIGHT.

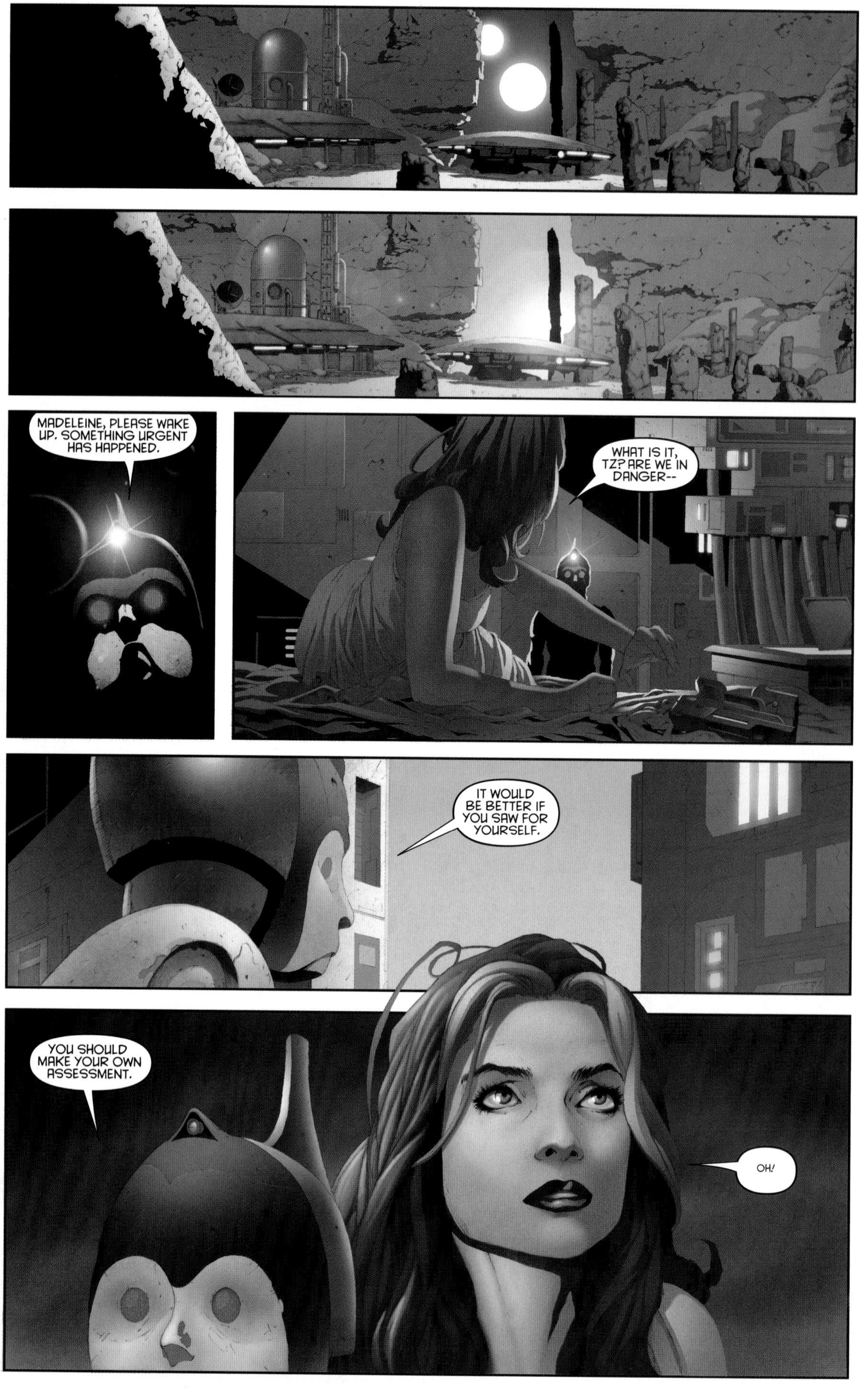
MADELEINE, PLEASE WAKE UP. SOMETHING URGENT HAS HAPPENED.
WHAT IS IT, TZ? ARE WE IN DANGER--
IT WOULD BE BETTER IF YOU SAW FOR YOURSELF.
YOU SHOULD MAKE YOUR OWN ASSESSMENT.
OH!

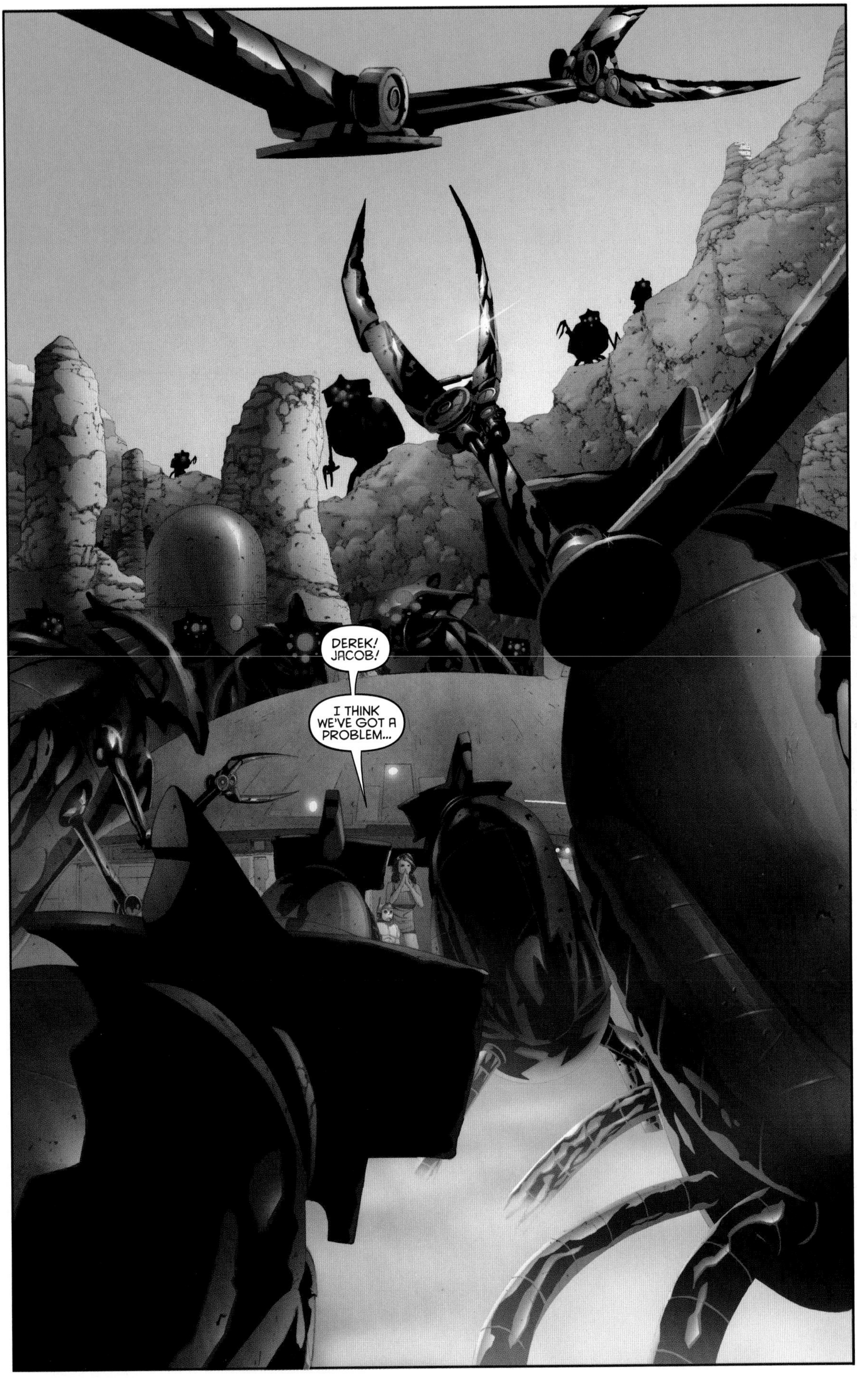

DEREK! JACOB!
I THINK WE'VE GOT A PROBLEM...

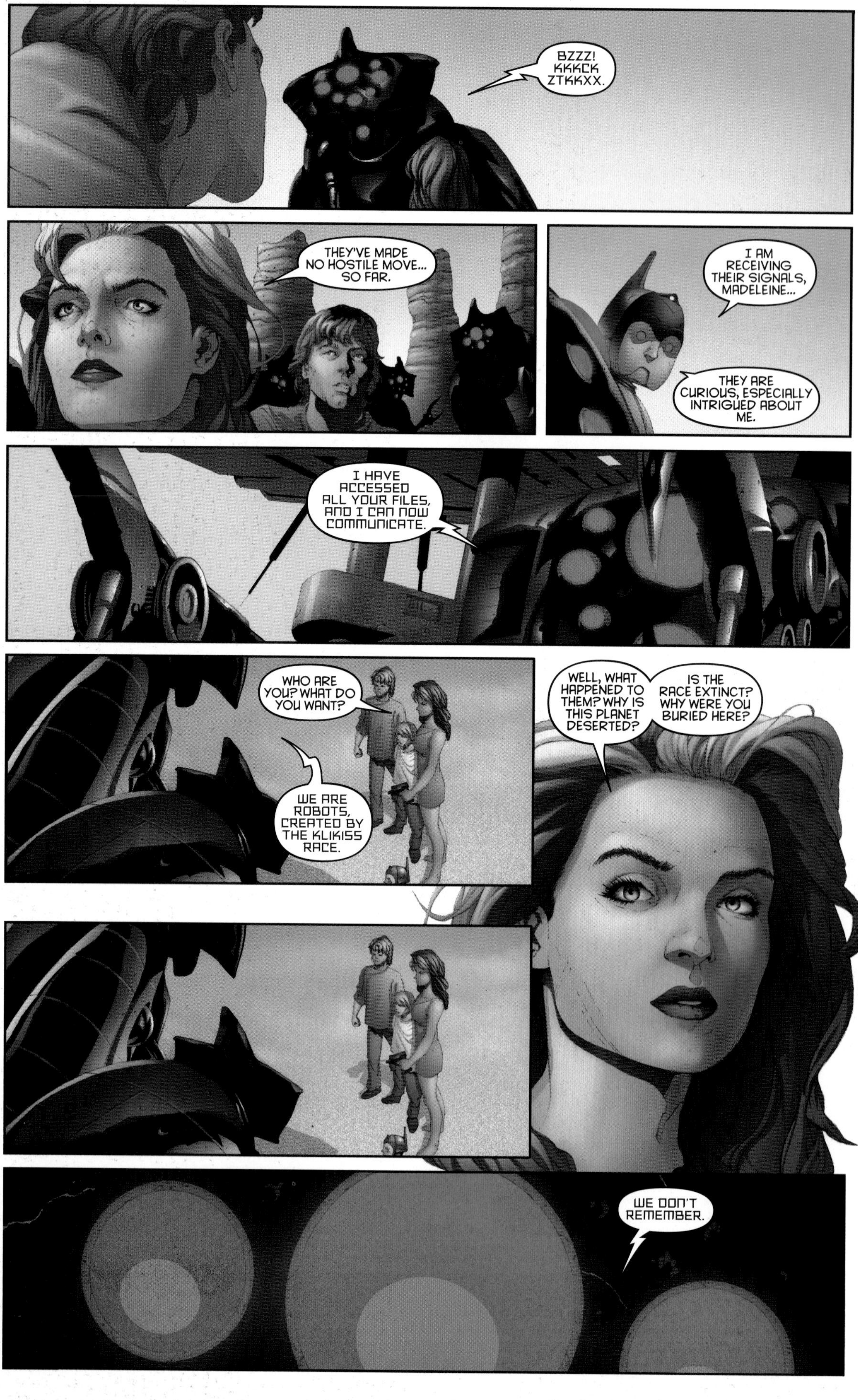
BZZZ! KKKCK ZTKKXX.
THEY'VE MADE NO HOSTILE MOVE... SO FAR.
I AM RECEIVING THEIR SIGNALS, MADELEINE...
THEY ARE CURIOUS, ESPECIALLY INTRIGUED ABOUT ME.
I HAVE ACCESSED ALL YOUR FILES, AND I CAN NOW COMMUNICATE.
WHO ARE YOU? WHAT DO YOU WANT?
WE ARE ROBOTS, CREATED BY THE KLIKISS RACE.
WELL, WHAT HAPPENED TO THEM? WHY IS THIS PLANET DESERTED?
IS THE RACE EXTINCT? WHY WERE YOU BURIED HERE?
WE DON'T REMEMBER.

THEROC

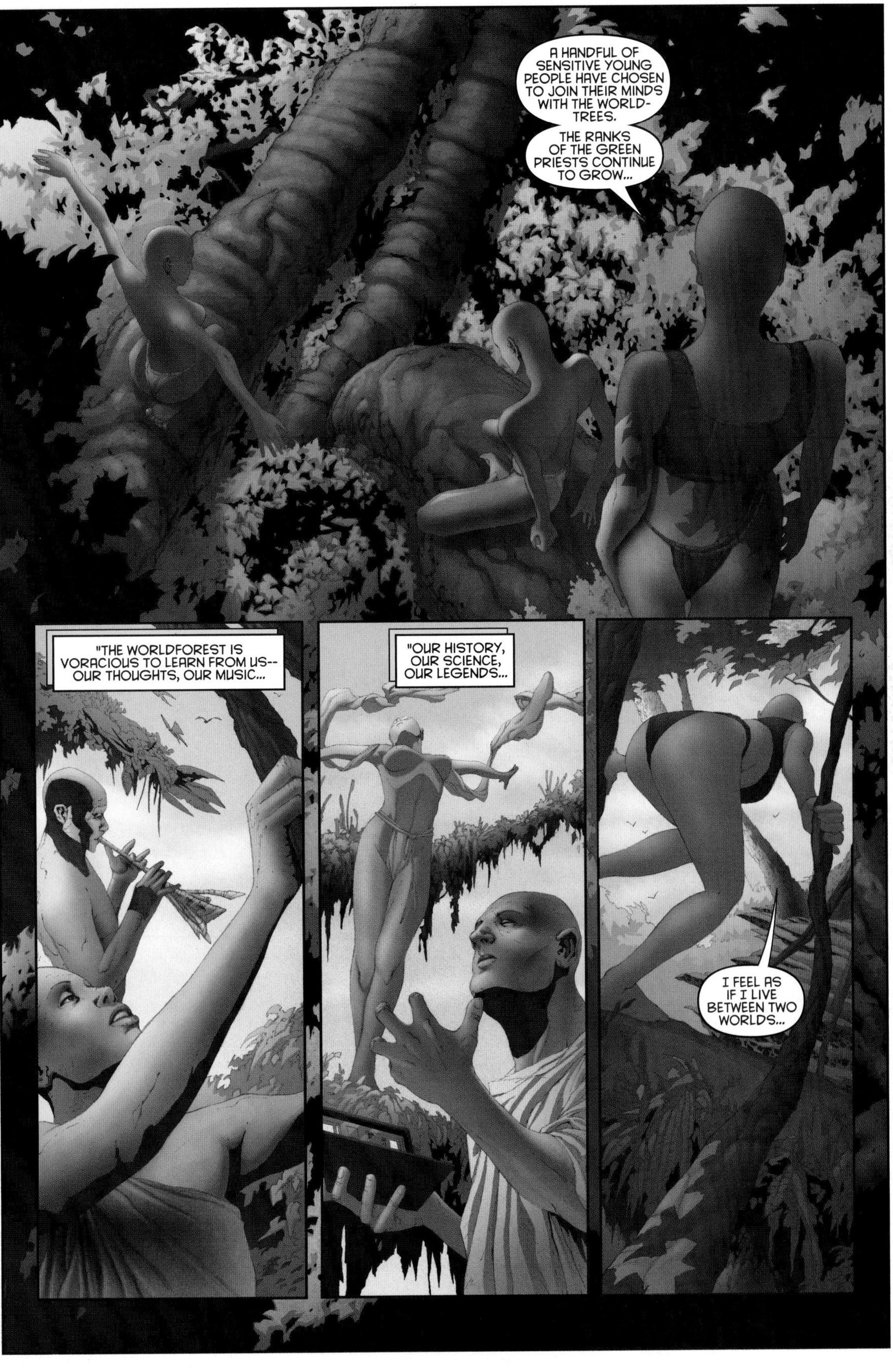
A HANDFUL OF SENSITIVE YOUNG PEOPLE HAVE CHOSEN TO JOIN THEIR MINDS WITH THE WORLD-TREES.
THE RANKS OF THE GREEN PRIESTS CONTINUE TO GROW...
"THE WORLDFOREST IS VORACIOUS TO LEARN FROM US-- OUR THOUGHTS, OUR MUSIC...
"OUR HISTORY, OUR SCIENCE, OUR LEGENDS...
I FEEL AS IF I LIVE BETWEEN TWO WORLDS...

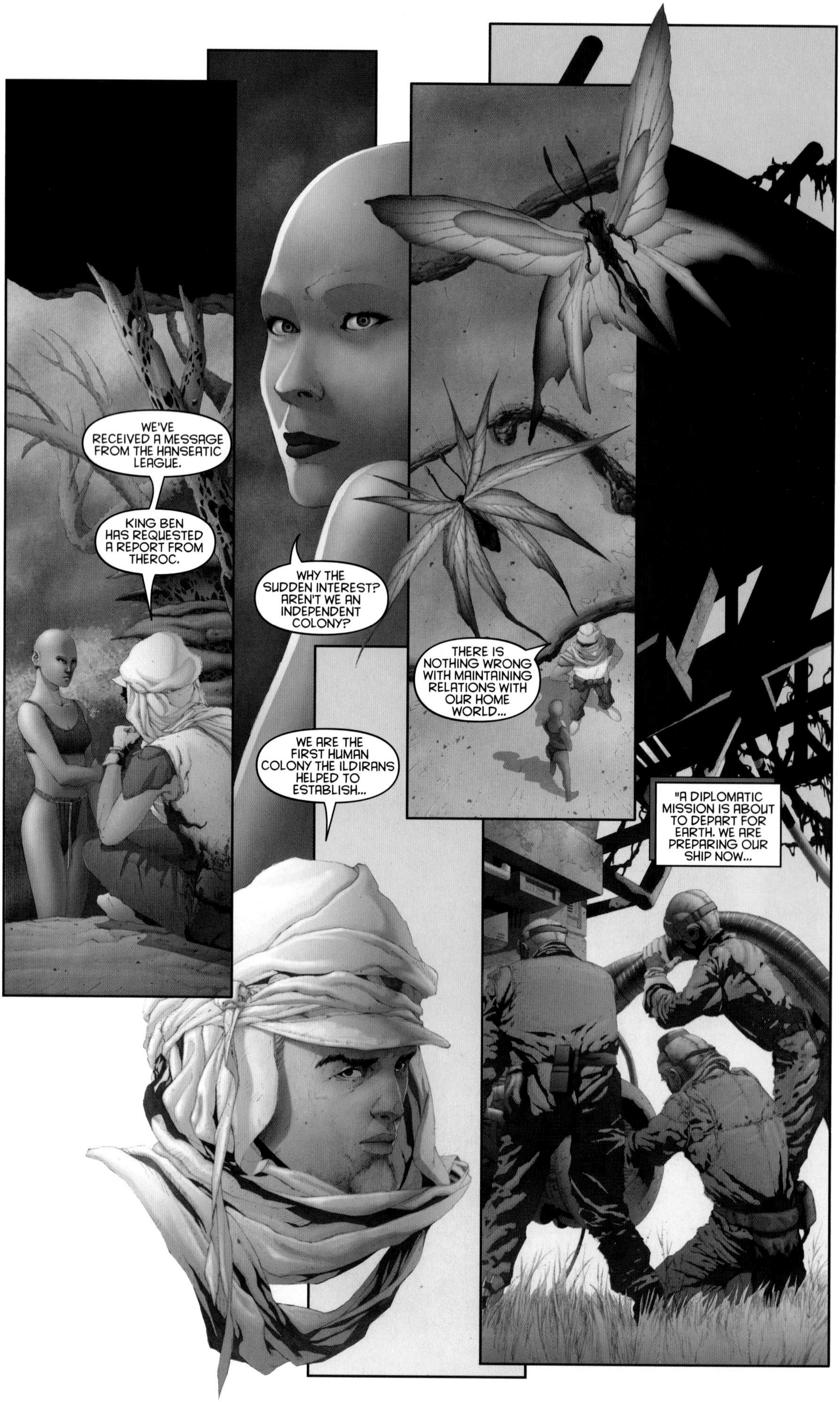

WE'VE RECEIVED A MESSAGE FROM THE HANSEATIC LEAGUE.
KING BEN HAS REQUESTED A REPORT FROM THEROC.
WHY THE SUDDEN INTEREST? AREN'T WE AN INDEPENDENT COLONY?
WE ARE THE FIRST HUMAN COLONY THE ILDIRANS HELPED TO ESTABLISH...
THERE IS NOTHING WRONG WITH MAINTAINING RELATIONS WITH OUR HOME WORLD...
"A DIPLOMATIC MISSION IS ABOUT TO DEPART FOR EARTH. WE ARE PREPARING OUR SHIP NOW...

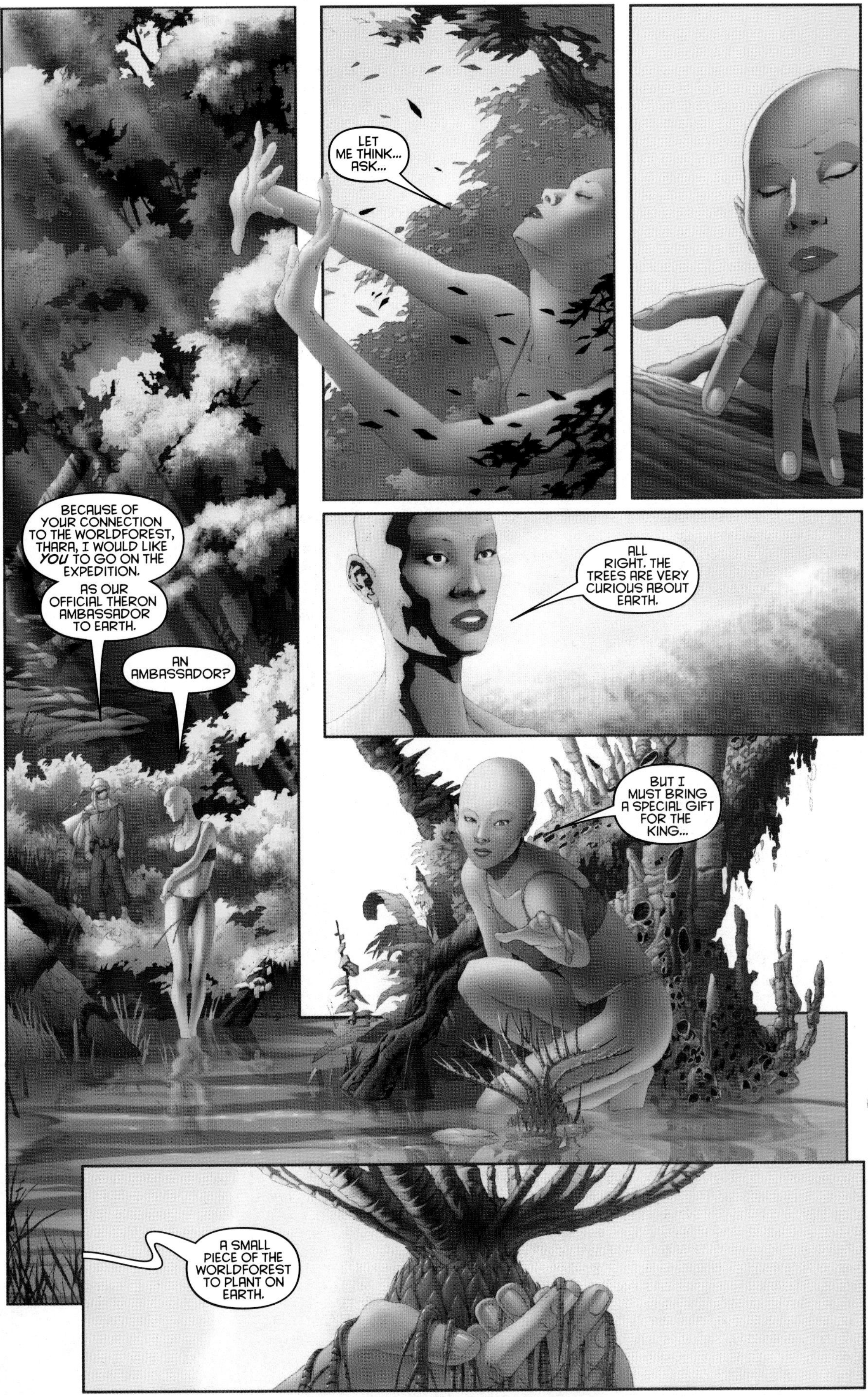
LET ME THINK... ASK...
BECAUSE OF YOUR CONNECTION TO THE WORLDFOREST, THARA, I WOULD LIKE *YOU* TO GO ON THE EXPEDITION.
AS OUR OFFICIAL THERON AMBASSADOR TO EARTH.
AN AMBASSADOR?
ALL RIGHT. THE TREES ARE VERY CURIOUS ABOUT EARTH.
BUT I MUST BRING A SPECIAL GIFT FOR THE KING...
A SMALL PIECE OF THE WORLDFOREST TO PLANT ON EARTH.

DOBRO

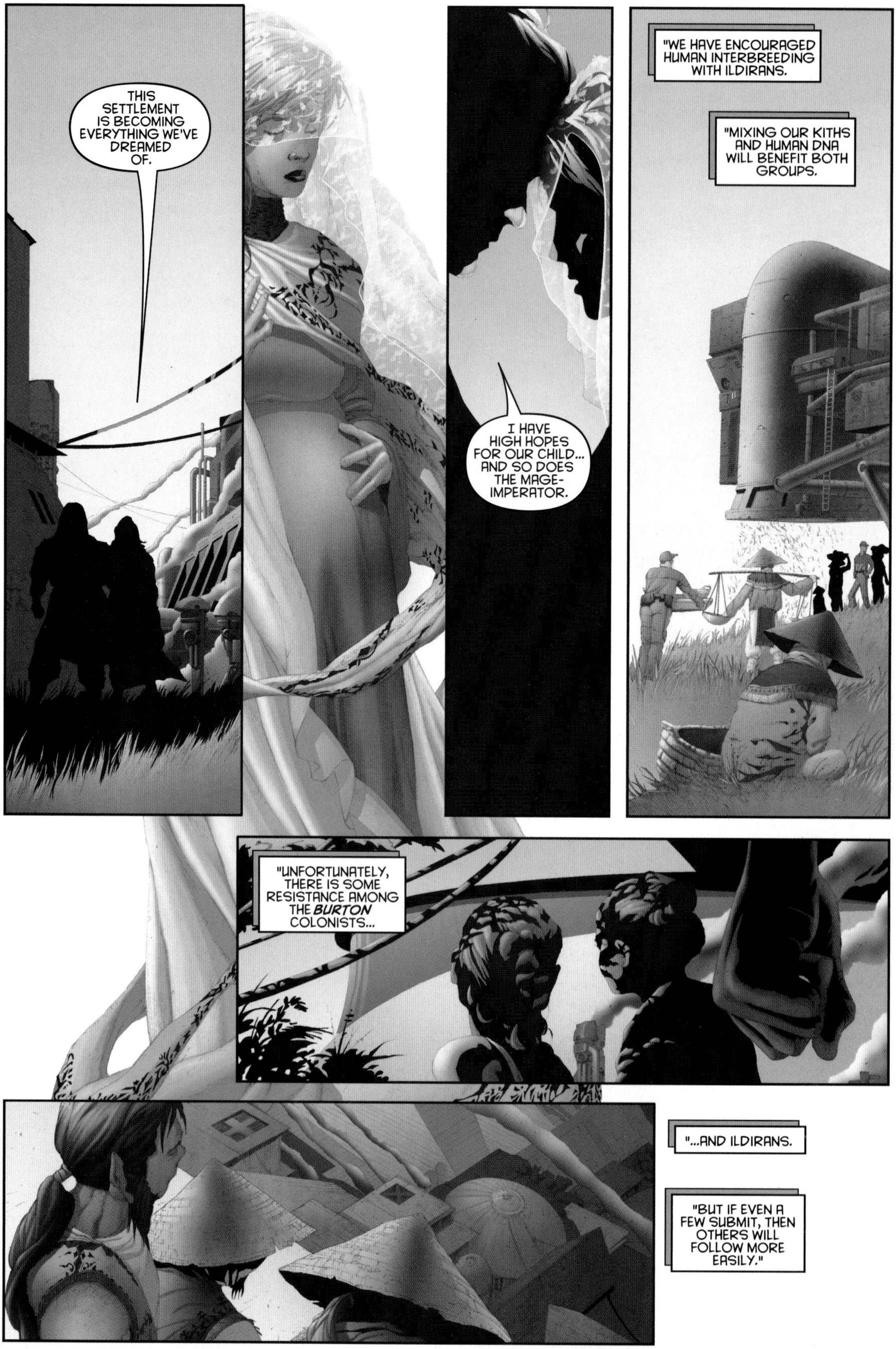
THIS SETTLEMENT IS BECOMING EVERYTHING WE'VE DREAMED OF.
I HAVE HIGH HOPES FOR OUR CHILD... AND SO DOES THE MAGE-IMPERATOR.
"WE HAVE ENCOURAGED HUMAN INTERBREEDING WITH ILDIRANS.
"MIXING OUR KITHS AND HUMAN DNA WILL BENEFIT BOTH GROUPS.
"UNFORTUNATELY, THERE IS SOME RESISTANCE AMONG THE *BURTON* COLONISTS...
"...AND ILDIRANS.
"BUT IF EVEN A FEW SUBMIT, THEN OTHERS WILL FOLLOW MORE EASILY."

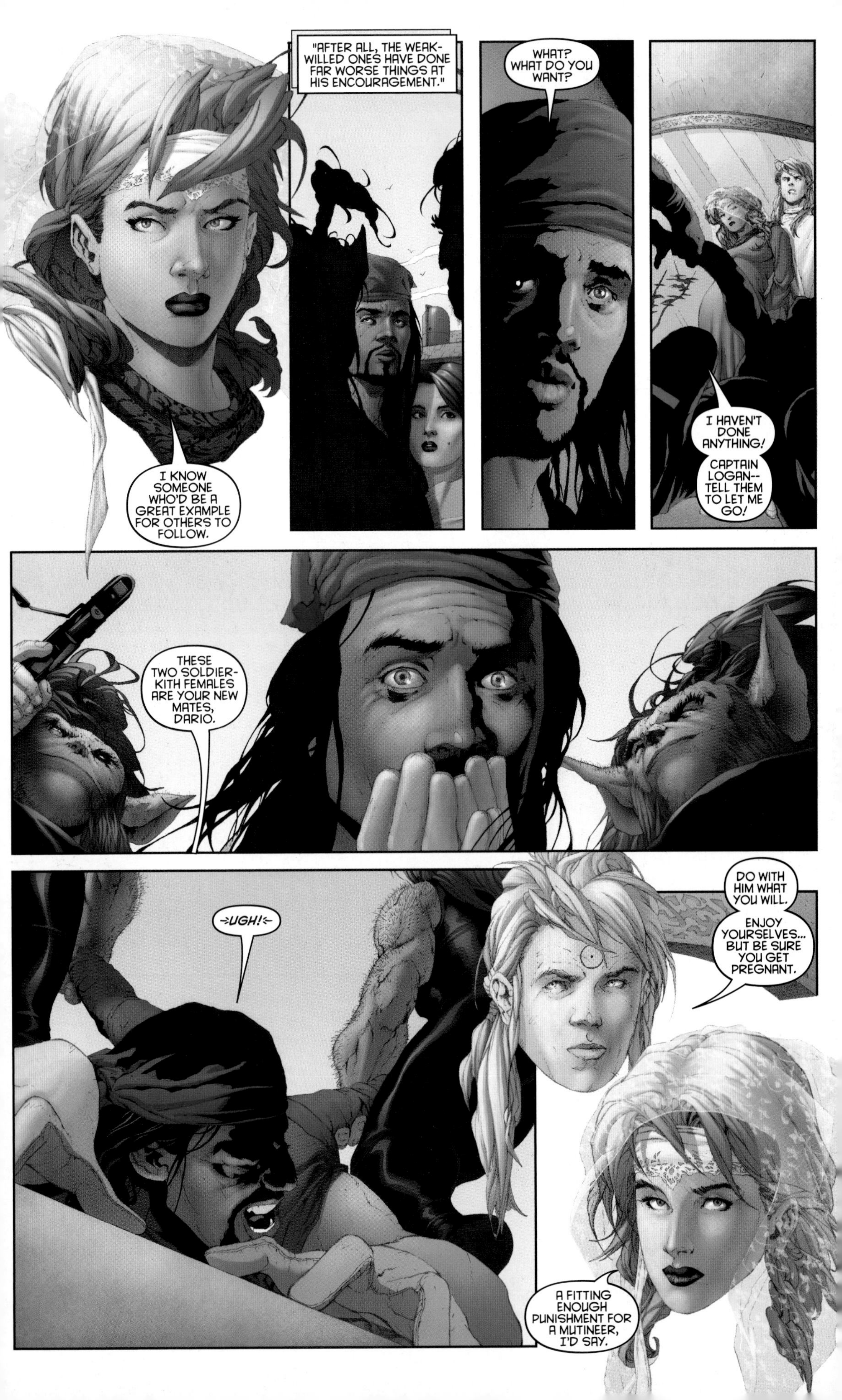
"AFTER ALL, THE WEAK-WILLED ONES HAVE DONE FAR WORSE THINGS AT HIS ENCOURAGEMENT."
I KNOW SOMEONE WHO'D BE A GREAT EXAMPLE FOR OTHERS TO FOLLOW.
WHAT? WHAT DO YOU WANT?
I HAVEN'T DONE ANYTHING!
CAPTAIN LOGAN-- TELL THEM TO LET ME GO!
THESE TWO SOLDIER-KITH FEMALES ARE YOUR NEW MATES, DARIO.
UGH!
DO WITH HIM WHAT YOU WILL.
ENJOY YOURSELVES... BUT BE SURE YOU GET PREGNANT.
A FITTING ENOUGH PUNISHMENT FOR A MUTINEER, I'D SAY.

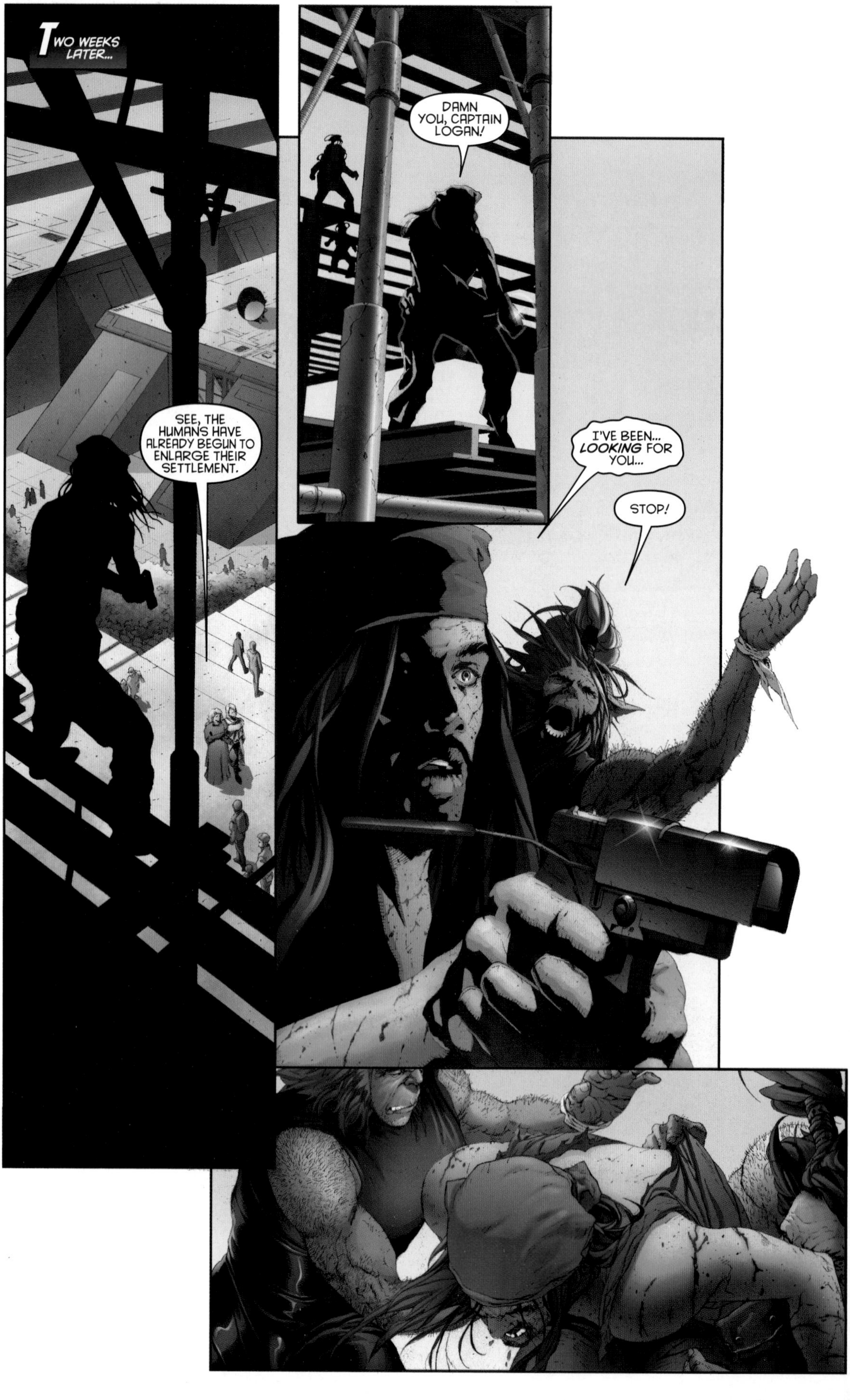
TWO WEEKS LATER...
SEE, THE HUMANS HAVE ALREADY BEGUN TO ENLARGE THEIR SETTLEMENT.
DAMN YOU, CAPTAIN LOGAN!
I'VE BEEN... LOOKING FOR YOU...
STOP!

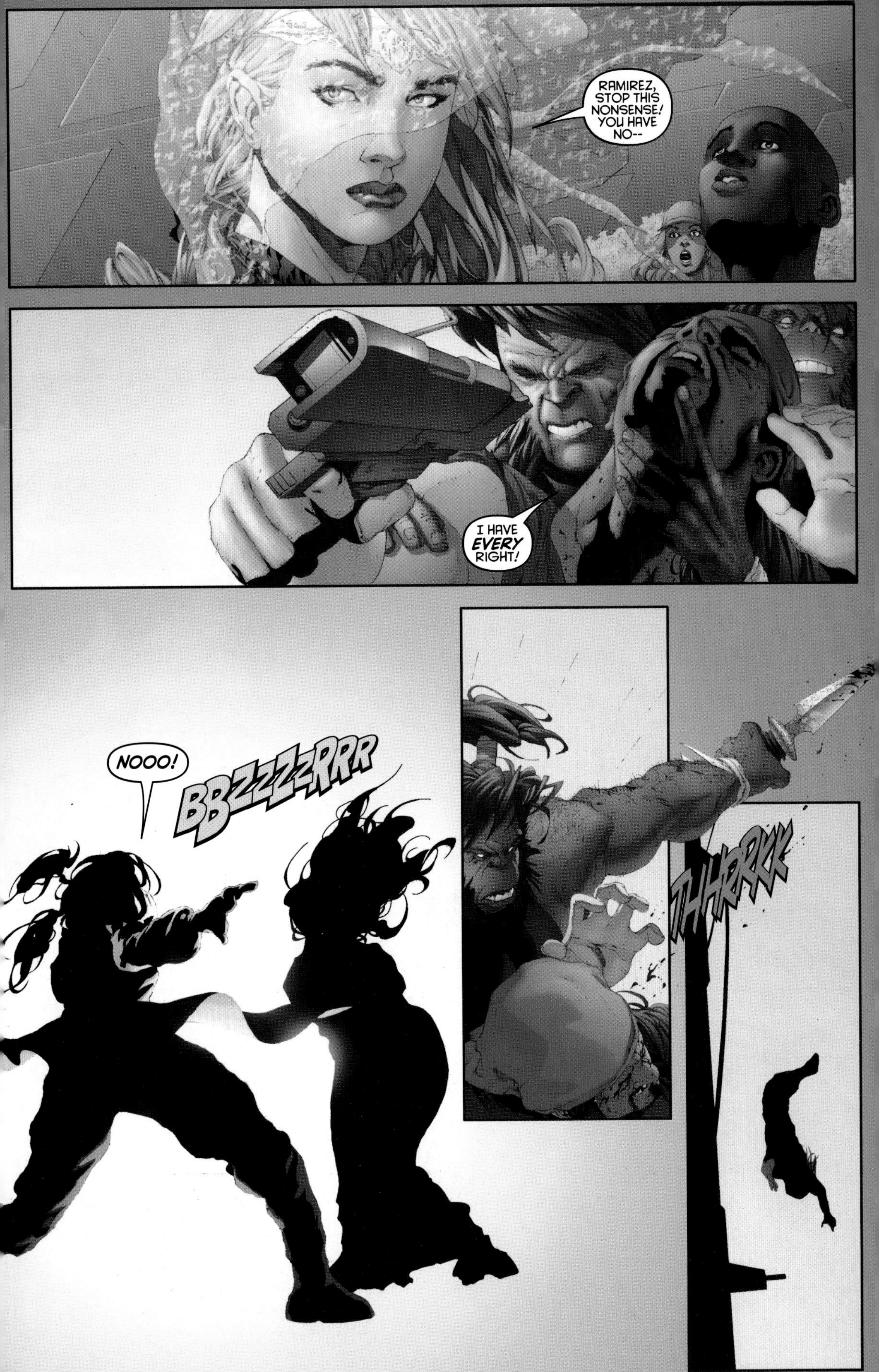
RAMIREZ, STOP THIS NONSENSE! YOU HAVE NO--
I HAVE EVERY RIGHT!
NOOO!
BBZZZZRRR
THHRKK

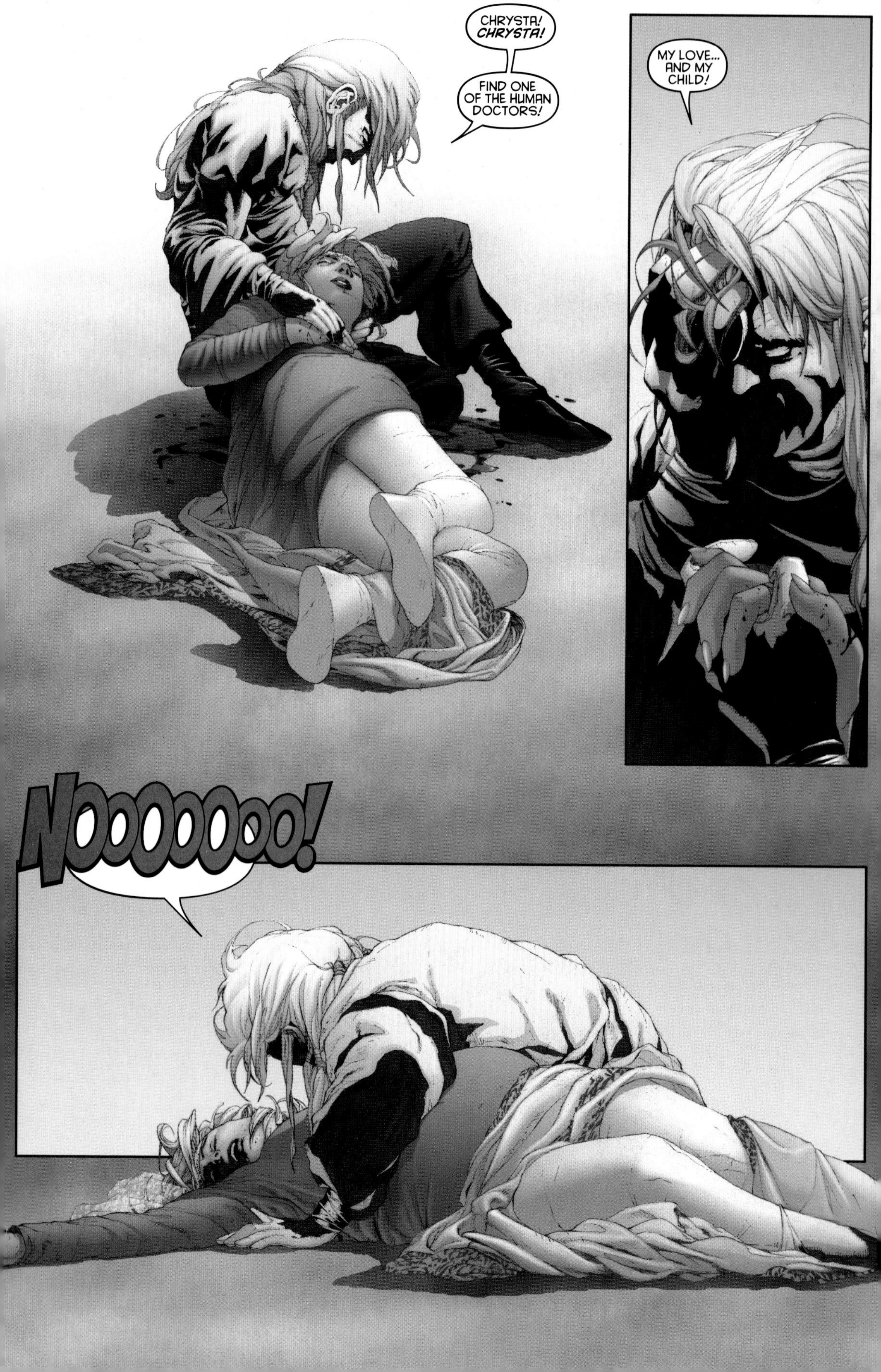
CHRYSTA! CHRYSTA!
FIND ONE OF THE HUMAN DOCTORS!
MY LOVE... AND MY CHILD!
NOOOOOOO!

DAYM

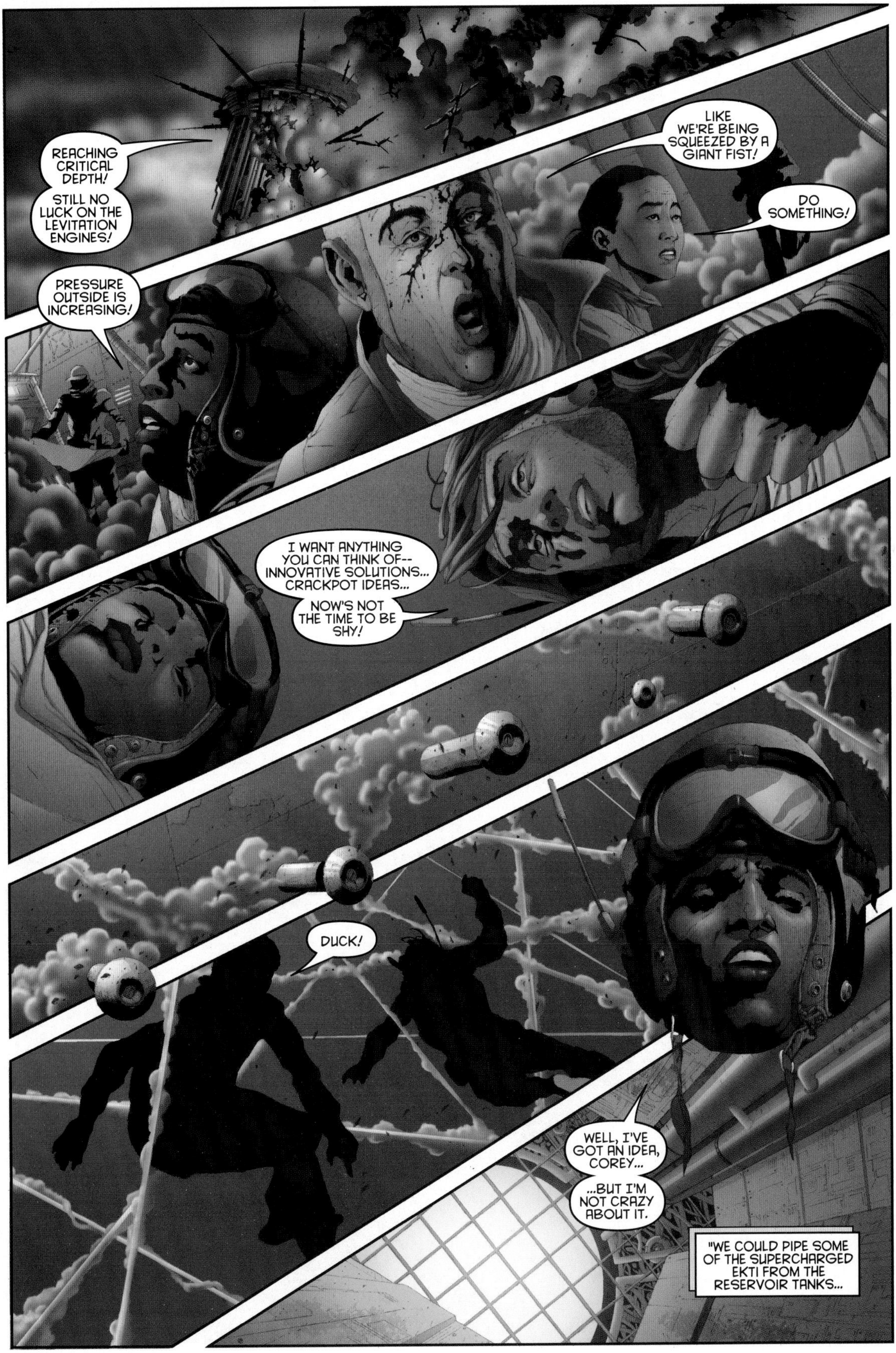

REACHING CRITICAL DEPTH!
STILL NO LUCK ON THE LEVITATION ENGINES!
LIKE WE'RE BEING SQUEEZED BY A GIANT FIST!
DO SOMETHING!
PRESSURE OUTSIDE IS INCREASING!
I WANT ANYTHING YOU CAN THINK OF-- INNOVATIVE SOLUTIONS... CRACKPOT IDEAS...
NOW'S NOT THE TIME TO BE SHY!
DUCK!
WELL, I'VE GOT AN IDEA, COREY...
...BUT I'M NOT CRAZY ABOUT IT.
"WE COULD PIPE SOME OF THE SUPERCHARGED EKTI FROM THE RESERVOIR TANKS...

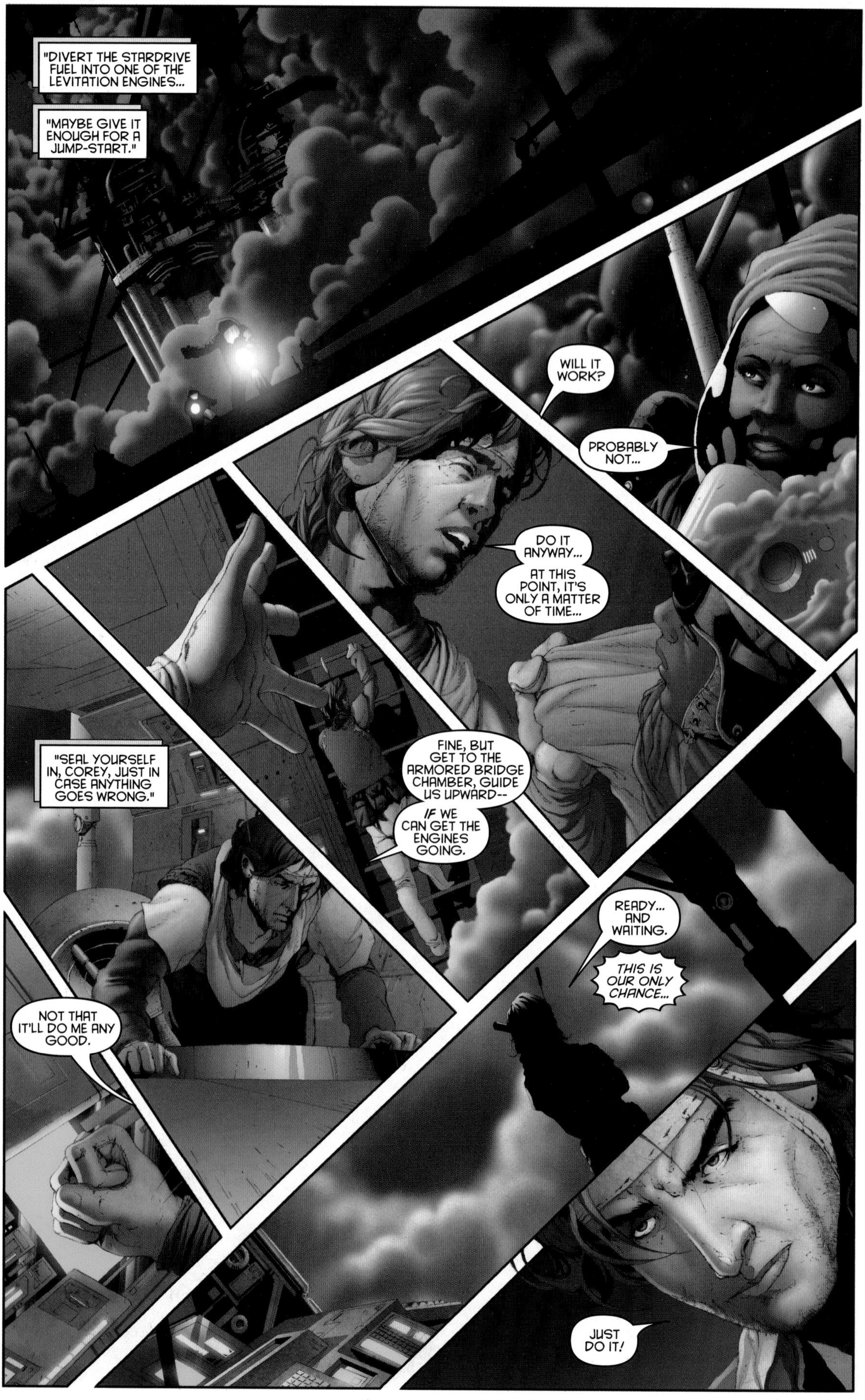
"DIVERT THE STARDRIVE FUEL INTO ONE OF THE LEVITATION ENGINES...
"MAYBE GIVE IT ENOUGH FOR A JUMP-START."
WILL IT WORK?
PROBABLY NOT...
DO IT ANYWAY...
AT THIS POINT, IT'S ONLY A MATTER OF TIME...
"SEAL YOURSELF IN, COREY, JUST IN CASE ANYTHING GOES WRONG."
FINE, BUT GET TO THE ARMORED BRIDGE CHAMBER, GUIDE US UPWARD--
IF WE CAN GET THE ENGINES GOING.
NOT THAT IT'LL DO ME ANY GOOD.
READY... AND WAITING.
THIS IS OUR ONLY CHANCE...
JUST DO IT!

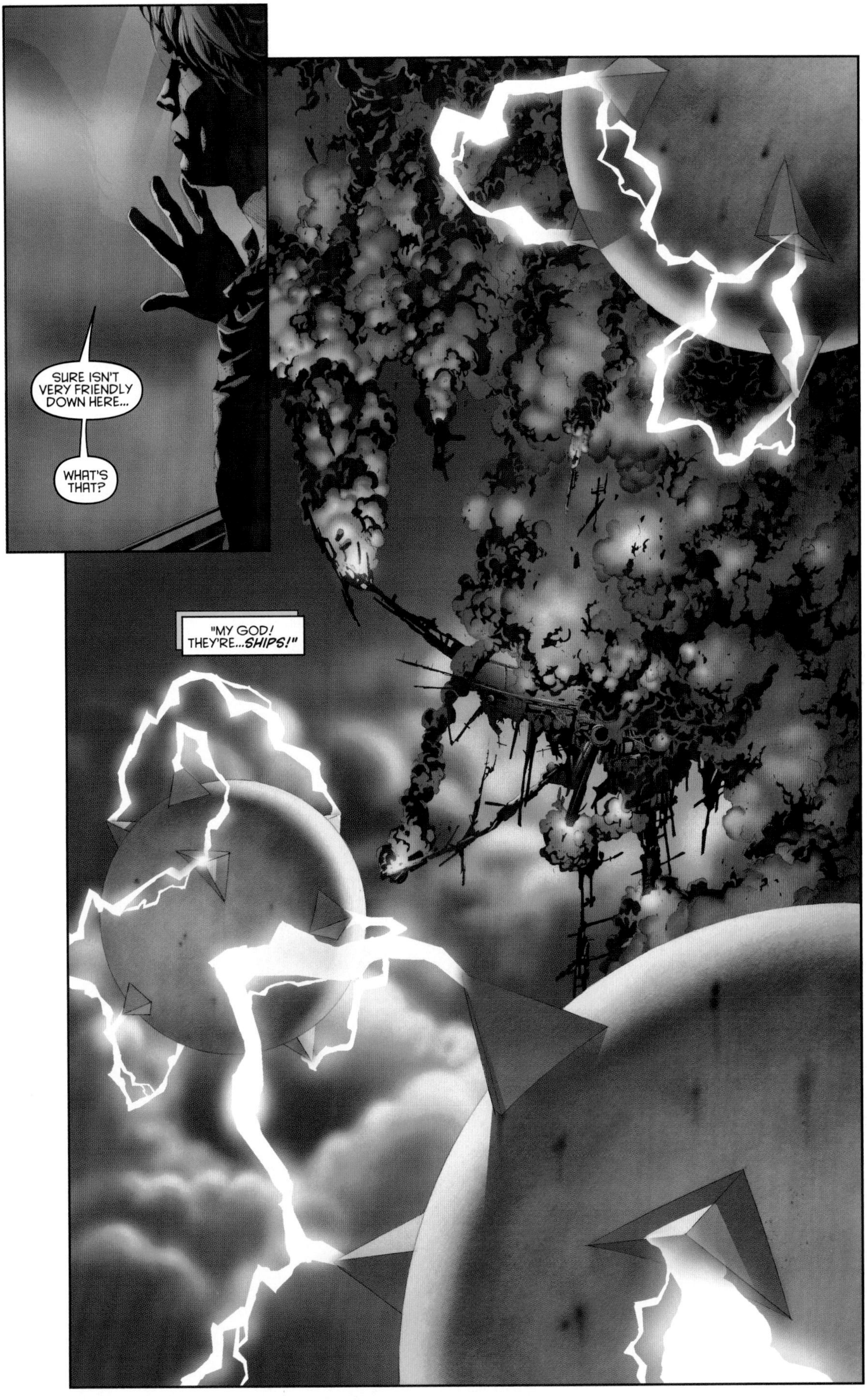
SURE ISN'T VERY FRIENDLY DOWN HERE...
WHAT'S THAT?
"MY GOD! THEY'RE...SHIPS!"

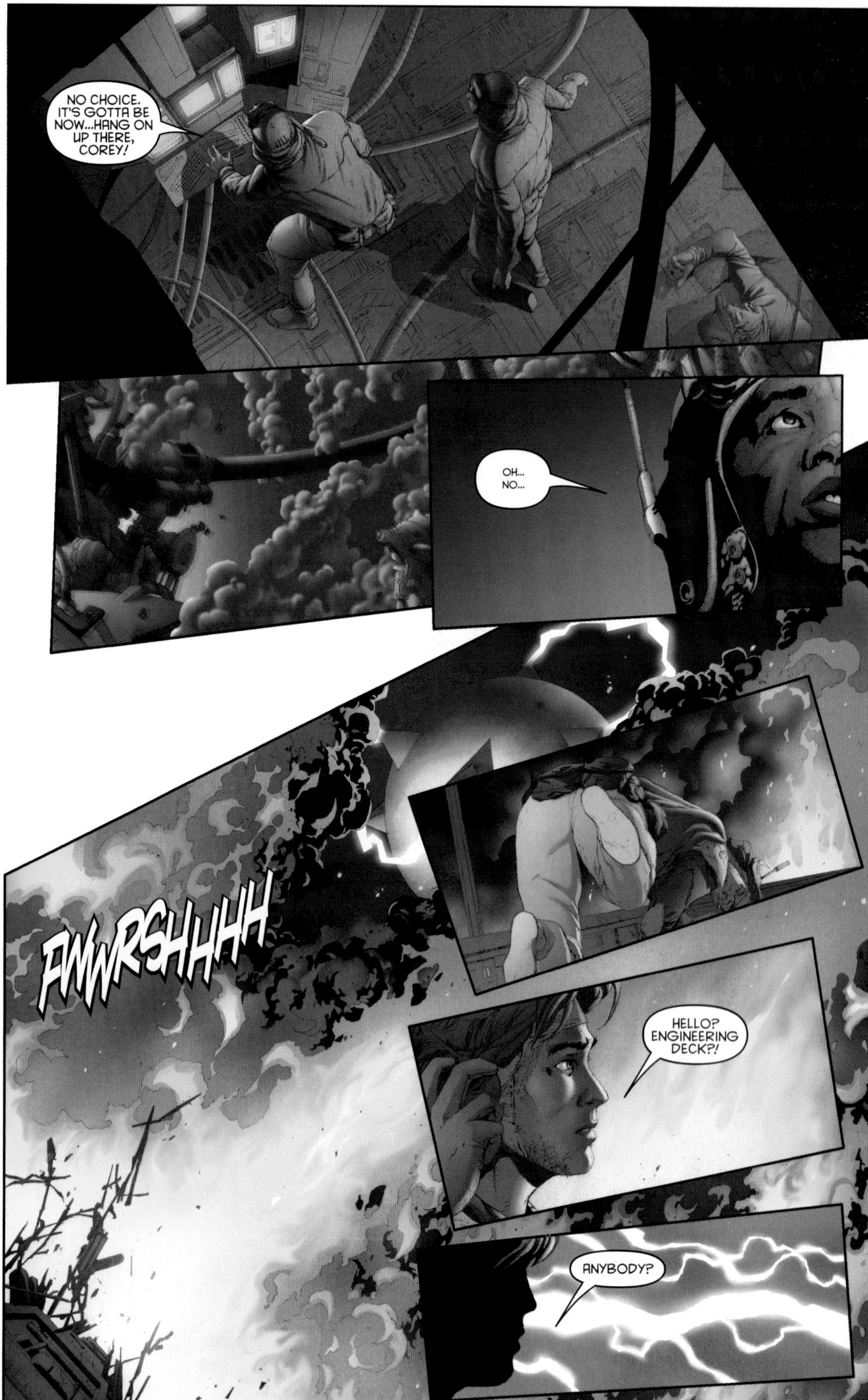
NO CHOICE. IT'S GOTTA BE NOW...HANG ON UP THERE, COREY!
OH... NO...
FWWRSHHHH
HELLO? ENGINEERING DECK?!
ANYBODY?

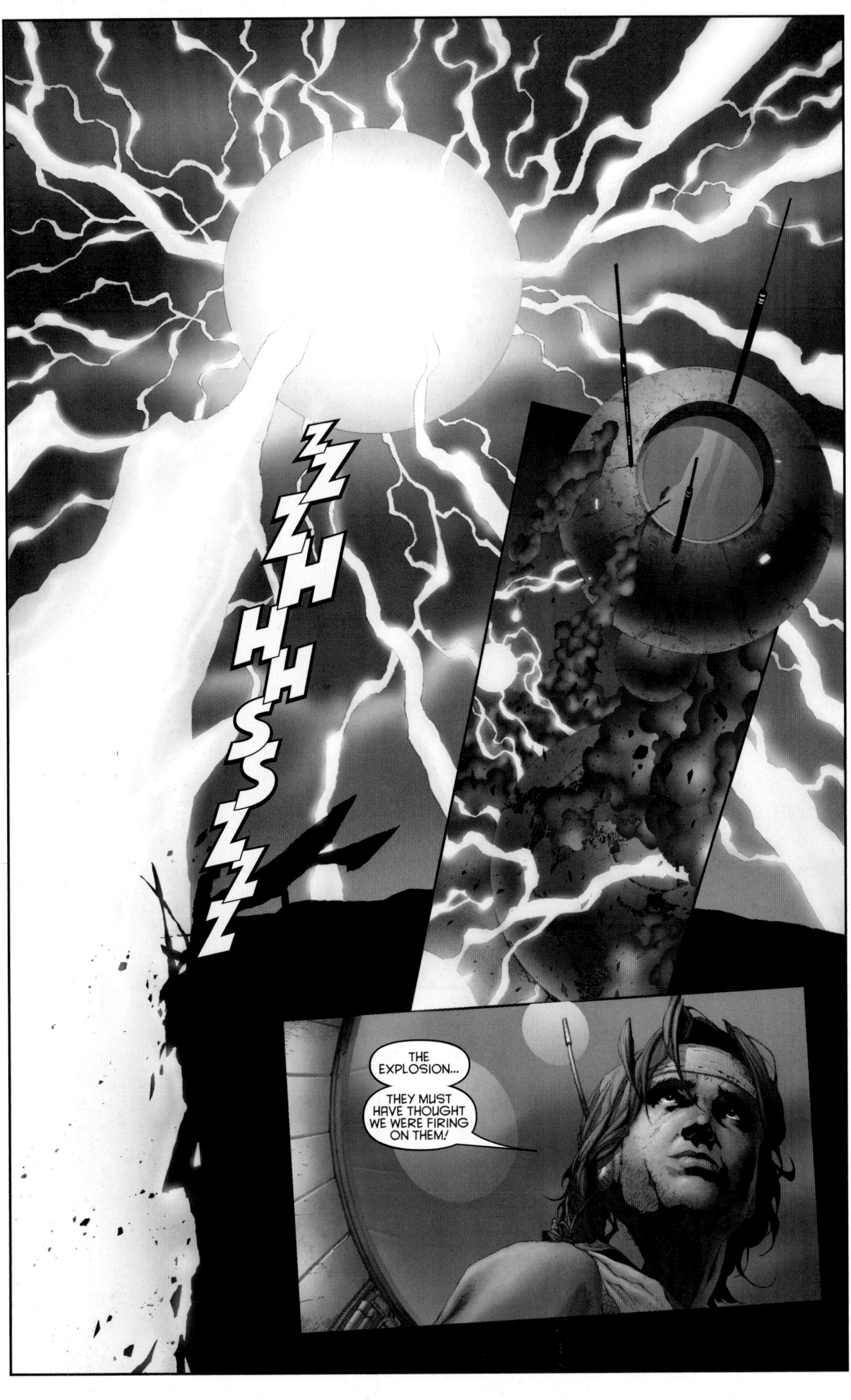
ZZZHHHHSSZZZZ
THE EXPLOSION...
THEY MUST HAVE THOUGHT WE WERE FIRING ON THEM!

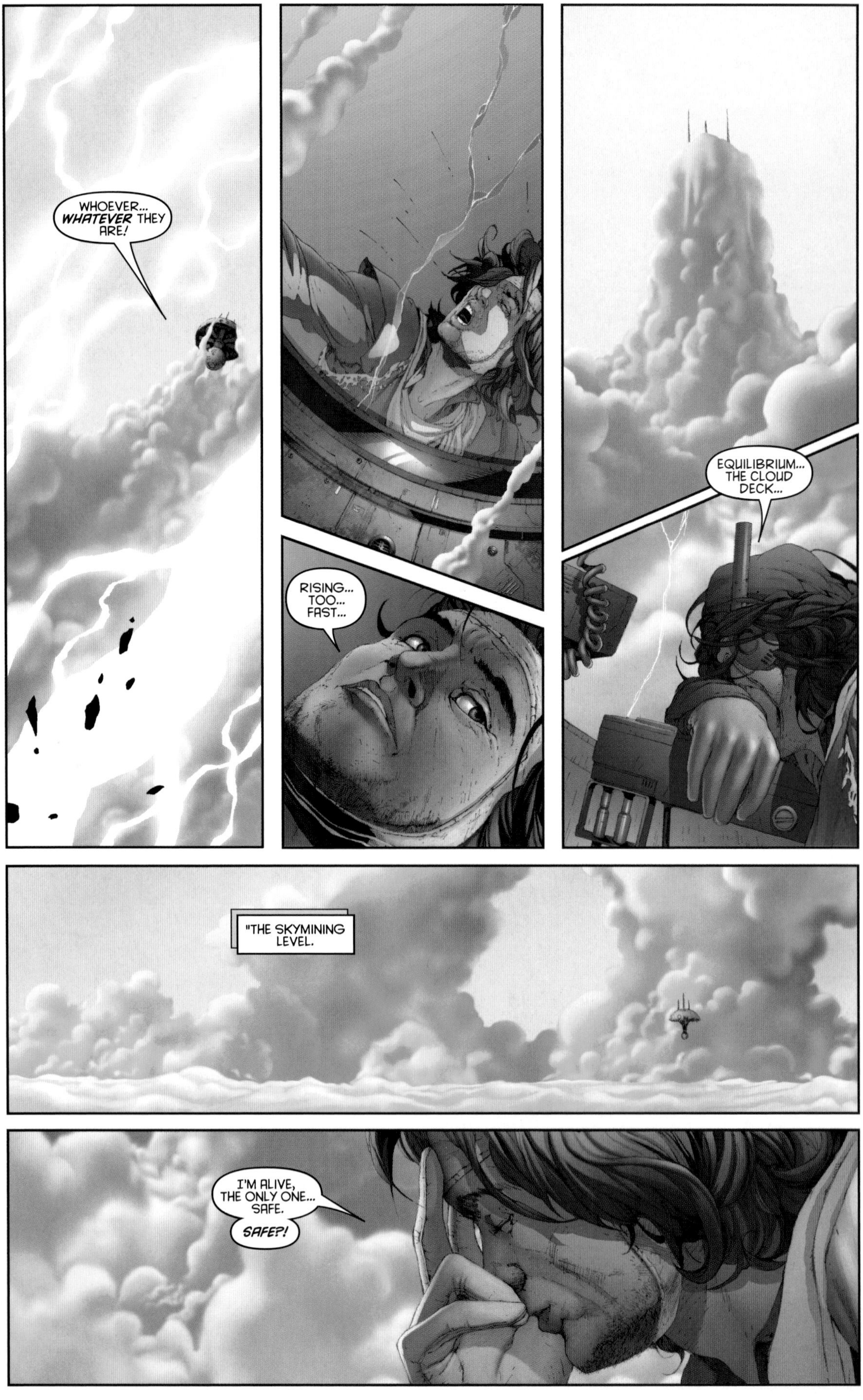
WHOEVER... *WHATEVER* THEY ARE!
RISING... TOO... FAST...
EQUILIBRIUM... THE CLOUD DECK...
"THE SKYMINING LEVEL.
I'M ALIVE, THE ONLY ONE... SAFE.
SAFE?!

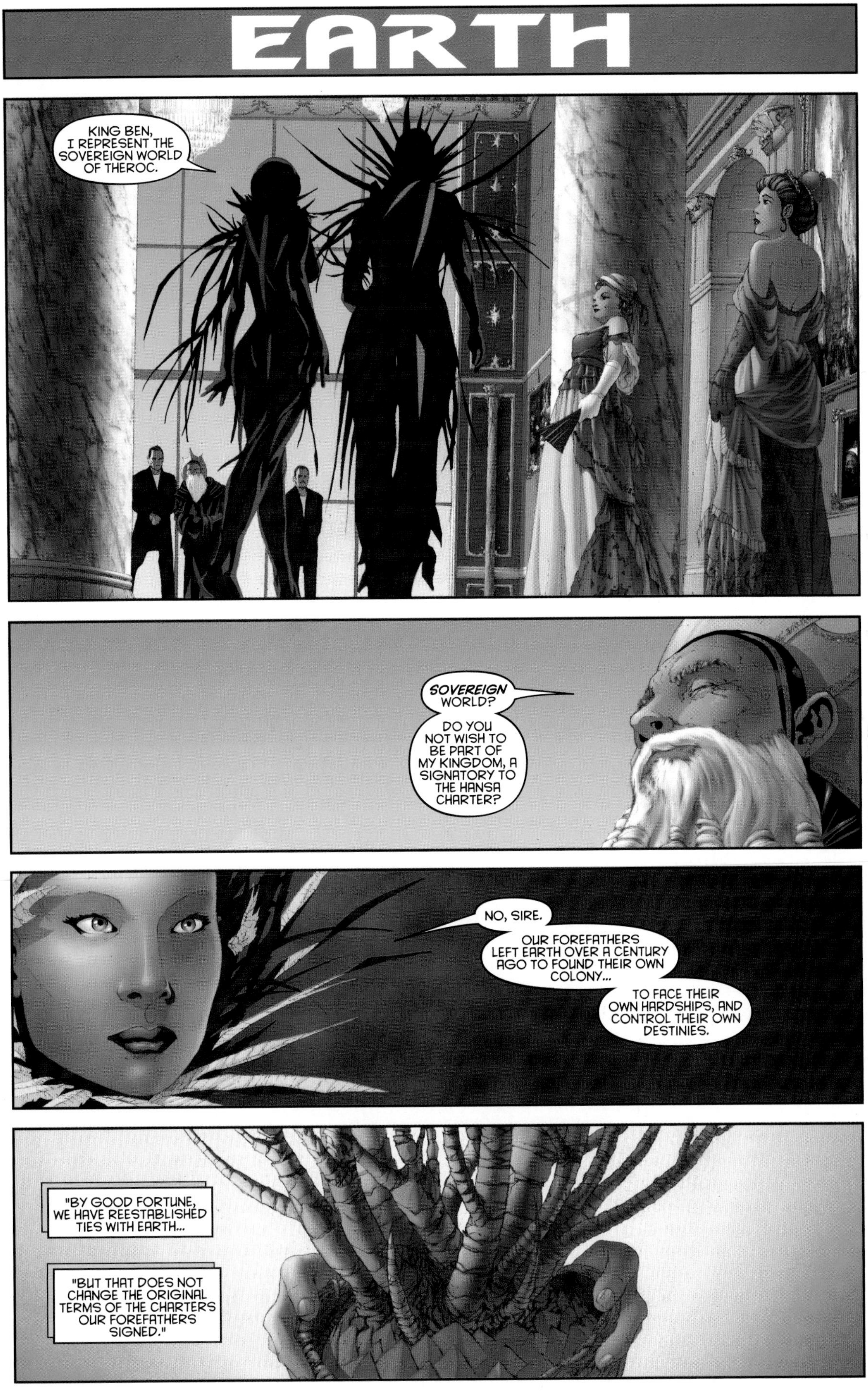
EARTH
KING BEN, I REPRESENT THE SOVEREIGN WORLD OF THEROC.
SOVEREIGN WORLD?
DO YOU NOT WISH TO BE PART OF MY KINGDOM, A SIGNATORY TO THE HANSA CHARTER?
NO, SIRE.
OUR FOREFATHERS LEFT EARTH OVER A CENTURY AGO TO FOUND THEIR OWN COLONY...
TO FACE THEIR OWN HARDSHIPS, AND CONTROL THEIR OWN DESTINIES.
"BY GOOD FORTUNE, WE HAVE REESTABLISHED TIES WITH EARTH...
"BUT THAT DOES NOT CHANGE THE ORIGINAL TERMS OF THE CHARTERS OUR FOREFATHERS SIGNED."

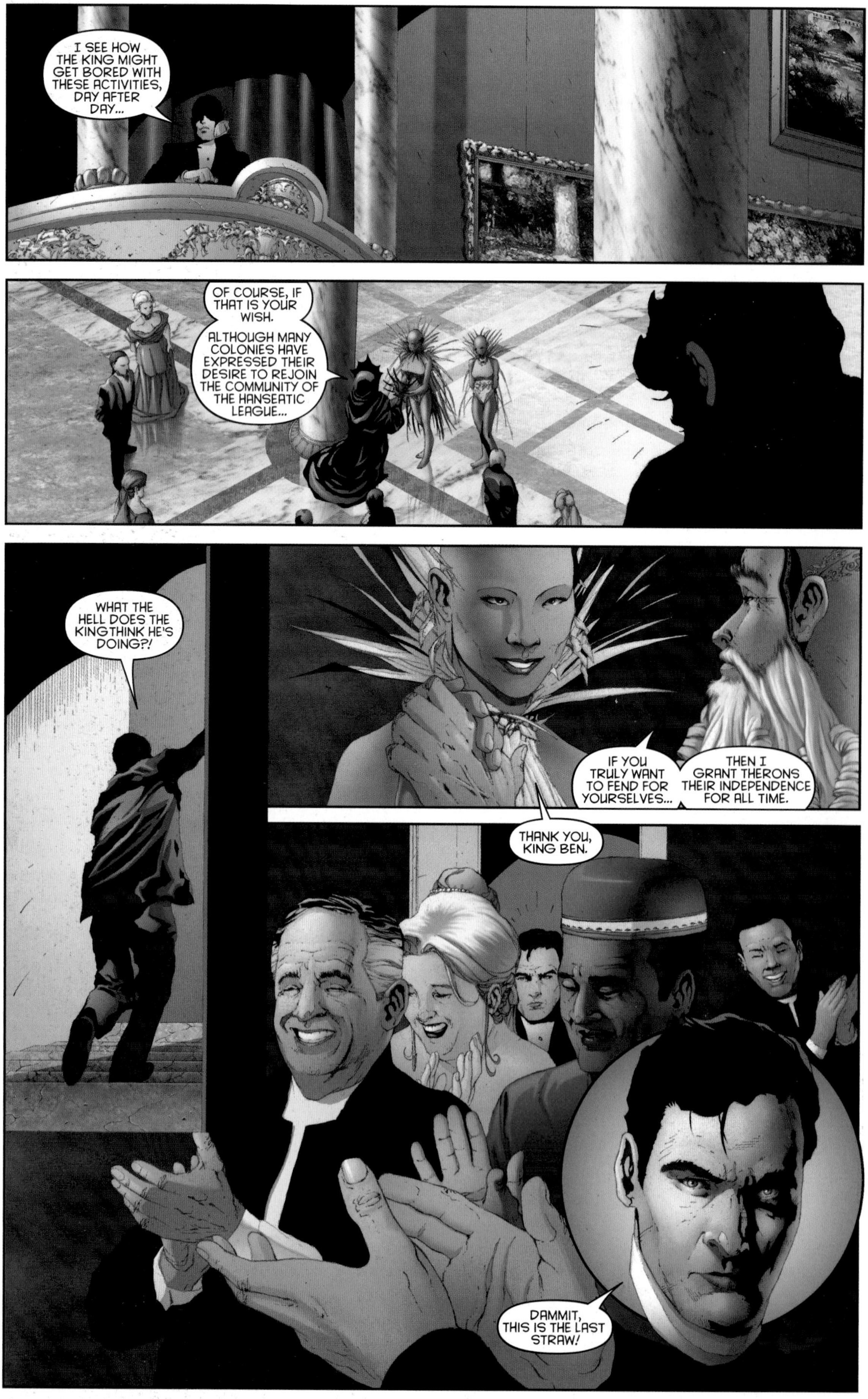
I SEE HOW THE KING MIGHT GET BORED WITH THESE ACTIVITIES, DAY AFTER DAY...
OF COURSE, IF THAT IS YOUR WISH.
ALTHOUGH MANY COLONIES HAVE EXPRESSED THEIR DESIRE TO REJOIN THE COMMUNITY OF THE HANSEATIC LEAGUE...
WHAT THE HELL DOES THE KINGTHINK HE'S DOING?!
IF YOU TRULY WANT TO FEND FOR YOURSELVES...
THEN I GRANT THERONS THEIR INDEPENDENCE FOR ALL TIME.
THANK YOU, KING BEN.
DAMMIT, THIS IS THE LAST STRAW!

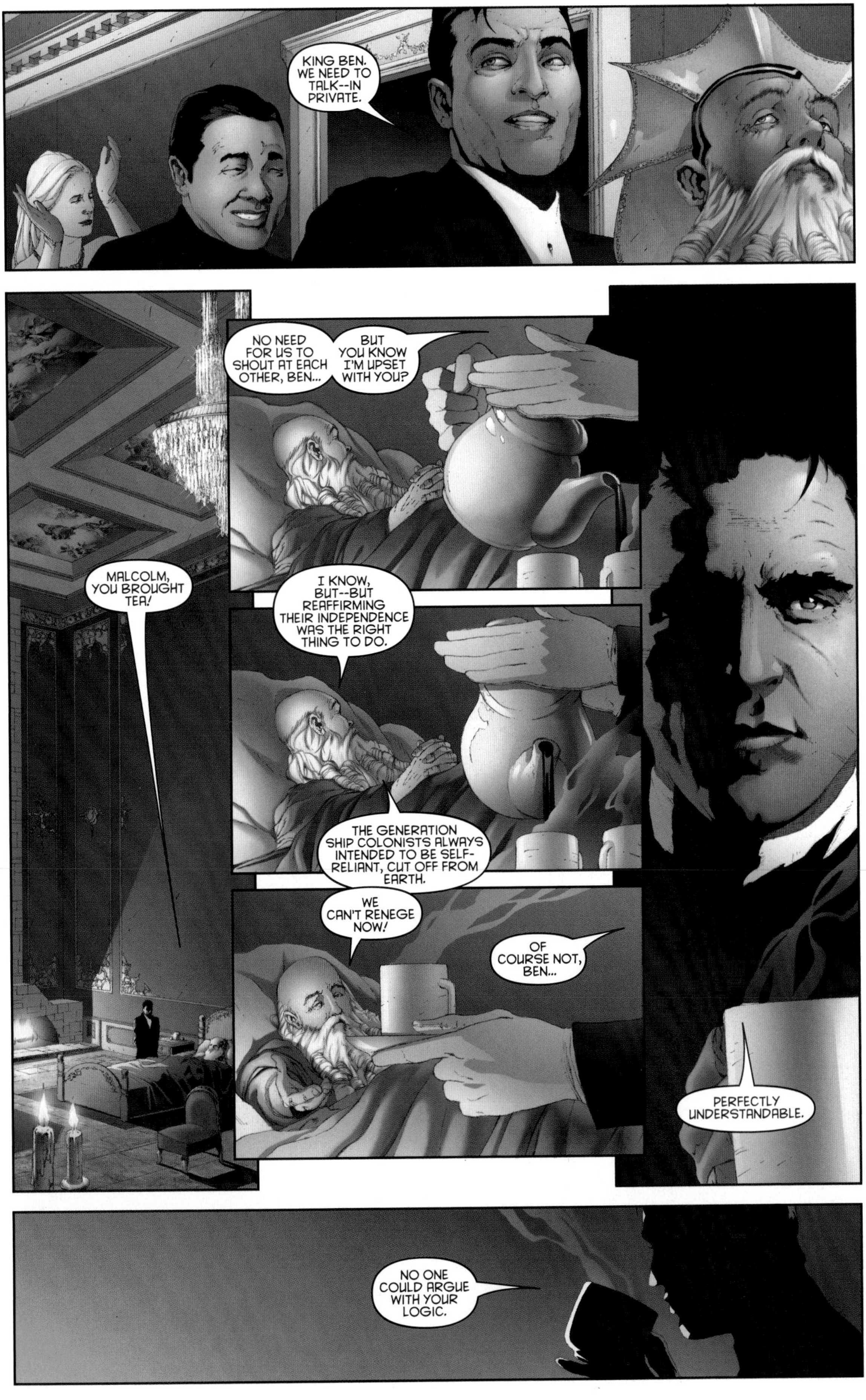
KING BEN. WE NEED TO TALK--IN PRIVATE.
NO NEED FOR US TO SHOUT AT EACH OTHER, BEN...
BUT YOU KNOW I'M UPSET WITH YOU?
MALCOLM, YOU BROUGHT TEA!
I KNOW, BUT--BUT REAFFIRMING THEIR INDEPENDENCE WAS THE RIGHT THING TO DO.
THE GENERATION SHIP COLONISTS ALWAYS INTENDED TO BE SELF-RELIANT, CUT OFF FROM EARTH.
WE CAN'T RENEGE NOW!
OF COURSE NOT, BEN...
PERFECTLY UNDERSTANDABLE.
NO ONE COULD ARGUE WITH YOUR LOGIC.

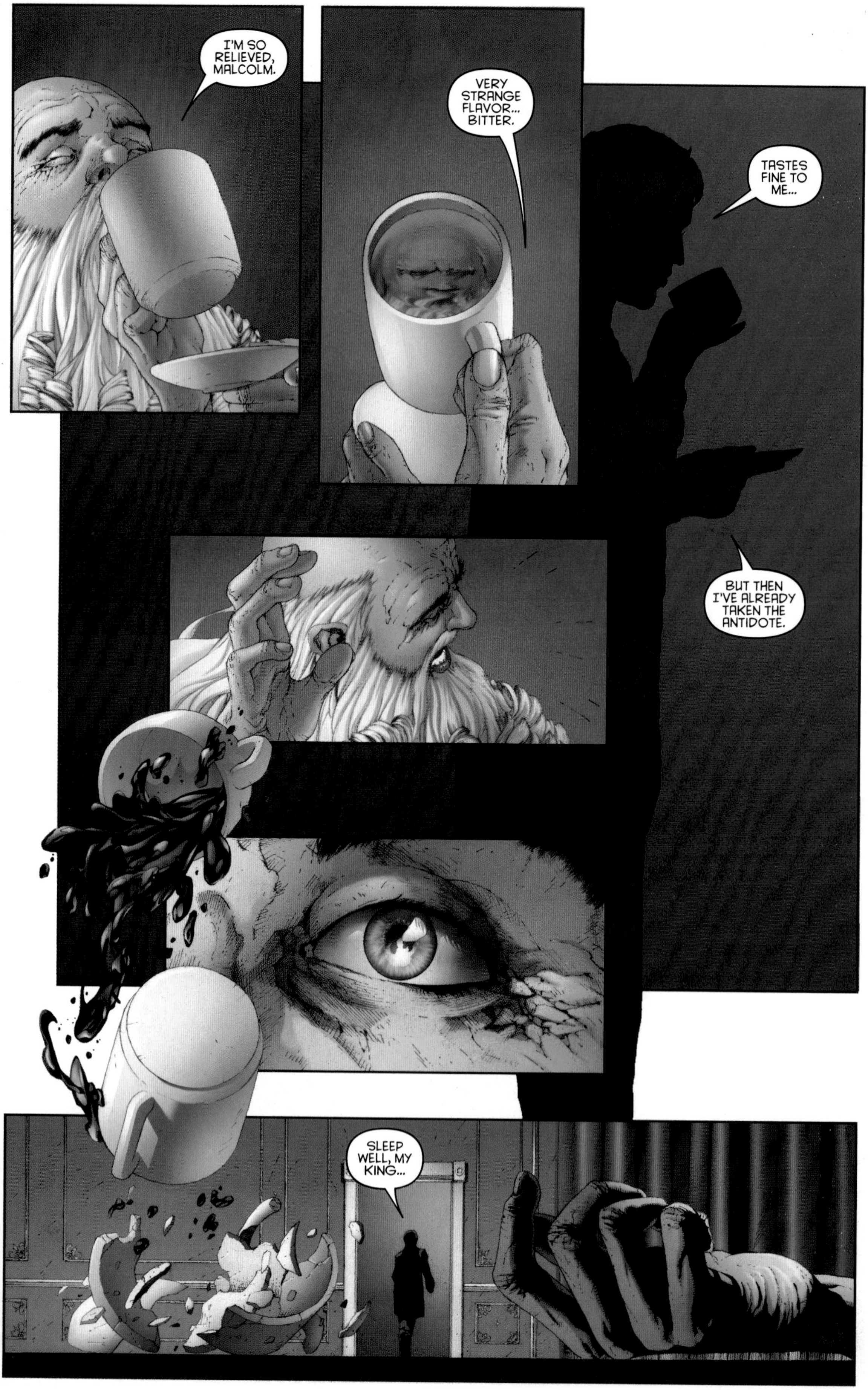
I'M SO RELIEVED, MALCOLM.
VERY STRANGE FLAVOR... BITTER.
TASTES FINE TO ME...
BUT THEN I'VE ALREADY TAKEN THE ANTIDOTE.
SLEEP WELL, MY KING...

LLARO

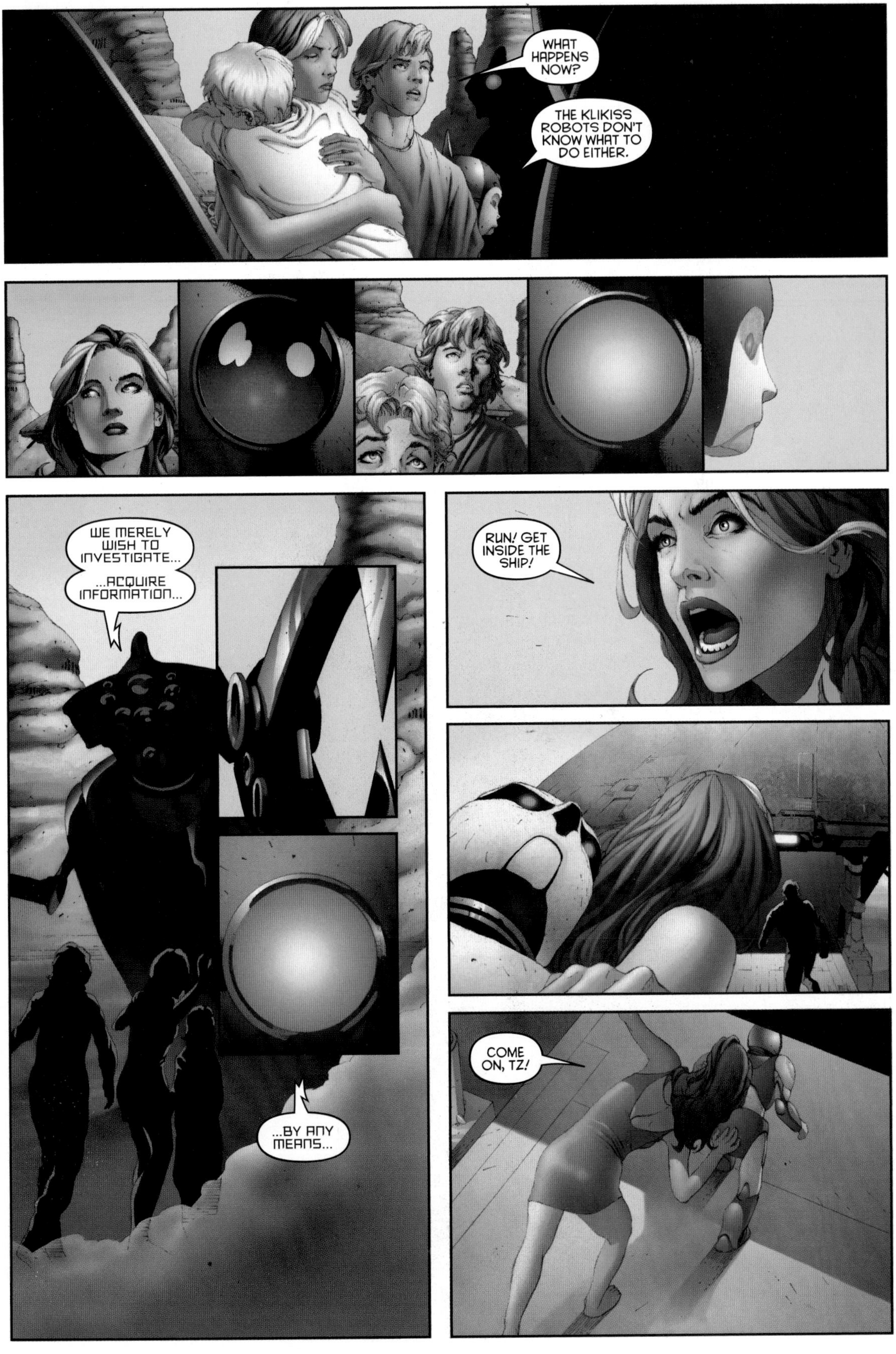
WHAT HAPPENS NOW?
THE KLIKISS ROBOTS DON'T KNOW WHAT TO DO EITHER.
WE MERELY WISH TO INVESTIGATE...
...ACQUIRE INFORMATION...
...BY ANY MEANS...
RUN! GET INSIDE THE SHIP!
COME ON, TZ!

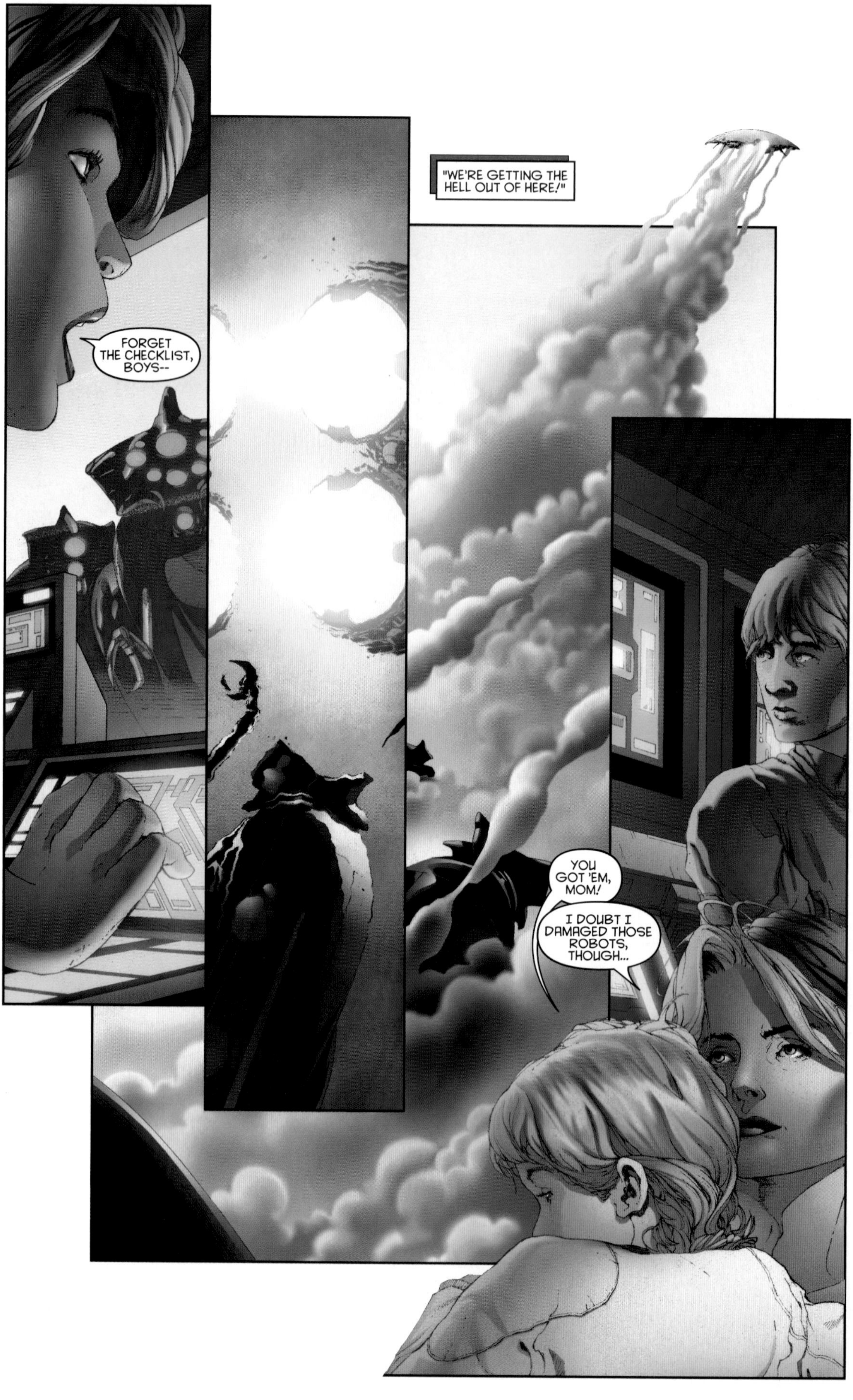
FORGET THE CHECKLIST, BOYS--
"WE'RE GETTING THE HELL OUT OF HERE!"
YOU GOT 'EM, MOM!
I DOUBT I DAMAGED THOSE ROBOTS, THOUGH...

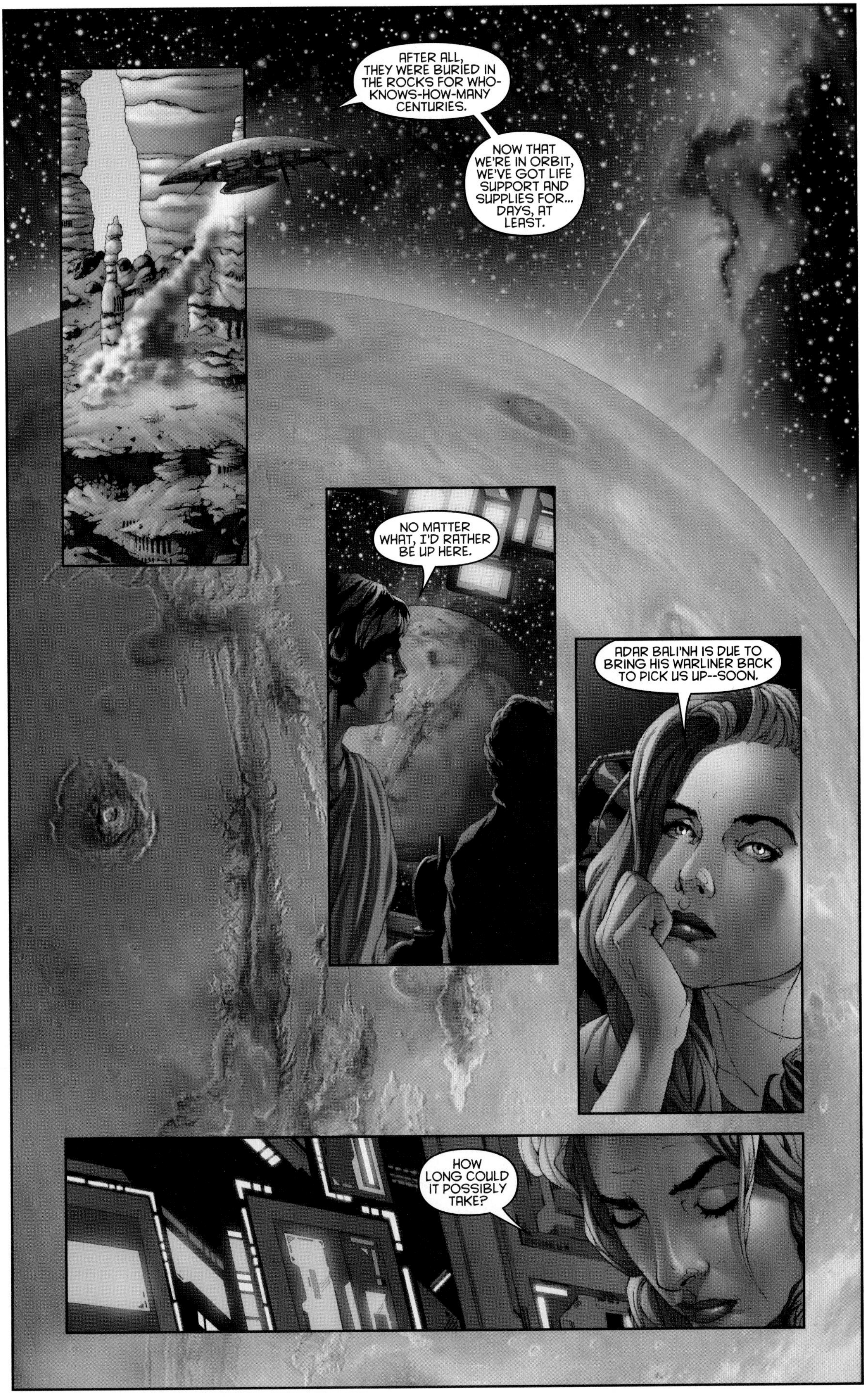
AFTER ALL, THEY WERE BURIED IN THE ROCKS FOR WHO-KNOWS-HOW-MANY CENTURIES.
NOW THAT WE'RE IN ORBIT, WE'VE GOT LIFE SUPPORT AND SUPPLIES FOR... DAYS, AT LEAST.
NO MATTER WHAT, I'D RATHER BE UP HERE.
ADAR BALI'NH IS DUE TO BRING HIS WARLINER BACK TO PICK US UP--SOON.
HOW LONG COULD IT POSSIBLY TAKE?

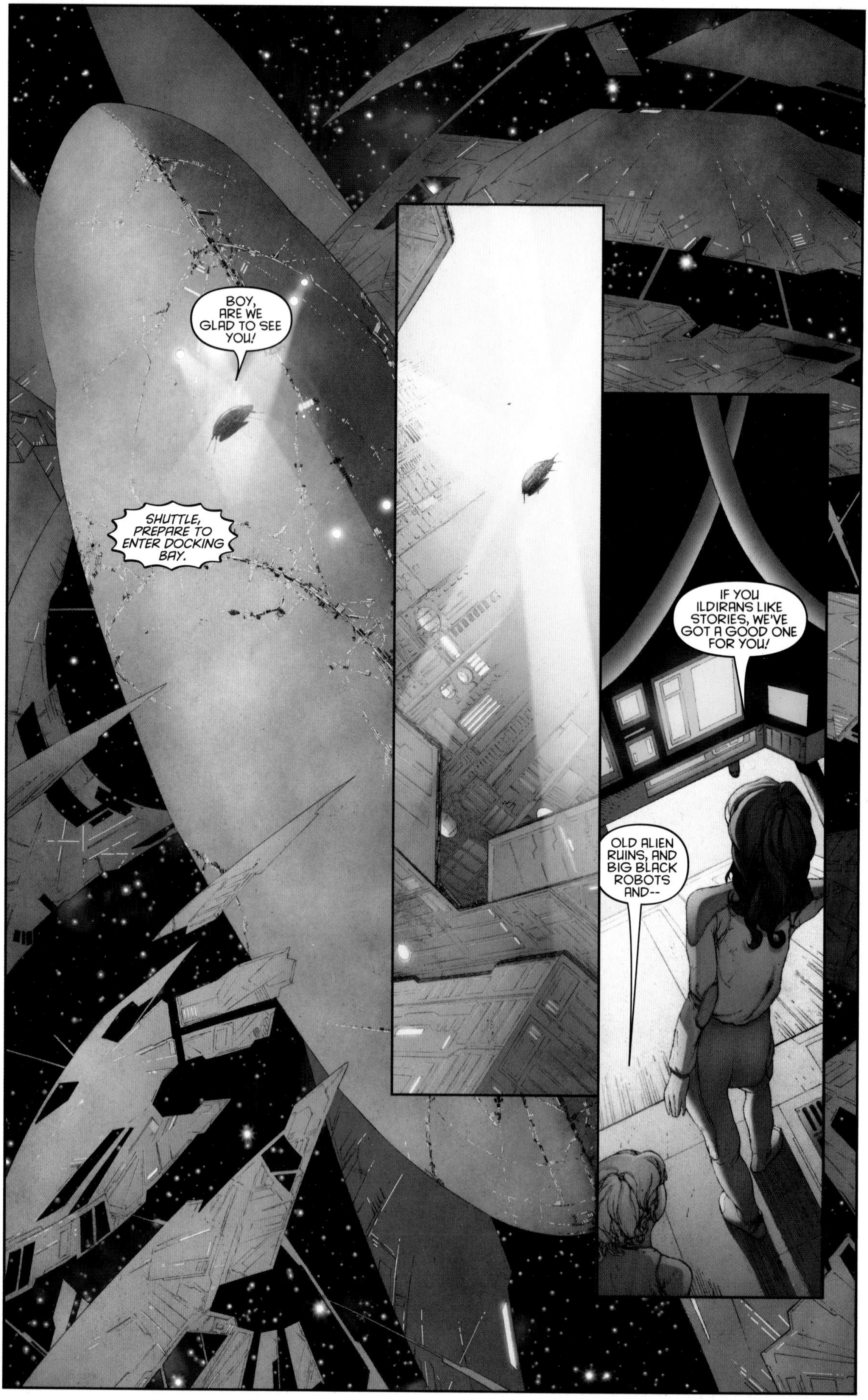
BOY, ARE WE GLAD TO SEE YOU!
SHUTTLE, PREPARE TO ENTER DOCKING BAY.
IF YOU ILDIRANS LIKE STORIES, WE'VE GOT A GOOD ONE FOR YOU!
OLD ALIEN RUINS, AND BIG BLACK ROBOTS AND--

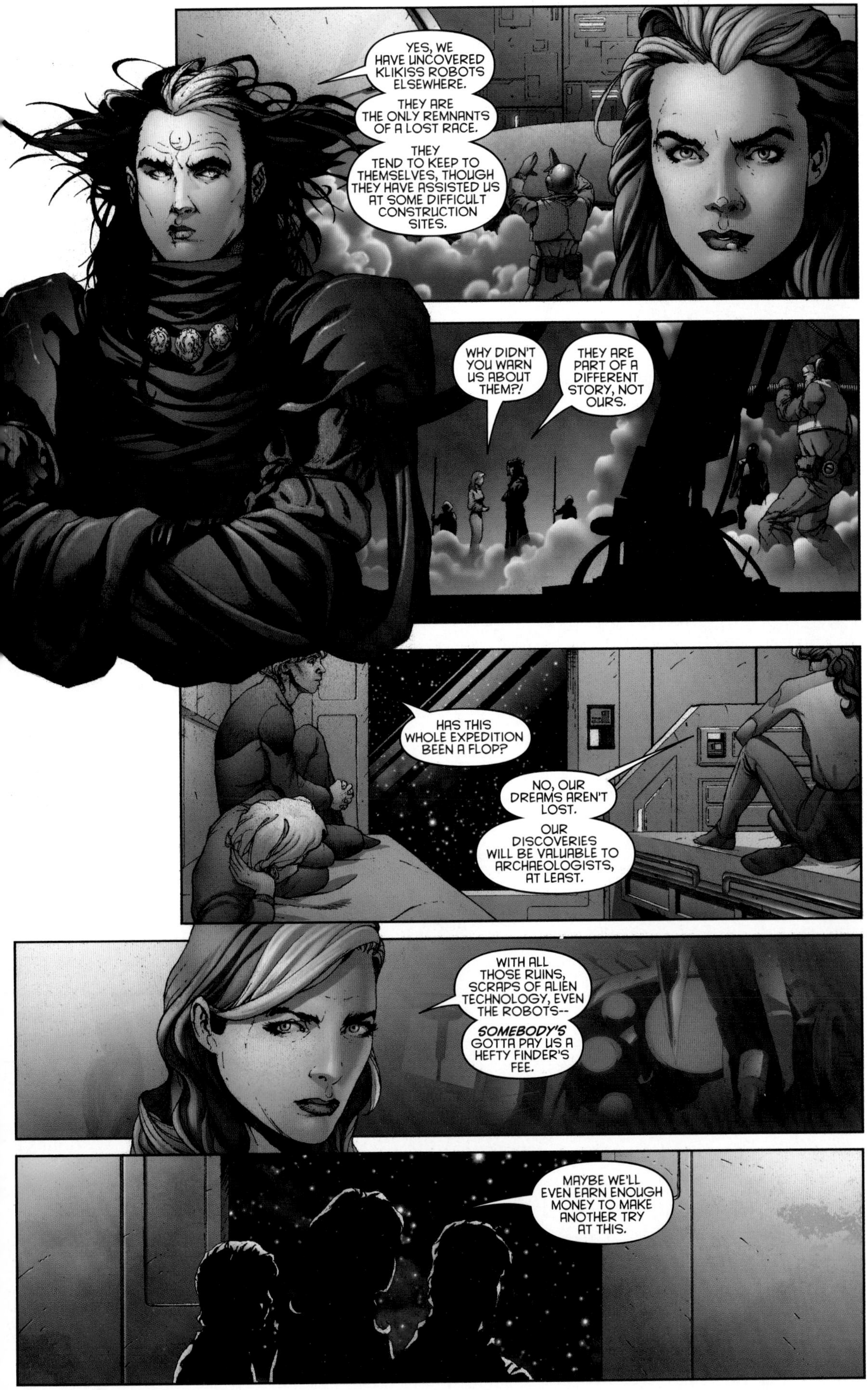
YES, WE HAVE UNCOVERED KLIKISS ROBOTS ELSEWHERE.
THEY ARE THE ONLY REMNANTS OF A LOST RACE.
THEY TEND TO KEEP TO THEMSELVES, THOUGH THEY HAVE ASSISTED US AT SOME DIFFICULT CONSTRUCTION SITES.
WHY DIDN'T YOU WARN US ABOUT THEM?!
THEY ARE PART OF A DIFFERENT STORY, NOT OURS.
HAS THIS WHOLE EXPEDITION BEEN A FLOP?
NO, OUR DREAMS AREN'T LOST.
OUR DISCOVERIES WILL BE VALUABLE TO ARCHAEOLOGISTS, AT LEAST.
WITH ALL THOSE RUINS, SCRAPS OF ALIEN TECHNOLOGY, EVEN THE ROBOTS--
SOMEBODY'S GOTTA PAY US A HEFTY FINDER'S FEE.
MAYBE WE'LL EVEN EARN ENOUGH MONEY TO MAKE ANOTHER TRY AT THIS.

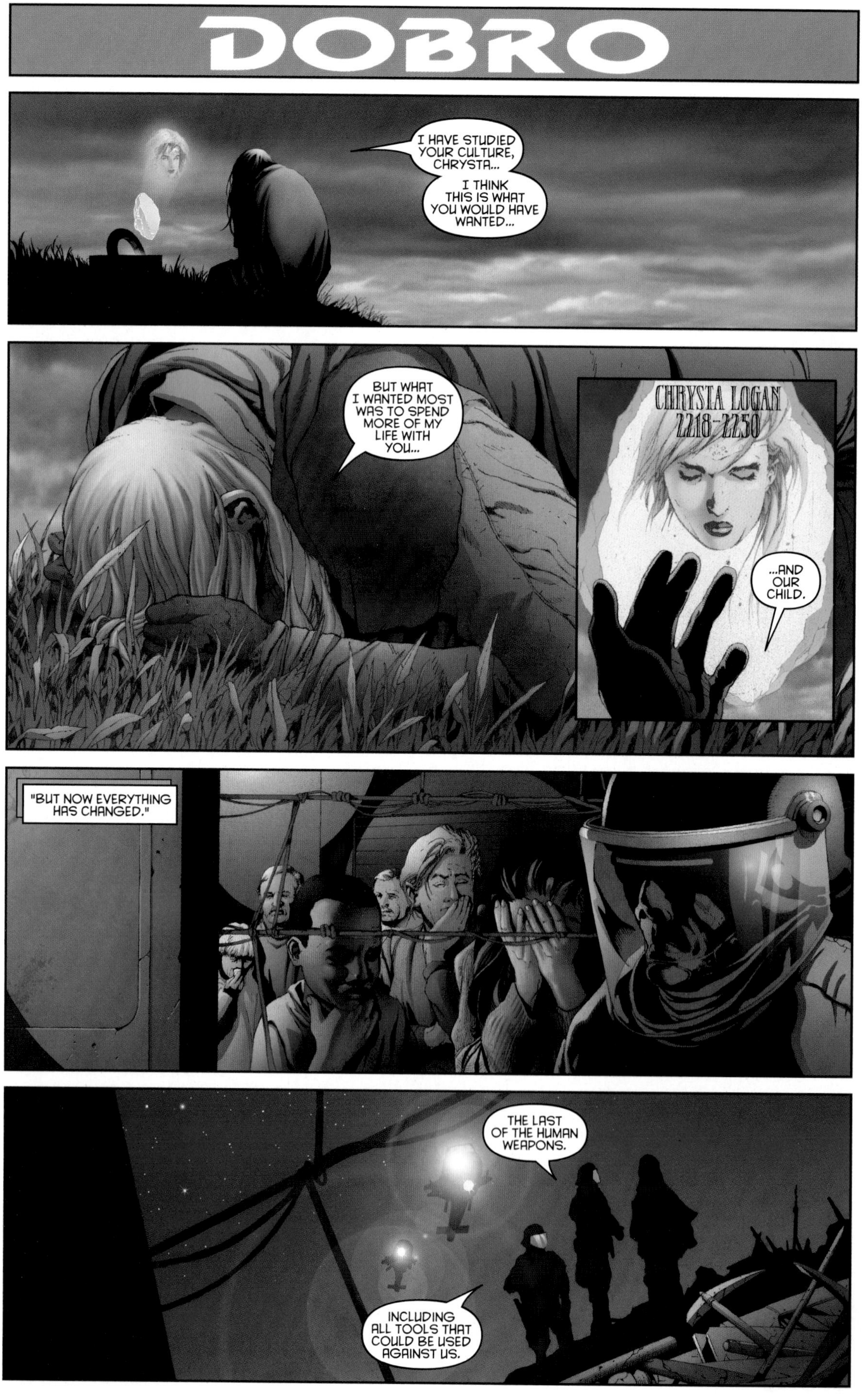
DOBRO
I HAVE STUDIED YOUR CULTURE, CHRYSTA...
I THINK THIS IS WHAT YOU WOULD HAVE WANTED...
BUT WHAT I WANTED MOST WAS TO SPEND MORE OF MY LIFE WITH YOU...
CHRYSTA LOGAN 2218-2250
...AND OUR CHILD.
"BUT NOW EVERYTHING HAS CHANGED."
THE LAST OF THE HUMAN WEAPONS.
INCLUDING ALL TOOLS THAT COULD BE USED AGAINST US.

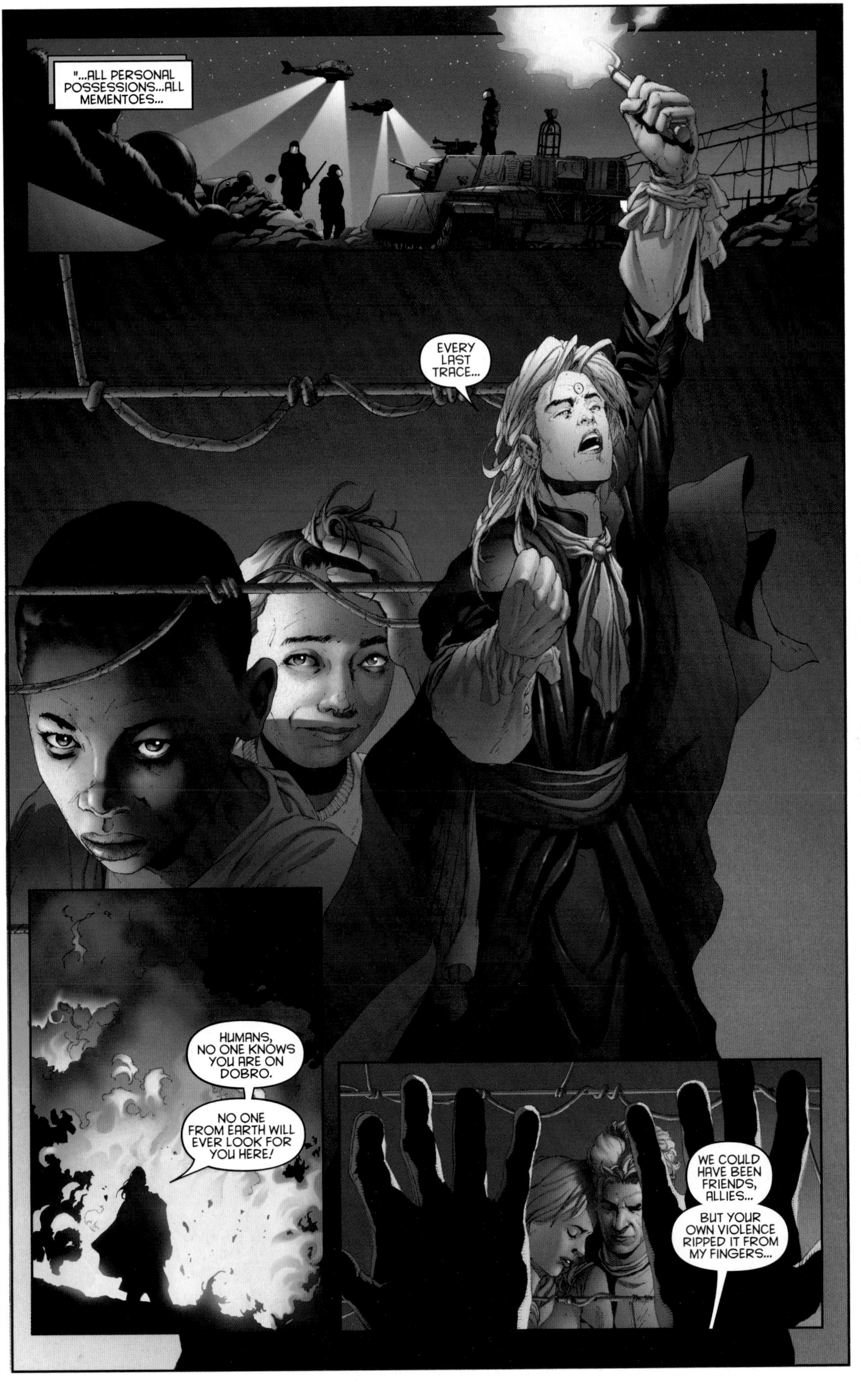
"...ALL PERSONAL POSSESSIONS...ALL MEMENTOES...
EVERY LAST TRACE...
HUMANS, NO ONE KNOWS YOU ARE ON DOBRO.
NO ONE FROM EARTH WILL EVER LOOK FOR YOU HERE!
WE COULD HAVE BEEN FRIENDS, ALLIES...
BUT YOUR OWN VIOLENCE RIPPED IT FROM MY FINGERS...

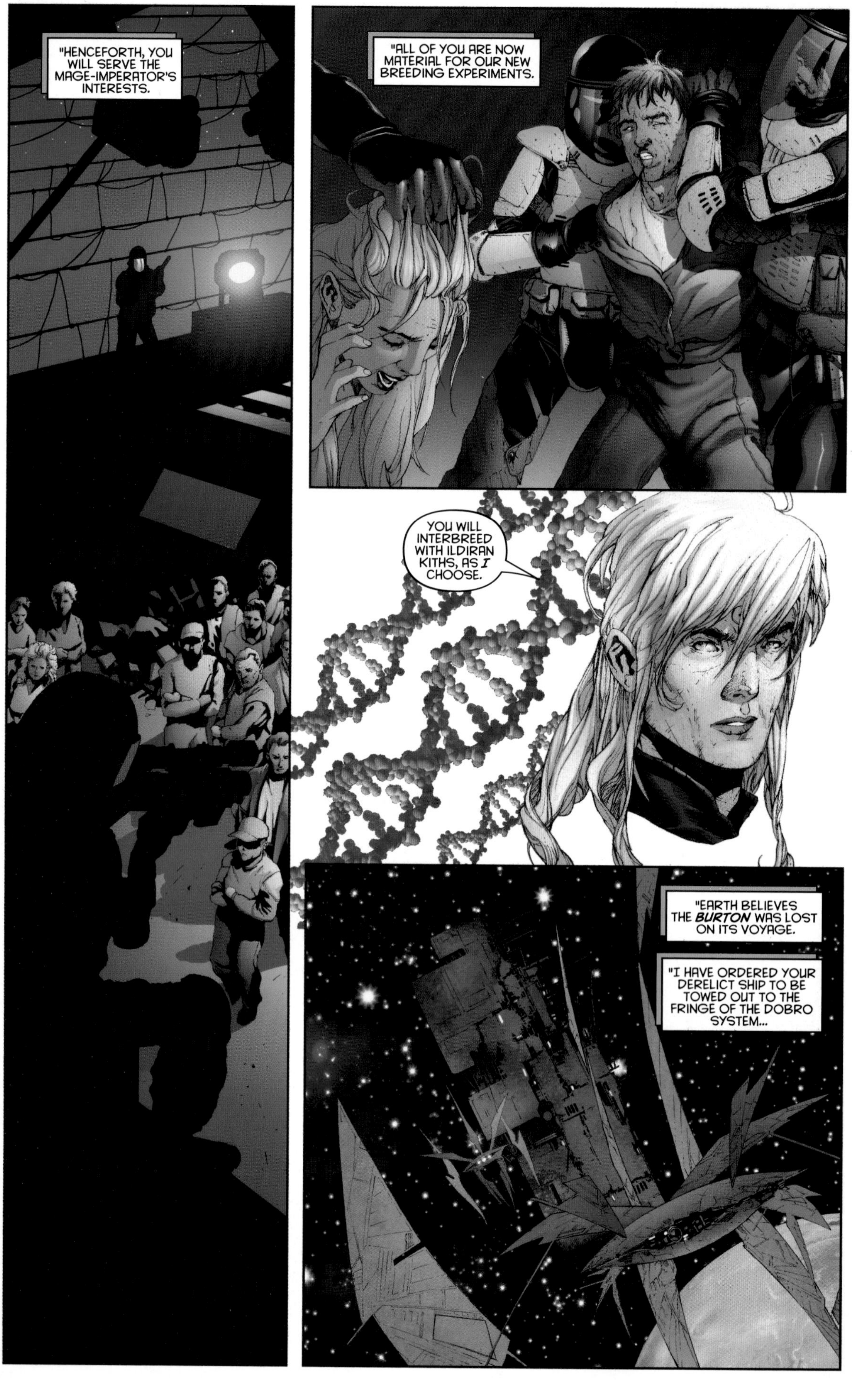
"HENCEFORTH, YOU WILL SERVE THE MAGE-IMPERATOR'S INTERESTS.
"ALL OF YOU ARE NOW MATERIAL FOR OUR NEW BREEDING EXPERIMENTS.
YOU WILL INTERBREED WITH ILDIRAN KITHS, AS *I* CHOOSE.
"EARTH BELIEVES THE *BURTON* WAS LOST ON ITS VOYAGE.
"I HAVE ORDERED YOUR DERELICT SHIP TO BE TOWED OUT TO THE FRINGE OF THE DOBRO SYSTEM...

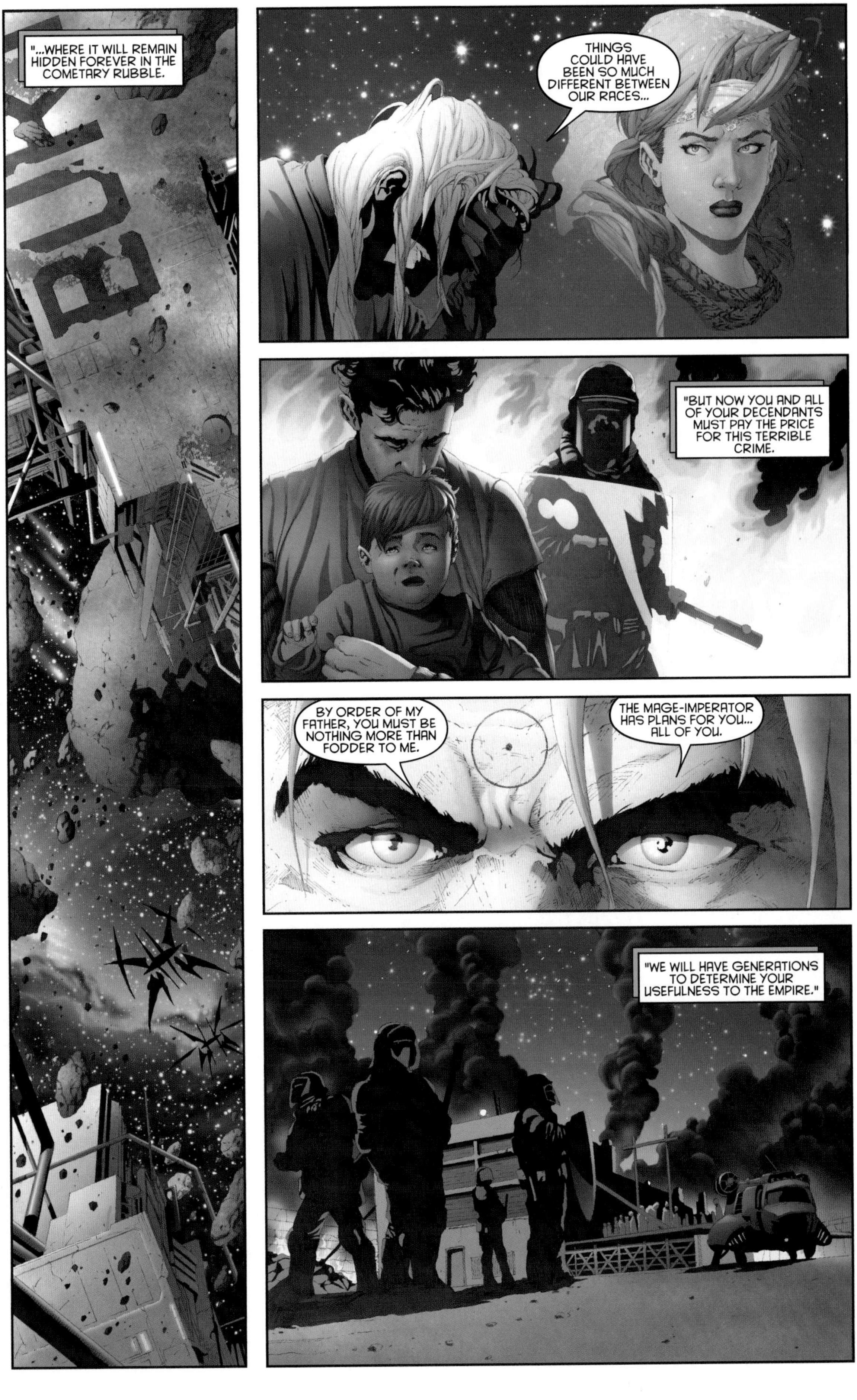
"...WHERE IT WILL REMAIN HIDDEN FOREVER IN THE COMETARY RUBBLE.
THINGS COULD HAVE BEEN SO MUCH DIFFERENT BETWEEN OUR RACES...
"BUT NOW YOU AND ALL OF YOUR DECENDANTS MUST PAY THE PRICE FOR THIS TERRIBLE CRIME.
BY ORDER OF MY FATHER, YOU MUST BE NOTHING MORE THAN FODDER TO ME.
THE MAGE-IMPERATOR HAS PLANS FOR YOU... ALL OF YOU.
"WE WILL HAVE GENERATIONS TO DETERMINE YOUR USEFULNESS TO THE EMPIRE."

DAYM

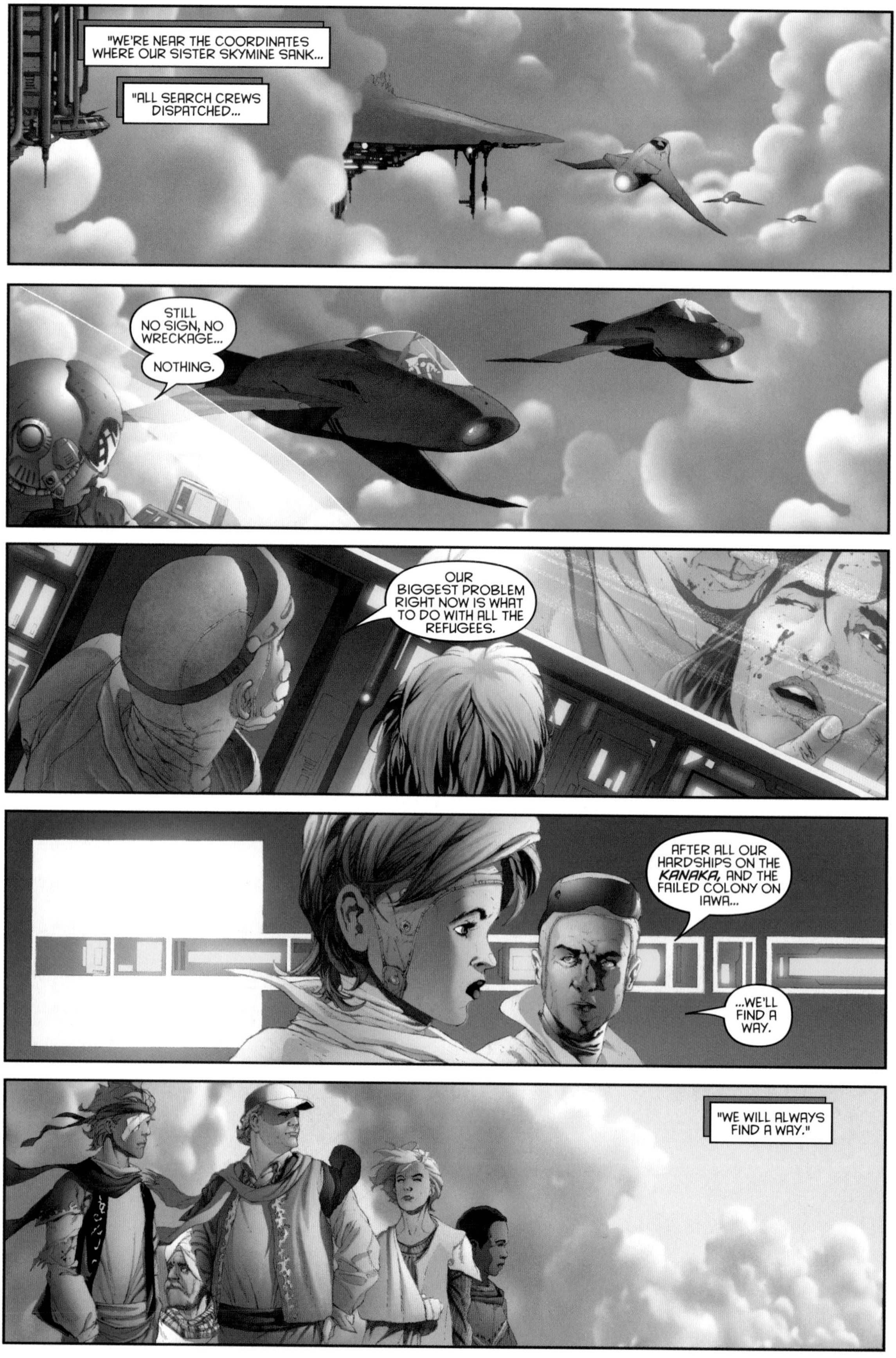

"WE'RE NEAR THE COORDINATES WHERE OUR SISTER SKYMINE SANK...
"ALL SEARCH CREWS DISPATCHED...
STILL NO SIGN, NO WRECKAGE...
NOTHING.
OUR BIGGEST PROBLEM RIGHT NOW IS WHAT TO DO WITH ALL THE REFUGEES.
AFTER ALL OUR HARDSHIPS ON THE *KANAKA,* AND THE FAILED COLONY ON IAWA...
...WE'LL FIND A WAY.
"WE WILL ALWAYS FIND A WAY."

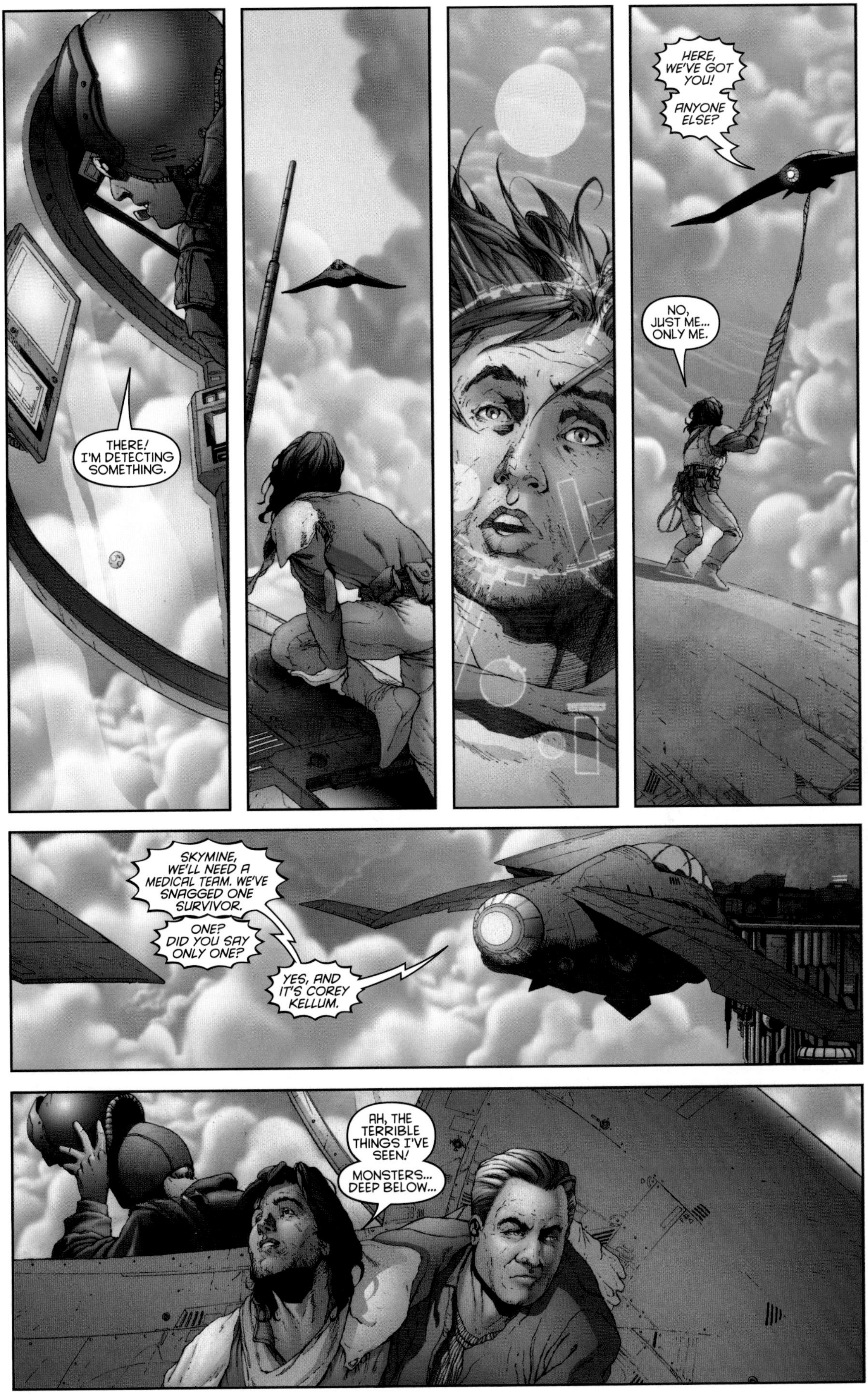
THERE! I'M DETECTING SOMETHING.
HERE, WE'VE GOT YOU!
ANYONE ELSE?
NO, JUST ME... ONLY ME.
SKYMINE, WE'LL NEED A MEDICAL TEAM. WE'VE SNAGGED ONE SURVIVOR.
ONE? DID YOU SAY ONLY ONE?
YES, AND IT'S COREY KELLUM.
AH, THE TERRIBLE THINGS I'VE SEEN!
MONSTERS... DEEP BELOW...

AND CITIES OR... SHIPS?

GIANT SPIKED SPHERES!

NOW, JUST CALM DOWN...

...YOU'RE ALL RIGHT NOW.

ALIEN SHIPS...OPENED FIRE--THEY DESTROYED THE SKYMINE!

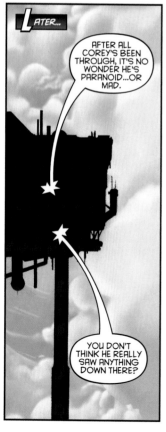

LATER...

AFTER ALL COREY'S BEEN THROUGH, IT'S NO WONDER HE'S PARANOID...OR MAD.

YOU DON'T THINK HE REALLY SAW ANYTHING DOWN THERE?

LOOK AT THOSE WEIRD LIGHTS DEEP BELOW. SWIRLING COLORS.

NEVER SEEN ANYTHING LIKE IT.

I CAN'T HELP THINKING WE MIGHT BE BETTER OFF WORKING SKYMINES ON OTHER GAS GIANTS.

MAYBE FROM NOW ON WE SHOULD JUST LEAVE DAYM *ALONE*...

EARTH

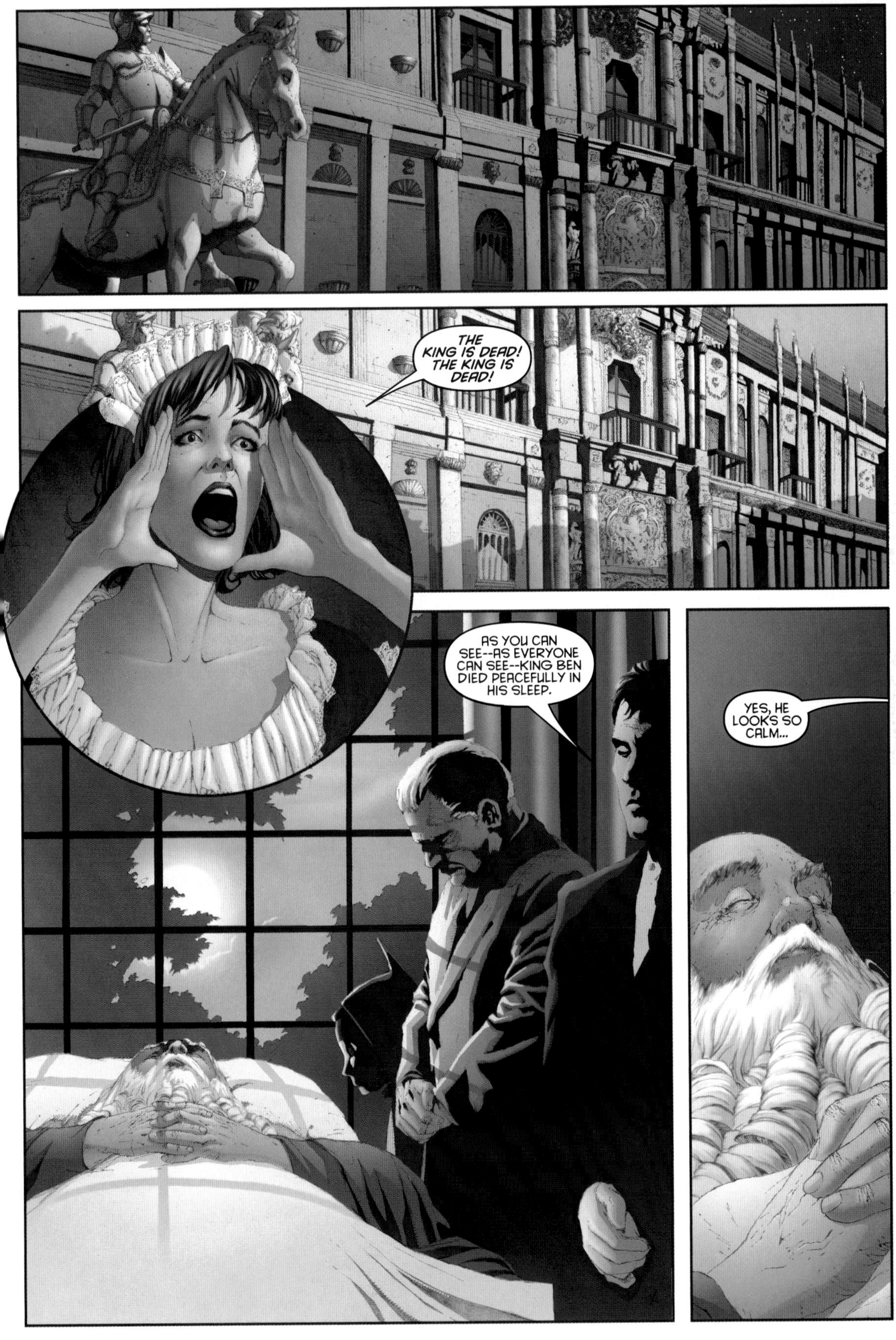
THE KING IS DEAD! THE KING IS DEAD!
AS YOU CAN SEE--AS EVERYONE CAN SEE--KING BEN DIED PEACEFULLY IN HIS SLEEP.
YES, HE LOOKS SO CALM...

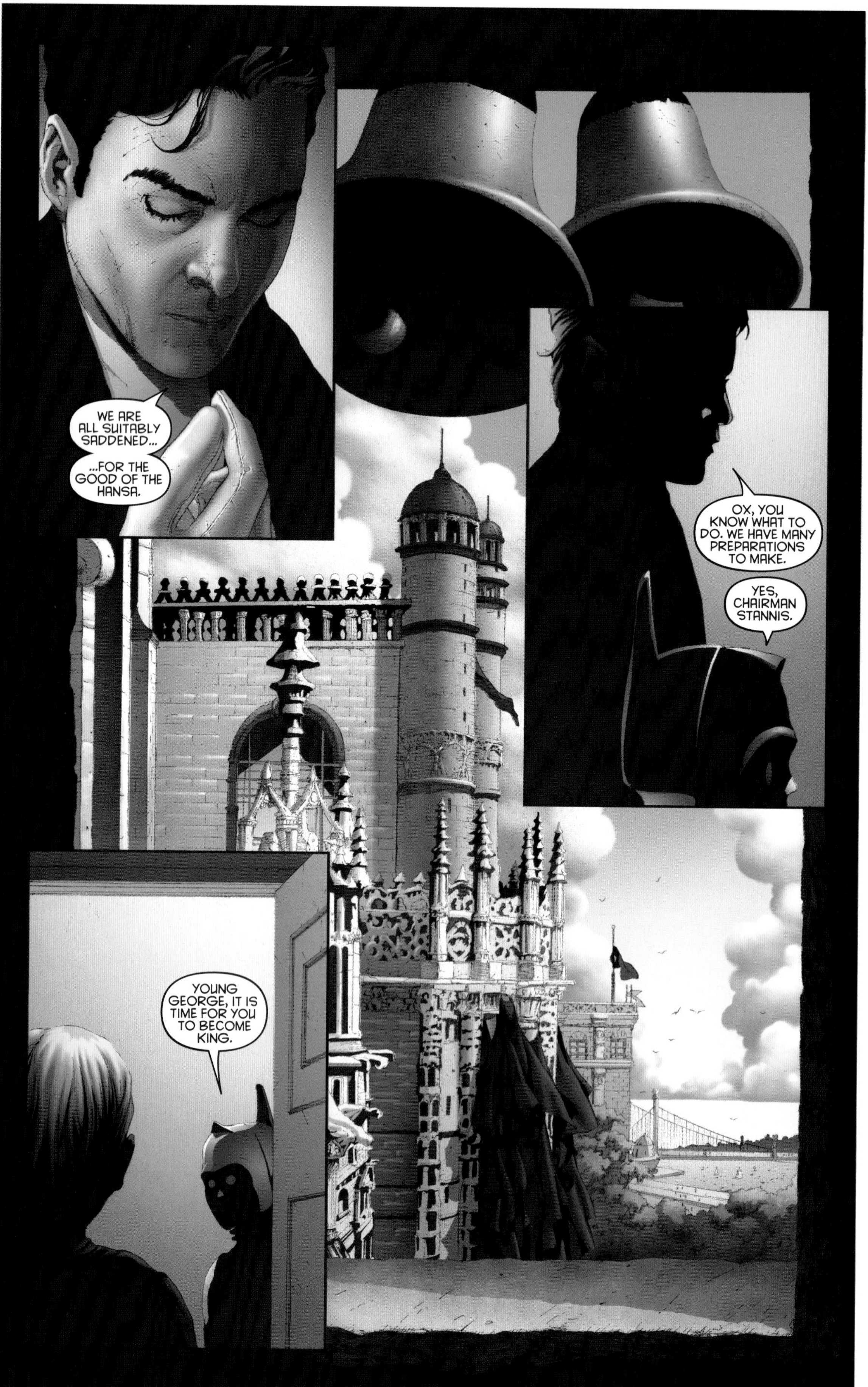
WE ARE ALL SUITABLY SADDENED...
...FOR THE GOOD OF THE HANSA.
OX, YOU KNOW WHAT TO DO. WE HAVE MANY PREPARATIONS TO MAKE.
YES, CHAIRMAN STANNIS.
YOUNG GEORGE, IT IS TIME FOR YOU TO BECOME KING.

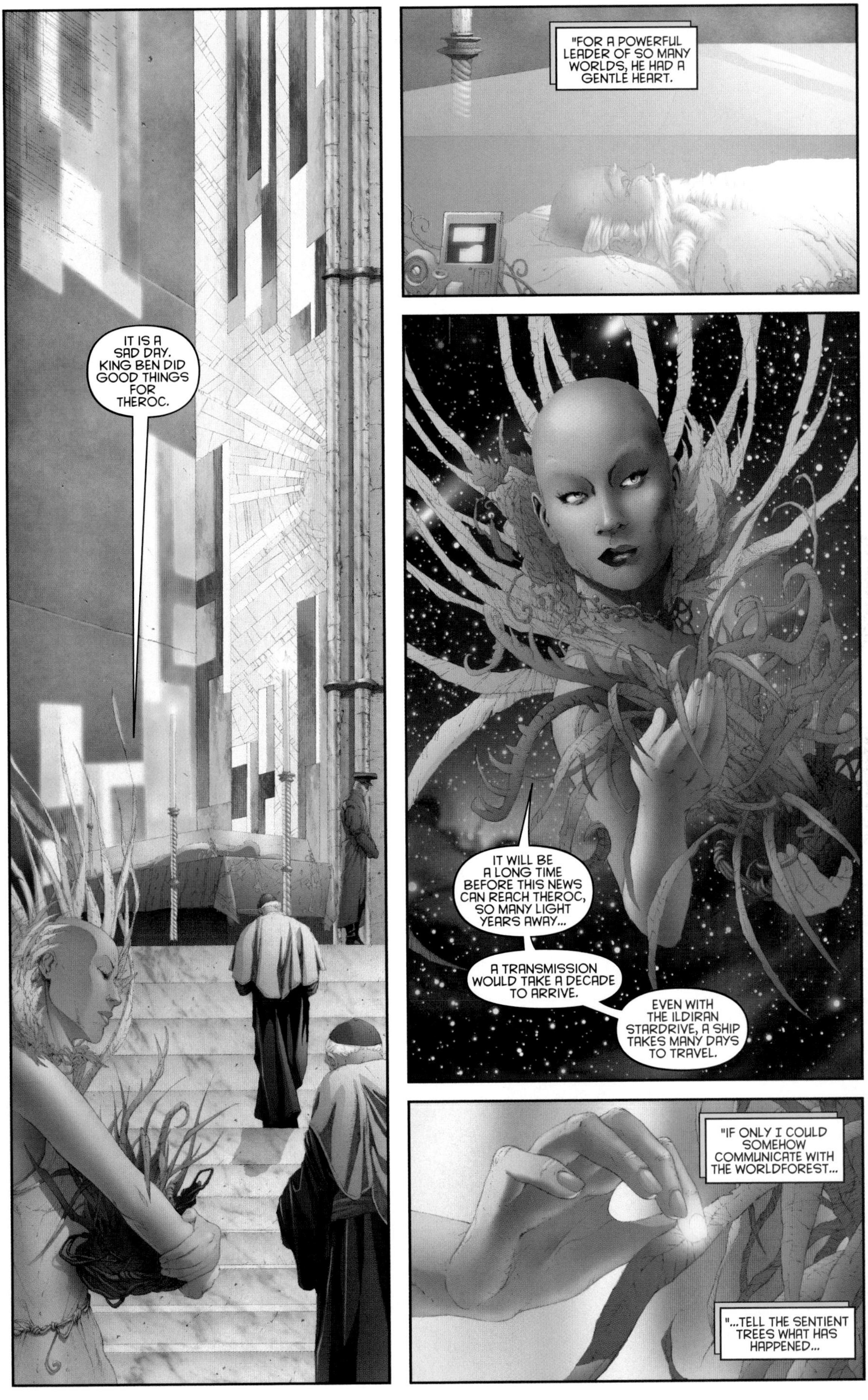
IT IS A SAD DAY. KING BEN DID GOOD THINGS FOR THEROC.
"FOR A POWERFUL LEADER OF SO MANY WORLDS, HE HAD A GENTLE HEART.
IT WILL BE A LONG TIME BEFORE THIS NEWS CAN REACH THEROC, SO MANY LIGHT YEARS AWAY...
A TRANSMISSION WOULD TAKE A DECADE TO ARRIVE.
EVEN WITH THE ILDIRAN STARDRIVE, A SHIP TAKES MANY DAYS TO TRAVEL.
"IF ONLY I COULD SOMEHOW COMMUNICATE WITH THE WORLDFOREST...
"...TELL THE SENTIENT TREES WHAT HAS HAPPENED...

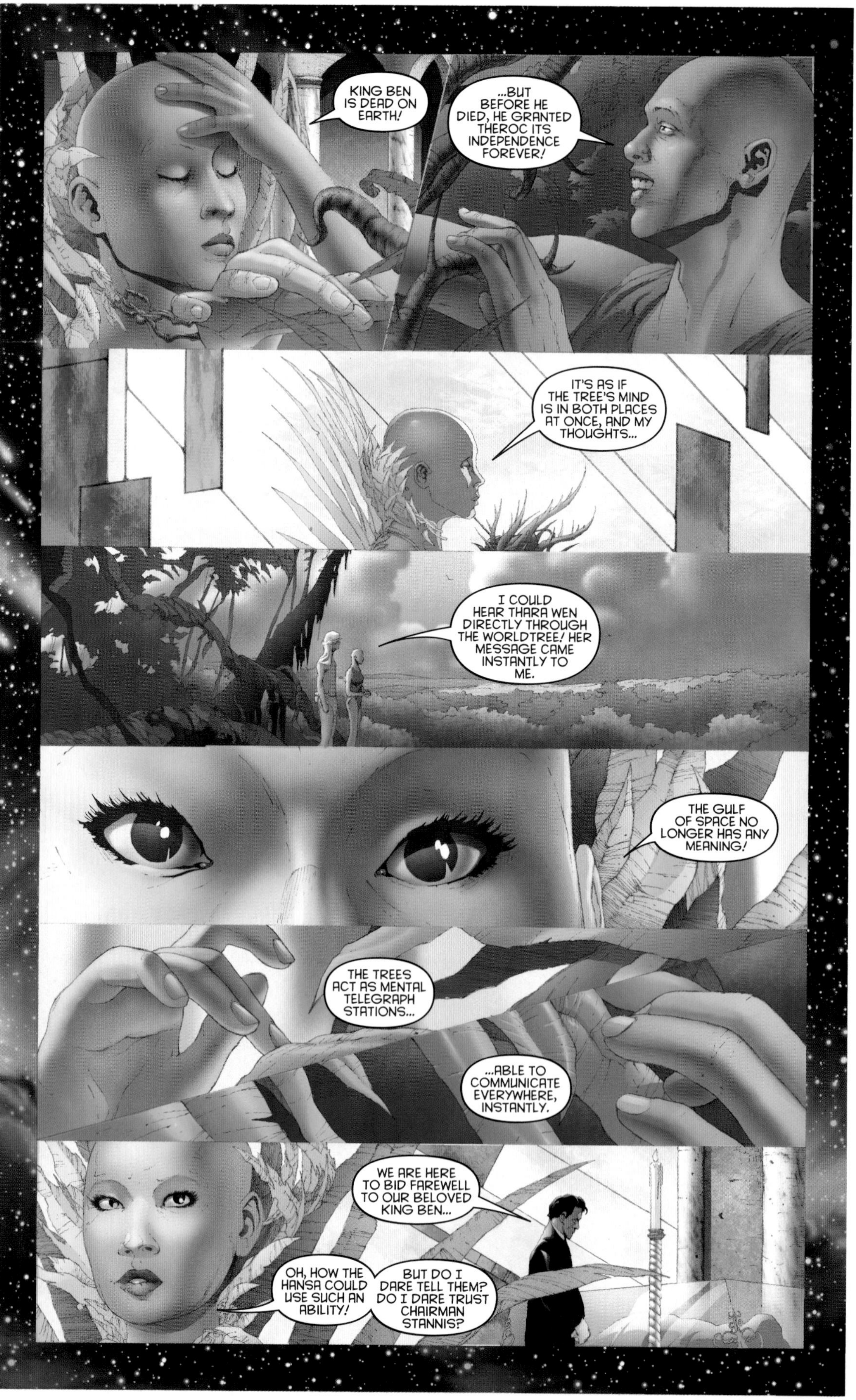
KING BEN IS DEAD ON EARTH!
...BUT BEFORE HE DIED, HE GRANTED THEROC ITS INDEPENDENCE FOREVER!
IT'S AS IF THE TREE'S MIND IS IN BOTH PLACES AT ONCE, AND MY THOUGHTS...
I COULD HEAR THARA WEN DIRECTLY THROUGH THE WORLDTREE! HER MESSAGE CAME INSTANTLY TO ME.
THE GULF OF SPACE NO LONGER HAS ANY MEANING!
THE TREES ACT AS MENTAL TELEGRAPH STATIONS...
...ABLE TO COMMUNICATE EVERYWHERE, INSTANTLY.
WE ARE HERE TO BID FAREWELL TO OUR BELOVED KING BEN...
OH, HOW THE HANSA COULD USE SUCH AN ABILITY!
BUT DO I DARE TELL THEM? DO I DARE TRUST CHAIRMAN STANNIS?

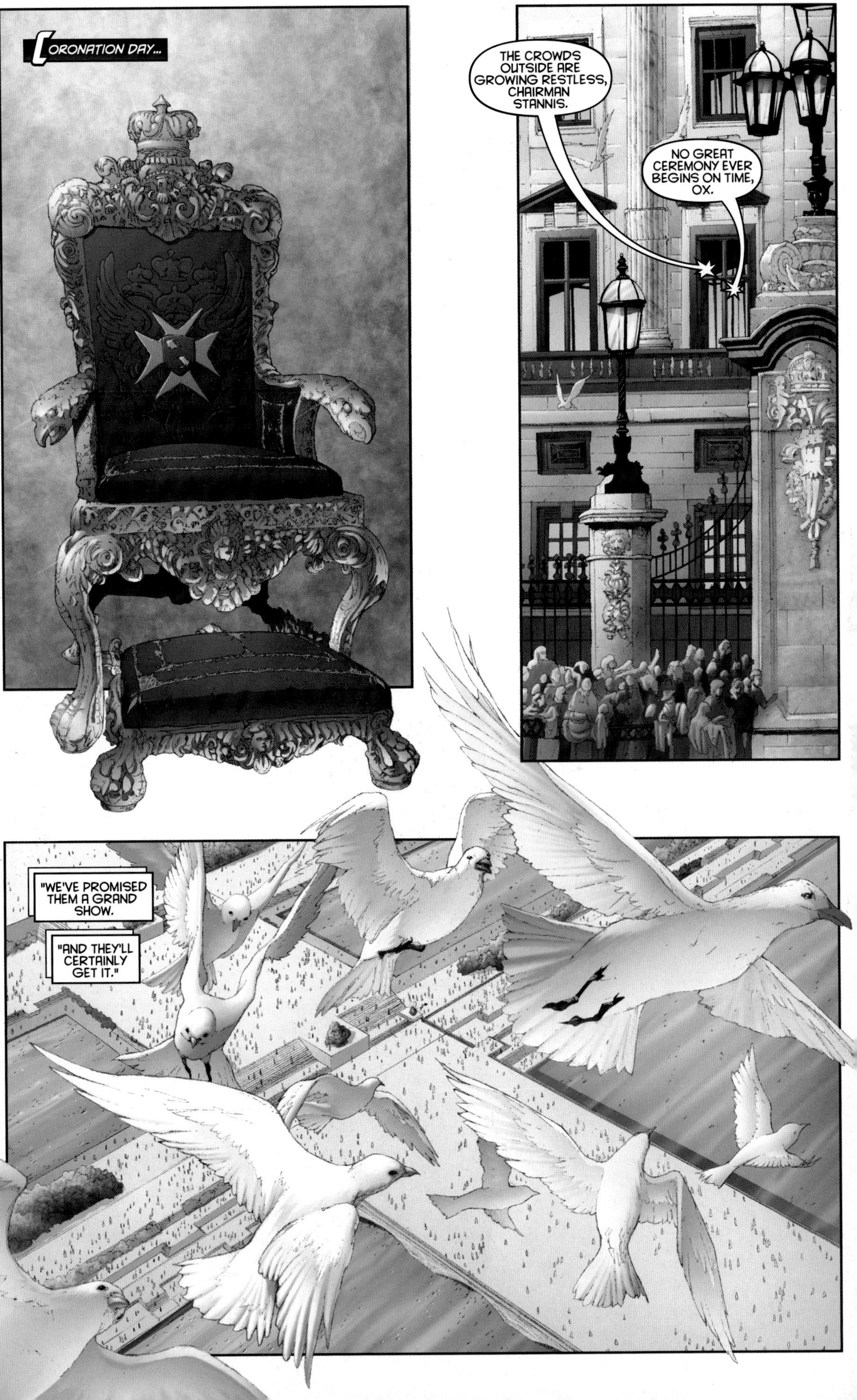
CORONATION DAY...
THE CROWDS OUTSIDE ARE GROWING RESTLESS, CHAIRMAN STANNIS.
NO GREAT CEREMONY EVER BEGINS ON TIME, OX.
"WE'VE PROMISED THEM A GRAND SHOW.
"AND THEY'LL CERTAINLY GET IT."

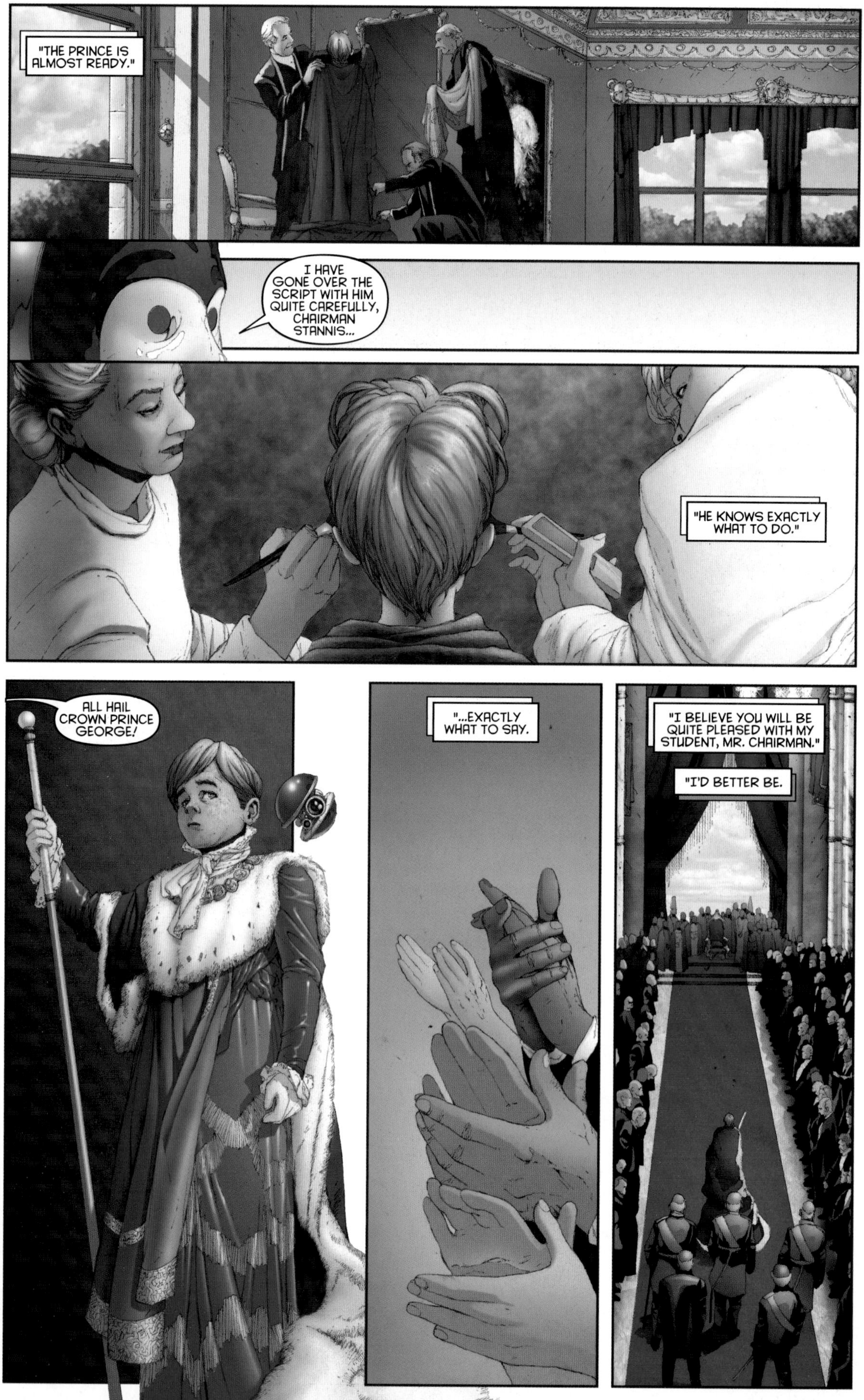
"THE PRINCE IS ALMOST READY."
I HAVE GONE OVER THE SCRIPT WITH HIM QUITE CAREFULLY, CHAIRMAN STANNIS...
"HE KNOWS EXACTLY WHAT TO DO."
ALL HAIL CROWN PRINCE GEORGE!
"...EXACTLY WHAT TO SAY.
"I BELIEVE YOU WILL BE QUITE PLEASED WITH MY STUDENT, MR. CHAIRMAN."
"I'D BETTER BE.

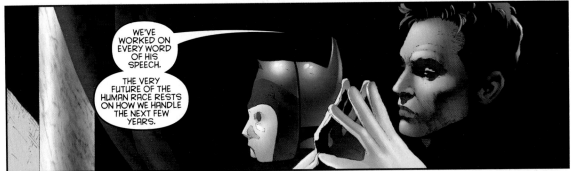

WE'VE WORKED ON EVERY WORD OF HIS SPEECH.

THE VERY FUTURE OF THE HUMAN RACE RESTS ON HOW WE HANDLE THE NEXT FEW YEARS.

MY MISSION IS TO KEEP THE HANSEATIC LEAGUE STRONG AND PROFITABLE...

...FOR THE GOOD OF ALL MANKIND, USING EVERY RESOURCE AVAILABLE.

YES, I THINK THIS NEW KING WILL HAVE A LONG AND SUCCESSFUL REIGN...

...IF HE CAN BEHAVE HIMSELF.

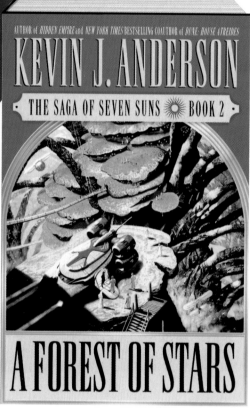
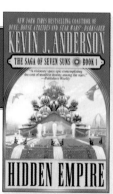
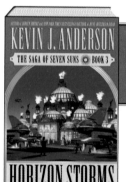